A SURVEY OF GRAMMATICAL STRUCTURES

by

Charles Peck

Summer Institute of Linguistics

1984

© 1981 by SIL International®

First Edition, 1981

Second Edition, 1984

Library of Congress Catalog No: 2017961193
ISBN: 978-1-55671-428-3

Printed in the United States of America

No part of this publication may be reproduced, stored in a retrieval system, or transmitted in any form or by any means—electronic, mechanical, photocopy, recording, or otherwise—without the express permission of SIL International®. However, short passages, generally understood to be within the limits of fair use, may be quoted without written permission.

Copies of this and other publications of SIL International® may be obtained through distributors such as Amazon, Barnes & Noble, other worldwide distributors and, for select volumes, www.sil.org/resources/publications:

SIL International Publications
7500 W. Camp Wisdom Road
Dallas, Texas 75236-5629 USA

General inquiry: publications_intl@sil.org
Pending order inquiry: sales_intl@sil.org
www.sil.org/resources/publications

This book was produced from a digitally scanned reproduction of the original publication.

Cover Design

Barbara Alber

Table of Contents

    Preface   xi
1. Introduction: the hierarchy of language   1
2. Taxonomic analysis procedures   3
  A. Outline of taxonomic analysis procedures   3
  B. Discussion of the outline   5
    1. Preliminary procedures   5
    2. Procedures for syntagmeme types   9
    3. Procedures for tagmemes   10
    4. Final procedures   12
3. Grammar write-up procedures   14
  A. Syntagmeme write-ups   14
  B. Conventions for displaying examples   21

4. Constituent trees   26
  A. Theory   26
  B. Example   26
    1. Arrays   27
    2. Trees   28
    3. Final tree   32

5. Stem-level structures   36
  A. Derived stems   36
    1. Derived verb stems   36
    2. Derived noun stems   37
    3. Derived adjective stems   40
    4. Derived adverb stem   41
    5. Embedding of derived stems   42
  B. Compound stems   42
  C. Reduplicated stems   44
  D. Reduplicated onomatopoeic stems   45
  E. Matrix of stem-level constructions   46
  F. Compound noun stems and attributive noun phrases   46
  G. Conclusion   46
    Bibliography   47

6. Word-level structures   48
  A. Non-verbs   48
    1. Noun words   48
    2. Kinship words   50
    3. Pronoun words   51
    4. Adjective words   52
    5. Preposition words and conjunction words   52
  B. Verbs   53
    1. Person marker affixes   53
    2. Tense affixes   55
    3. Aspect affixes   56
    4. Voice affixes   59

    5. Mood affixes   60
    6. Relationals and medial verbs   60
  Bibliography   62

7. Allomorphs   63
  A. Assimilation   63
  B. Reduction   64
  C. Metathesis   65
  D. Fusion   65
  E. Harmony   66
  F. Replacement   66
  G. Epenthesis   66
  H. The three parts of an allomorph description   67
  I. Grammatically conditioned allomorphs   67
  J. The place of allomorph statements in a grammar paper   68
Bibliography   68

8. Phrase-level structures   69
  A. Noun phrases   69
    1. Description noun phrase   69
    2. Possession phrases in English   73
    3. Possession phrases in other languages   75
    4. Qualifying prepositional phrase   76
    5 Attributive noun phrase   77
    6. Coordinate noun phrase   77
    7. Serial noun phrase   79
    8. Alternate noun phrase   80
    9. Appositional noun phrase   82
   10. Reduplicated noun phrase   83
   11. Replacive noun phrase   84
   12. Compound noun phrase   85
  B. Other (noun-verb) phrases   85
    1. Phrase search matrix   85
    2. Kinship phrases   86
    3. Pronoun phrases   88
    4. Name phrases   89
    5. Number phrases   93
    6. Adjective phrases   95
    7. Time phrases   99
    8. Location phrases   102
  C. Prepositional phrases   104
    1. Location prepositional phrase   105
    2. Time prepositional phrase   106
    3. Instrument prepositional phrase   106
    4. Accompaniment prepositional phrase   107
    5. Manner prepositional phrase   107
    6. Benefactive prepositional phrase   108
    7. Object prepositional phrase   108
    8. Subject prepositional phrase   109
    9. Complex prepositional phrases   109
   10. Inflected prepositions   110
   11. Distribution matrix   111
  D. Verb phrases   113
    1. English verb phrase   114
    2. Manner modifiers   114

3. Motion auxiliaries   115
   4. Desiderative auxiliaries   116
   5. Do-plus-infinitive verb phrase   116
   6. Give verb phrase   117
   7. Aspectual auxiliaries   117
   8. Idiomatic compound verb phrase   118
      Bibliography   120

9. Clause-level structures   121
   A. Verbal clauses   121
      1. Bitransitive or ditransitive clause   121
      2. Transitive clause   124
      3. Intransitive clause   127
      4. Ambient clause   129
   B. Verbless clauses   130
      1. Descriptive clause   130
      2. Equational clause   131
      3. Possession clause   132
      4. Location clause   132
      5. Name clause   133
      6. Existential clause   133
   C. Clause constituents   134
      1. Predicate tagmeme   134
      2. Subject tagmeme   134
      3. Object tagmeme   135
      4. Indirect object tagmeme   135
      5. Benefactive tagmeme   136
      6. Time and location tagmemes   136
      7. Manner tagmeme   137
      8. Negative tagmeme   137
      9. Instrument tagmeme   137
     10. Purpose tagmeme   138
     11. Reason tagmeme   138
     12. Accompaniment tagmeme   138
     13. Summary of clause syntagmeme   138
   D. Voice   139
      1. Accusative versus ergative languages   139
      2. Passive and object advancement   139
      3. Antipassive and subject enhancement   140
      4. Object-incorporation and object-demotion   141
      5. Instrument advancement   142
      6. Other advancements   143
   E. Moods   143
      1. Declarative   143
      2. Interrogative   144
      3. Command clauses   146
      4. Optative and desiderative   146
   F. Nominalized clauses   147
   G. Relativized clauses   150
   H. Dependent clauses   151
   I. Other dependent clauses   152
   J. Clause-search matrix   154
   K. Cohesion in clauses   154
      Bibliography   155

10. Case grammar   156
A. Lexical decomposition of verbs   156
B. Scope and structure   157
C. Lexical properties of nouns   159
D. Semantic derivations   160
E. Case grammar   162
F. Case matrices   164
G. Longacre's case system   166
H. Conclusion   171
  Bibliography   172

11. Sentence-level structures   173
A. Outer-periphery margin tagmemes   173
   1. Sentence introducer margin   173
   2. Sentence modifier margin (performatives)   173
   3. Exclamation margin   173
   4. Vocative margin   173
   5. Response margin   173
   6. Disclaimer margin   173
   7. Summary   174
B. Inner-periphery tagmemes   175
   1. Time margins   175
      a. Prior-time margin   175
      b. Simultaneous-time margin   176
      c. Subsequent-time margin   177
      d. Indefinite-time margin   177
   2. Condition margins   177
      a. Condition margin   177
      b. Circumstance margin   178
      c. Concessive margin   178
   3. Logical margins   179
      a. Reason or cause margin   179
      b. Purpose margin   179
      c. Result margin   180
      d. Contrast margin   180
      e. Similarity margin   180
   4. Other margins   181
      a. Sentence topic margin   181
      b. Location margin   182
      c. Benefactive margin   182
      d. Afterthought margin   182
      e. Tag question   183
   5. Summary   183
C. Nuclear tagmeme clusters   186
   1. Simple sentences   186
      a. Simple sentence   186
      b. Juxtaposed sentence   187
   2. Time-oriented sentences   187
      a. Narrative sentence   187
      b. Simultaneous sentence   189
   3. Quotation oriented sentences   189
      a. Direct quotation sentence   190
      b. Indirect quotation sentence   190

     c. Sensation sentence   191
     d. Perceived description sentence   193
     e. Indirect quotation sentence   193
   4. Logical structure sentences   195
     a. Coordinate sentence   195
     b. Antithetical sentence   196
     c. Alternative sentence   197
     d. Conditional sentence   198
     e. Contrafactual sentence   199
     f. Concessive sentence   200
     g. Reason sentence   201
     h. Result sentence   201
     i. Caution sentence   202
   5. Parallel-structure sentences   202
     a. Parallel sentence   202
     b. Paraphrase sentence   203
     c. Recapitulation sentence   204
     d. Amplification sentence   204
     e. Covariant sentence   205
     f. Comparative sentence   206
     g. Evaluation and summary sentences   208
   6. Equation-structure sentences   210
     a. Pseudocleft sentence   210
     b. Cleft sentence   211
     c. Evaluation cleft sentence   212
   7. Merged sentences   213
     a. Manner merged sentence   213
     b. Conative merged sentence   214
     c. Predispositional merged sentence   215
     d. Obligation merged sentence   216
     e. Passive merged sentence   216
     f. Telic merged sentence   217
     g. Aspectual merged sentence   218
     h. Reciprocal merged sentence 219
     i. Causative merged sentence   220
     j. Sensation merged sentence   221
   8. Dependent sentences   223
     a. Relator-axis dependent sentences 223
     b. Embedded sentences 224
   Bibliography   224

12. Propositional Calculus   225
 A. Basic deep structures   226
   1. Conjoining without sequencing   226
   2. Conjoining with sequencing   230
 B. Rhetorical elaborations   234
   1. Nonreportative   234
   2. Reportative   236
 C. Frustration   238
   1. Basic frustration   238
   2. Rhetorical frustration   239
   3. Frustrated modality   240
 D. Definition of terms   240
   1. Predicates with terms   240

    2. Predicates with predicates   241
    3. Terms   241
    4. Roles   242
    5. Apparatus   242
  Bibliography   243

13. Paragraph-level structures   244
  A. Paragraph boundaries   244
    1. In chronological discourses   244
    2. In logical discourses   245
  B. Discourse-like paragraphs   245
    1. Narrative paragraph   245
    2. Explanatory paragraph   248
    3. Procedural paragraph   249
    4. Hortatory paragraph   252
    5. Embedding of paragraphs   255
  C. Repartee paragraphs   256
    1. Dialogue paragraph   256
    2. Compound dialogue paragraph   258
    3. Dramatic paragraph   259
    4. Compound dramatic paragraph   261
  D. Structures unique to paragraph level   262
    1. Simple paragraph   262
    2. Comment paragraph   263
    3. Description paragraph   264
    4. Induction paragraph   265
    5. Warning paragraph   266
    6. Exemplification paragraph   267
    7. Execution paragraph   268
    8. Stimulus-response paragraph   269
    9. Rheotorical question-answer paragraph   270
    10. Hypothetical paragraph   271
  E. Sentence-like paragraphs   272
    1. Alternative paragraph   272
    2. Contrast paragraph   272
    3. Parallel paragraph   273
    4. Simultaneous paragraph   274
    5. Reason paragraph   275
    6. Result paragraph   275
    7. Quotation paragraph   277
  F. Cyclical paragraphs   278
  G. Paragraph cohesion   279
  Bibliography   281

14. Discourse level   282
  A. Narrative discourse   282
  B. Expository discourse   284
  C. Procedural discourse   285
  D. Hortatory discourse   286
  E. Dramatic discourse   288
  F. Activity discourse   289
  G. Epistolary discourse   290
  H. Surface-structure matrices of discourse types   291
    1. Longacre's matrices   291

    2. Forster's matrices   292
 I. Deep-structure matrix of discourse types   294
 J. Encoding matrix   296
 K. Determining constituent boundaries   296
 L. Overlay structures   297
    Bibliography   300

15. Discourse features   301
 A. Grimes's types of information in discourse   301
    1. Events   301
    2. Participants   302
    3. Identification   302
    4. Setting   303
    5. Background   303
    6. Evaluation   303
    7. Collateral   303
    8. Performative   304
 B. Other features   304
    1. Aspects and tenses   304
    2. Ranking of information   305
    3. Grouping, coherence and prominence   305
    4. Themes   305
    5. Constituents and threads   306
 C. Recent studies   306
    1. Transitivity   306
    2. Participant references   307
    3. Pecking order   309
 G. Discourse charting   309
    1. Basic charting   309
    2. Span charts   310
    3. Thurman charts   310
    4. Longacre-Levinsohn chart   310
    5. Summary   314
  Bibliography   314
  Index   315

Preface

This book has grown out of my lectures to the advanced grammar classes of Summer Institute of Linguistics in Brisbane and Sydney, Australia and in Norman and Dallas in the United States of America. The material was originally developed in response to the request from the Papua New Guinea S. I. L. Branch that the material taught be more practical. These notes, I hope, will indeed be useful for S.I.L. advanced classes and for practicing linguists on the field.

No new theories are presented. The theoretical stance is tagmemic, drawn from Robert E. Longacre and Kenneth L. Pike. This is not intended to disparage other theories. Other theories can give insights and understanding that a taxonomic approach cannot. But a taxonomic approach is the easiest to understand for practicing linguists with a minimum of training who are more interested in learning a language than in working on a theory.

The chapters in this book are arranged in a logical order but probably should not be read in that order. The casual reader should begin with chapter five and procede through the book, or begin with chapter fifteen and read the chapters in a reverse order.

Many have helped and encouraged me in the development of these materials. My assistants at various times include Bob Conrad, Steve Echerd, Bill Leal, and David Frank, each of whom has helped. My colleagues, Alan Healey and Bruce Hooley, helped shape my thinking somewhat in the early days. Terry Sullivan read the manuscript and made many valuable comments. And of course, my students have helped in many ways. My thanks to all of them. Heidi Aschmann typed an early version, and Yolanda Yoque keyboarded it.

The present volume represents my current thinking. I expect to change and add to my ideas. And so I will appreciate any constructive feedback from readers and students. Feel free to send your comments to me, and thank you, in advance.

Dallas, 1981   C. Peck

Chapter 1

Introduction

The hierarchy of language

We know that spoken language comes in a temporal sequence, and we read and write in temporal sequences. But when we analyze the patterns of a language, we find that the best approach is to view it as patterns of different sizes on different levels. We are accustomed to seeing written language broken up into paragraphs, sentences, and words. As linguists, we want to examine language for its paragraph patterns, sentence patterns, clause patterns, phrase patterns, word patterns, and stem patterns. And as we look at the different levels, we will see that each level has its own particular characteristic patterns and flavor.

Each grammatical pattern (at any level) comprises a sequence of pattern-points. The pattern is called a 'syntagmeme' and the pattern-points 'tagmemes'. For example, a transitive clause comprises a subject, a predicate, an object, and possibly a time or a location. The transitive clause is a 'syntagmeme' and the components such as subject, predicate, object, time, and location are 'tagmemes'. So a syntagmeme consists of an ordered sequence of tagmemes.

A tagmeme is a binary construct consisting of a function label, such as 'subject,' 'predicate,' and 'location,' and a set of one or more category labels, such as syntagmeme names and morpheme-class names, that describe all the various pieces of language that expound that function. So a tagmeme is a combination of a function name and a set of exponent class names.

The symbol for a tagmeme has other parts, also. Foremost is an indication of whether the tagmeme is obligatory or optional, + or $\pm$. Other features of the tagmeme such as its place on a wave (margin versus nucleus) and its coherence features such as agreement may also be added.

So a subject tagmeme might look like

a) + Subject (as actor): pronouns, proper nouns, noun phrases,

```
or                    | pronouns
b)                    | proper nouns
            subject   | noun phrases
       +    ─────────────────────────
            actor     | affixes on verb
                      | must agree in
                      | person and number
                      | with the actual
                      | exponent of this
                      | tagmeme
```

```
or          ┌─────────────────────────┐
c)          | + Subject               |
            |─────────────────────────|
            |   actor                 |
            |─────────────────────────|
            |   pronouns              |
            |   proper nouns          |
            |   noun phrases          |
            |─────────────────────────|
            |   agreement             |
            |   with verb             |
            |   affixes in            |
            |   person and number     |
            └─────────────────────────┘
```

Example a), above, is the older way of writing tagmemes, b) is Pike and Pike's system, and c) is Longacre's system which we will use in this book. We choose system c) 'bidimensional arrays', because it gives more room for exponent names and presents the sequence of tagmemes that constitute a syntagmeme in a more readily accessible form.

Note that syntagmemes are exponents of tagmemes and syntagmemes consist of tagmemes. The bounds, or beginning and end, of a syntagmeme are determined by the bounds of a tagmeme that it expounds. For example, we can tell where a noun phrase begins and where it ends because it expounds, say, the subject of a clause. We can tell where the subject of a clause begins and ends when we analyze a clause. As a general rule, syntagmemes are delimited by the tagmemes they expound.

In chapter 2, we will discuss actual procedures for analyzing language data into syntagmemes and tagmemes. The concepts presented very briefly here will become clearer as we proceed.

Chapter 2

Taxonomic analysis procedures

(The material in this chapter is taken from Robert E. Longacre: 1964, Grammar Discovery Procedures.)

Taxonomic analysis is a guess-and-check procedure. The analyst makes tentative constituent breaks and assigns tentative labels to the constructions and their parts. Then as he (or she) works out the analysis, some of the tentative decisions will be confirmed, and others will have to be changed. When the analysis is done and written up, the linguist has to see if he can live with it as he progresses in his language learning and further analysis. It may have to be modified when further analysis is done. This is the nature of a guess and check procedure.

This book is aimed at giving the analyst an inventory of linguistic concepts and labels that will help him in his initial guesses. Naturally, this inventory cannot be exhaustive, and most analysts will have to make up new terms to fit new phenomena. This book should give them some leads on how to proceed.

A. First, we will give the outline of the procedure, then we will discuss each point more fully.

An Outline of Taxonomic Analysis Procedures

1. Preliminary.

   a. Define the grammatical level (or phonological level) you plan to analyze. Take various texts and mark off the syntagmas of that level.

   b. Copy (or cut out and paste) each syntagma onto a file card (14 x 21 cm is a good size). Mark any residue left in the texts, (with, perhaps, a wavy underline).

   c. Tentatively identify the tagmas in each syntagma on each card, writing your analysis on each card.

   d. Sort the file cards; first, by the filler of the nuclear slot to see if there is any correlation of syntagma structure with the class of nuclear filler; and secondly, by any other structural feature. Note each correlation on the affected file cards. Several sortings and searches may be needed to find all the various correlations.

   e. Decide how many different etic syntagma types you have, and copy the syntagmas belonging to each different type onto a separate workchart.

2. Analytic procedures for syntagmeme types.

   a. Distinguish the nuclear tagmas on each workchart from the peripheral tagmas.

   b. Examine the workcharts, looking for systematic structural differences.

   c. Separate workcharts with two or more differences, one of which must involve the nuclear tagmas. Consider the separated workcharts as being separate emic syntagmemes.

   d. Combine workcharts with fewer than two differences (or with no differences in nuclear tagmas) as single emic syntagmemes.

   e. Arrange the syntagmemes in a systematic matrix and look for empty boxes or multiple box fillers and consider reanalyzing some of the syntagmemes to fill up the cells of the matrix.

3. Analytic procedures for tagmeme types.

   a. Make a complete list of all the fillers of each tagma and write a summary of each list.

   b. Check pairs of suspect tagmas for differences in function, filler class, and distribution. Be sure contrastive tagmas have contrastive names and noncontrastive tagmas have noncontrastive names.

   c. Look for tagmas (especially peripheral ones) that may be repetitions of a single tagmeme, and label them appropriately.

   d. Look for sequences of tagmas that may be the result of a needless cut. Combine such tagmas into one tagmeme and note the filler class of more complex syntagmas.

   e. Look for tagmas with awkward fillers that might benefit from another cut. Cut such fillers at an appropriate place and replace the tagma with two or more tagmas corresponding to the new filler classes.

   f. When all tagmas are analyzed, consider them to be tagmemes.

4. Final procedures.

   a. Reexamine the residue to see how much of it can be accounted for by your analysis. Perhaps a bit more analysis will account for most or all of the residue.

   b. Write up your tentative analysis.

c. Check your analysis against more text material.

d. Revise your write-up as needed, include lots of examples, "be kind to the reader" paragraphs, a good table of contents, a list of abbreviations, and data on the language speakers, location, time, and so on.

B. Now let's go through the outline, point by point.

1. Preliminary procedures: getting started

a. In analyzing grammatical constructions, the first thing to do is to decide which grammatical level you wish to analyze. There are two reasons for this decision. First, it is too big a job to analyze more than one level at a time. It is so big that most people get lost in it. Second, if you stick to one level, the constructions do not usually overlap and hence can be clearly separated. If you try to analyze more than one level, the constructions of one level are always included inside the constructions of the other level. (Even on a single level, we get embedding.)

We work with texts, generally, because they are more natural speech. But you can use individually elicited constructions as well, so long as you have not unconsciously brow-beaten your language helper into following your patterns; that is, we want structures natural to the language.

By texts, we mean monologues that you have recorded on tape, have transcribed on paper, and have had your language helper edit out the false starts and wrong usages.

Some language helpers may edit out too much. They may think that the vernacular should conform to the structure of a trade language, or they may have idiosyncratic ideas about style. One language helper in Papua New Guinea would edit out all repetitions, for example. Also a language helper may feel he hasn't done his job if he hasn't changed something.

Remember, everyone makes false starts and wrong usages or structures, and it will complicate our analysis if we leave them in the texts.

Elicited data is always suspect. In most cultures, individuals have been taught not to disagree and not to cause friction. Such language helpers will often let you murder the language and tell you it is all right. You may have to train your helper to disagree and be critical, but he must trust you first, because it is a big step for him. The way to get around elicited material is to tape-record long monologues such as stories, debates, arguments, sermons, and so on, and transcribe them with a language helper's help.

When you have gathered your data, it is best to work with only a small amount of them at first. For example, on the field we say, "Bring in enough texts to give us several hundred examples of the constructions you want to analyze." In the workshop we begin with a text or part of a text that will give us around a hundred examples. We analyze the hundred examples as a pilot project. When it is finished, we scan all the rest of the texts for examples that fill out our analysis and for examples that do not fit what we have done, so that we can incorporate them into the analysis.

There are two reasons for this approach. First, it cuts the size of the project down to comprehensible proportions. You do not get lost in the forest.

And, second, at any grammatical level there are a few constructions that are used over and over, and often they will account for the bulk of the data. You can get lots of examples of these even in the pilot project. And once you have analyzed them in the pilot project, you do not have to pay so much attention to them in the rest of the material. The total analytic load is reduced.

Having chosen the text(s) for your pilot project, begin by marking off the constructions you find in it. If you are working at higher-than-clause level, there will be very little of the text that is not a part of a construction. At lower levels, there may be much of the text that is not included.

One caution is in order here. If, in your first hundred examples, a large portion of them are the shortest and simplest forms, it might be well to stop and examine the short examples; write yourself some notes on them; and then ignore any further similar examples in your search for the one-hundred examples. For example, if you are studying clauses and you start with a narrative text in which most clauses are just (large) verbs, with no other words or phrases, you should examine the verbs, see what tenses and aspects they take, then continue looking for clauses with more than just verb constituents. Or, if you are studying verbs, and most of your initial examples are minimal verbs, examine them, and then ignore further minimal verbs. Collect only larger, more complex verbs.

In marking out the constructions, you may encounter things that look like the other constructions or there may be constructions that look very difficult. Leave them in residue by underlining them with a wavy line.

One rule in linguistic analysis is, "Do the easy parts first." Do not be afraid to leave a lot of residue. You can approach it later to see if you can do something with it.

In beginning a language project, you should keep a grammar notebook with a page or several pages for each kind of grammatical construction you find. If you keep such a notebook, it can substitute for the slips and sorting that is described here.

Now you have your data, the next step is to get it out where you can manipulate it.

b. Copy the constructions out onto file cards or slips. (Three-by-five slips are small. An octavo size sheet (half the size of this page or around fourteen by twenty-one centimeters or ten by fifteen centimeters) makes a convenient size.) An alternative is to take a (carbon or photocopy) copy of the text and cut the constructions out and paste them on slips. What is important is that the constructions be put onto slips that can be compared, sorted, marked up, and stacked. It will make for an easier job for both the analyst and consultant.

This work of copying or cutting-and-pasting always seems like uninteresting, repetitious busywork. But it is essential to proper analysis and cannot be bypassed. You can reduce the load by copying only the constructions you are studying. Then when you write your paper, go back to the source text and get the whole clause or sentence to put into your report.

Since it is so routine, you might get a computer to do it for you. You would still have to cut up the printout to make the slips.

In one workshop, the consultees refused to make slips or cards. The result was that they and the consultant wasted a lot of time while they flipped through notebooks looking for the examples they had found earlier.

On each slip or card, you should have the vernacular construction, a morpheme-by-morpheme gloss, a free translation, and a note about where the construction was found, that is, notebook number, page number, line number. The vernacular construction should be located near the center of the slip or card, so that you have room to write things above it.

c. Make a tentative analysis of the parts of the construction such that each part is a construction from another level or is a single morpheme. In other words, break each construction up into its constituent parts, and note your breaks and tentative labels for the constituents on the slips, above the vernacular constructions. We make these breaks and tentative labels in order to facilitate the sorting of similar constructions.

Most of the rest of this course will be aimed at giving you the vocabulary you need for these labels.

d. When you have all the constructions on slips and tentatively analyzed, begin sorting the slips into piles.

One important early sort should bring together constructions with the same filler of the nuclear slot, for example: noun, verb, conjunction, and so on. Then examine the patterns of constituents to see if certain nucleus fillers take one pattern and others take a different pattern of accompanying constituents.

This procedure would separate count versus mass versus kinship versus abstract nouns; or transitive versus intransitive verbs or clauses; or coordinate versus antithetical versus alternative versus juxtaposed sentences.

The next sorts should be made on the basis of some other features, such as how the construction is used, how it begins or ends, the length of the construction, the occurrence of certain constituents. Make as many sorts as you can think of. Some will be significant, some insignificant, and the results are usually worth the trouble. The kinds of things to look for at each level will be the topic of much of the rest of this course.

After each significant sort, add notes to the slips telling which pile they fell into. At the end, each slip may have two, three, four or more notes.

Sample sorted slip

```
                    | III.28.7                                           |
notes on            |                                    tr    raq       |
sortings            |                                 motion   pon       |
                    |         Pred              Pred          obj        |
                    |   iš-   pon           ri-  raq  taqe    winak      |
                    |   comp- arrive.there  he.II- find plural  man      |
                    |                                                    |
                    |              'He met the men.'                     |
other               |     transitive clause — with raq                   |
notes               |     verb phrase, apparently                        |
                    |     subject absent — OK                            |
```

(example courtesy Theodor Engel)

e. On the basis of the notes on the slips, put the slips into piles such that each pile has slips having the same notes. Then copy the slips in each pile onto workcharts, one workchart for each pile.

A workchart is a chart with columns labeled with the tentative constituent labels, and a vernacular construction on each line with its constituents spaced out into the columns. The purpose of this step is to bring similar constructions together so you can inspect them rapidly.

Sample workchart

possessor owner	body part or innate possession
wunduri-∅ bush.turkey-nom	djalu -∅ wing -nom
muwada -na canoe -loc	nuru-na bow-loc
ya:rama -wanji horse -erg	mani-wanji djalu -wanji hoof -erg foreleg -erg
nana-nganji miya-nji that-refr snake-ref	wayu-nji snake.track-refr

and others

(data courtesy Ted Furby)

This completes the preliminary procedures. Although they seem like busywork, stick to it until you are through. The mobility of sorting slips will make the work enjoyable.

2. We turn now to the procedures for dealing with the workcharts with a view to reducing the number of separate charts. We want to find the set of 'emic' construction types or syntagmemes.

a. The most useful first procedure is to distinguish nuclear tagmas (columns in the workcharts) from peripheral ones. Longacre lists the following rules for determining which tagmas are nuclear:

1) All obligatory tagmas are nuclear, that is, any column that is filled in every row is probably nuclear.

2) Tagmas whose fillers are cross-referenced to the fillers of nuclear tagmas are also nuclear. That is, if there is any agreement or collocation requirements between the fillers of a tagma/column which is full (obligatory) and the fillers of another tagma/column which is not full, hence 'optional', then the second tagma is also nuclear.

3) Tagmas that are distinctive to some constructions may also be nuclear; for example, transitive clauses, where object tagma would be distinctive and nuclear.

4) Nuclear tagmas are usually contiguous, not scattered throughout the constructions. So be suspicious of a 'nuclear' tagma that is off by itself, separated from the others; it may or may not be nuclear.

5) Nuclear tagmas tend to be filled with large, open classes of fillers.

6) Nuclear tagmas are usually diagnostic, that is, they are different or have different fillers in different constructions types. They are not the same in all the workcharts.

These criteria may be conflicting in some instances. For example, on sentence level, the conjunctive links are diagnostic, but are expounded by very small closed classes of conjunction morphemes. Analysts differ here, but I would give rule six more weight and would include the link as a nuclear tagmeme. Others will look at the closed class and rule five and say that the link is not nuclear.

b. Compare the workcharts, looking for systematic structural differences. Significant systematic structural differences include such things as:

1) different numbers of tagmas, especially of nuclear tagmas, that is, a construction with two nuclear tagmas enjoys at least one difference from a construction with three.

2) different order of tagmas, that is, a construction with a structure ABC as (nuclear) tagmas enjoys at least one difference from a construction with CBA as (nuclear) tagmas.

3) different filler classes, that is, a structure with tagmas +A:a +B:b has at least one difference from a structure with tagmas +A:c +B:b, where a, b, and c are filler classes of morphemes or syntagmemes, and a and c are different filler classes.

c. Separate workcharts with two or more differences, one of which involves a nuclear tagma, that is, if two workcharts have only one difference between them or no difference between the nuclear tagmas, you should not count them as separate.

d. After separating the ones that need to be separated, combine those charts that are not to be separated. These workcharts are now allosyntagmas of a single syntagmeme. Choose the workchart with the most columns as the normal form, and the others as variants of it, with some optional tagmas.

Any workchart that remains alone is also a syntagmeme, but with no variants.

We now have our set of syntagmemes for the level of the hierarchy we chose in the first step.

e. As a check, arrange the syntagmemes into a systematic matrix and look for empty matrix cells and cells with multiple fillers. Recheck your analysis to see if you can fill or simplify the bad cells.

A matrix may be a 2x3, a 2x4, a 2x5, a 2x6, a 2x7, a 3x3, a 3x5, a 3x6, a 3x7, a 4x4, a 4x5, a 4x6, a 5x5, and so on. You need to experiment with several arrangements and see which gives the most consistent rows and columns. (See R. E. Longacre: Philippine Languages, vol. II, p. 192-218, for some examples at sentence level.) (In the following chapters, we will suggest possible matrices for each level.)

3. We have our syntagmemes, but we still need to check the tentative labels on the constituents of the syntagmemes. Section 3 deals with checking these labels.

a. The first step in examining the constituents is to sort, classify, and assemble into subclasses the filler class of each constituent. Take the items in a column in a workchart, plus the items in the corresponding columns of workcharts combined with the first one and arrange them in classes of similar items and give names to the classes and subclasses.

Make a new workchart for each collection of workcharts, but this time, write in the names or labels for the subclasses of the filler class. Be sure the labels you give to filler subclasses are consistent. If a subclass occurs in more than one place, it should have the same name wherever it occurs. And different subclasses should have different names.

The advantage of replacing the filler class lists with subclass names is that it makes comparisons of filler classes much easier in the next step.

This is an appropriate time to discuss labels. In grammatical analysis, there are two distinct kinds of labels: function labels and category labels. And it is best to keep them separate and not to confuse them. Category labels are the names of syntagmemes and of morpheme classes. They are the names of linguistic chunks. Function labels are concerned with the cohesion of a syntagmeme. Individual tagmas/tagmemes have function labels, and the assemblage of the function labels of the constituents of a syntagma/syntagmeme tells how the constituents of that construction are related to each other.

Again, the purpose of this course is to learn some of these labels and to learn how to create new labels.

b. This next step is rechecking the tentative constituent labels you assigned back in step c of the preliminary procedures. First you look at constituents that have the same tentative label. Do they have the same or similar function and the same filler class? If they do, they should have the same label. If they don't, the labels should be different: perhaps they need contrasting modifiers in their labels. Now look at pairs of tagmas with different labels. If their filler classes are different, and/or their function is different, leave the contrasting labels. But if filler classes are the same and the function is the same, then the labels should be the same.

c. Look for tagmas (especially peripheral ones) that may be repetitions of a single tagmeme and label them the same way. Such repetitions might be times or locations in a clause, modifiers in a phrase, coordinate/alternative/serial bases in a sentence, or buildups and expositions in a paragraph.

The next two steps are to check your constituent breaks. Perhaps you have too few or too many columns in your workcharts, and you need to change the decisions you made back in step c of the preliminary procedures. This kind of analysis is a guess-and-check method, which gives you an opportunity to recheck your earlier decisions. Early decisions do not have to be completely correct.

d. Look for sequences of tagmas that may be the result of a needless constituent cut. Combine such tagmas (erase the line between the two columns in the workcharts) and revise the list of fillers (many of the fillers are more complex now). This often happens when stem-level constituents are treated at word level and when phrase-level constituents are accidentally treated at clause level.

Sometimes there is real ambiguity here and a decision has to be made. For example, in a clause, is the manner phrase a constituent of the clause or is it a constituent of a verb phrase expounding the predicate of the clause? Or, is a phonologically brief possessive pronoun a constituent of a phrase or is it a constituent of a possessed noun (word) expounding the head of the phrase? Such questions sometimes require an arbitrary decision. In other cases, one decision or the other will simplify the overall analysis and make it more elegant. Here, we can only say, try it both ways and see how it comes out.
(The terms in the above paragraph will become clearer as the course proceeds.)

e. Look for tagmas with awkward fillers that might benefit from another cut.

Perhaps in making your initial workcharts you noticed a column with fillers that seemed to be made of two parts, or the fillers involved two disparate things. If so, try drawing another vertical line in the workchart, making two columns out of one, and distribute the fillers into the two slots appropriately. If it seems to work better this way, then relabel the columns and go back to a.

f. When you have completed all the above steps you have the syntagmemes and their constituent tagmemes for your data at that level.

4. Next come the final procedures in which you complete the pilot project, scan the rest of the data, complete the analysis and write the final report.

a. Reexamine the residue to see how much of it fits into your analysis. You may be surprised to see how it fits in, or it may require additional construction(s) or it may remain as residue.

b. Write up your analysis. The method for writing will be covered later in the next chapter. The advantage of writing is that it makes you express your thinking and makes you clarify some points that may have been fuzzy or inconsistent.

c. Check your analysis against the rest of your texts. Look for better examples of what you already have. Look for longer more complex examples, and collect any and all examples that do not fit your analysis. They may be variants of syntagmemes you already have, or they may require the adding of syntagmemes to your analysis.

d. Now, complete the write-up, adding lots of transitional paragraphs, introductory paragraphs, and explanatory paragraphs, all of which may be called 'be kind to the reader' paragraphs.

Lastly, have a colleague read your report to see if he can understand it.

Bibliography

Longacre, Robert E. 1964. Grammar discovery procedures. Janua Linguarum Series Minor 33. The Hague: Mouton and Co.

_____. 1968. Discourse, paragraph, and sentence structure in selected Philippine languages. Santa Ana: S.I.L.

Chapter 3

Grammar write-up procedures

In the final procedure (part 4) of the taxonomic discovery procedures chapter you were told to write up your analysis of your level of the grammatical hierarchy. In this chapter, we will discuss one simple but effective way to write up an analysis.

First, you should draw up a summary chart for each syntagmeme, combining all the consolidated workcharts which make up that syntagmeme. The summary chart may have more columns than any one workchart, or it may have the same number of columns as your widest workchart. Put the (contrastive) tagmeme labels at the tops of the columns and in the columns put the (contrastive) exponent subclass names. You now have the basic part of a bidimensional array for that syntagmeme.

A. For each syntagmeme we make a chapter or a section of the chapter by using the following outline:

1. introduction to the syntagmeme,

2. the name of the syntagmeme and its bidimensional array, with its notes on agreement, permutations, and such,

3. a discussion of the various interesting features of the syntagmeme, its structure or usage,

4. and, examples of the exponent sequences of the syntagmeme.

1. The introduction to the syntagmeme should be one or more well-constructed paragraphs telling the distinctive features of the syntagmeme, its possible variants, and how the syntagmeme is used in speech or in discourse (sentences, paragraphs, and discourse).

Here is a good example of an introduction to a syntagmeme, by Mr. and Mrs. Furby (with some adaptations):

3.4. Associative noun phrase

The associative noun phrase has a basic meaning of association in that it has an obligatory element which can best be translated as 'having'. The associative noun phrase is used to describe method of travel, such as 'horse-having', 'motor-car-having', 'boat-having'. This construction indicates temporary possession of horse, car or boat, but it is not used with aeroplane since ownership is not so clearly defined. Its use also includes accompaniment such as 'man with a boy', 'child with mother', but here again possession is implied as it would not be used for 'boy with a man.' It would, however, be used for 'boy with his father.' Similarly, possession is just as strongly implied when the phrase indicates instrument, as in 'they fought each other, sticks-having.'

The associative noun phrase comprises an optional head and an obligatory association. As is seen in the bidimensional array in chart 10, the exponents of the head are limited to the modified noun phrase or a personal pronoun, while the association is expounded only by the concomitant noun phrase. Both tagmemes are inflected for case.

The associative noun phrase may occur embedded within the appositional and coordinate phrases and may expound the head tagmeme of the location modification noun phrase. The associative noun phrase may expound the subject, object, referent, locative, allative, ablative, topic and comment tagmemes of the clause.

(Note how the first paragraph tells what the syntagmeme is used for, its meaning; and the second paragraph tells how the syntagmeme is constructed. The third paragraph tells where this syntagmeme is used.)

A well-constructed explanatory paragraph has a leading statement and succeeding reinforcing or supporting statements. Three statements, each about something different, do not make a good paragraph.

You may find the introductory paragraphs difficult to write at first; if so, leave them to the end and write them all as you finish the paper. Then you can make sure they make proper transitions and do emphasize what needs to be emphasized about each syntagmeme.

2. The display of the syntagmeme in a bidimensional array has the following form:

*Figure xx. Name of syntagmeme

+ Tagmeme-1	+ Tagmeme-2	± Tagmeme-3	± Tagmeme-4
Exponent subclass-a	Exponent subclass-f	Exponent subclass-j	Exponent subclass-p
Exponent subclass-b and others	Exponent subclass-g and others	Exponent subclass-k and others	Exponent subclass-q and others
Notes on above exponents	Notes on above exponents	Notes on above exponents	Notes on above exponents
Notes on agreement, cooccurrence restrictions, permutations, cohesion, and so on.			

*Figure XX. Name of syntagmeme

Rule 1.

    2.

    3.

*The figure number and the name of the syntagmeme should appear immediately above or immediately below the bidimensional array.

The various notes and rules may overlap a bit, but try to avoid too much redundancy. The various notes and rules are where you tell the reader about the cohesion, conditioned variability, free variability, agreement, cooccurrence restrictions, limitations in certain contexts, and so on.

The '+' means 'optional', that is, that tagmeme may be absent in some examples. The '+' means 'obligatory'; the tagmeme must always be present in all examples. A '±' means that the presence or absence of the tagmeme is controlled by a rule stated below. Sometimes you may need to use a grouping of tagmemes, such as ± (+...+...) where the sequence is optional, but if it occurs, the first tagmeme must occur.

Some of you may be familiar with the four-box tagmeme of Pike and Pike, which has the following form:

±	Place on wave	Exponent
	Role	Cohesion

We are using a three-box tagmeme in this class, omitting the upper left box of the Pike and Pike tagmeme. (However, on clause level, we do not omit any box.)

The reason we omit the upper left box is that it contains only 'nucleus' and 'margin'. As you analyze various levels, the distinction between nucleus and margin will be quite clear in some places, but quite unclear in others. In these other places, the choice becomes a forced choice and is quite meaningless. And in any case, the nucleus vs. margin distinction is not especially interesting or relevant.

The problem is different on clause level where we have enough words in English for Pike and Pike to have enough labels for the two left-hand boxes, so they put labels such as subject, predicate, object, and adjunct in the upper left-hand box, and put role labels such as actor, undergoer, scope, item, and statement in the lower left-hand box. We will use similar but more extensive function labels, and a similar but more extensive list of roles. (On pages 39 and 40, Pike and Pike show a bidimensional array, which, if we omit their section of examples, looks very much like what we will do here.)

At this point, it may be well to discuss function labels versus category labels. Function labels are concerned with the cohesion of a syntagmeme. Each tagmeme in a syntagmeme is given a function name that tells how that tagmeme relates to the rest of the syntagmeme. A function name by itself is meaningless except as a hypostasis from one or more syntagmemes. That is, we can talk about 'subject' but in doing so, we are lifting it out of the syntagmemes where it occurs and are abstracting from those contexts some meaning that we attribute to the isolated label 'subject'.

Category labels are the names of syntagmemes and classes of morphemes. Thus 'noun' is the name of a class of words, of which the noun 'trees' is a member. 'Clause' is the name of a syntagmeme, of which the clause 'Joe saw Mary' is an example. Labels like 'noun' and 'clause' are category names. The analyst should avoid confusing functions labels with category labels.

It is usually necessary to abbreviate the glosses of functor morphemes. These abbreviations will tax the reader's memory less if they are long enough to suggest the whole word or words. Thus 'DISTR' is better than just 'D' for 'distributive' and 'TRANS' is better than just 'TR' for 'transitive'.

3. Following the bidimensional array of a syntagmeme and its notes and rules, it is often helpful to put into prose, in well-constructed explanatory paragraphs, some of the things that will help the reader understand better what the notes and rules mean. Or this may be the place to amplify some parts of the introduction to the syntagmeme.

4. Following the array and its explanations and discussions, you should give half a dozen good examples in context. Often the reader will not understand all your preceding material until he studies the examples. And often, good, full-context examples will answer a reader's question that you didn't think to answer.

Thus if you are displaying words or phrases, give them with the whole clauses in which they occur. If you are illustrating clauses, give full sentence examples. It is often helpful to illustrate sentences in the contexts of other sentences. At sentence level and higher, it is good to include an illustrative text, with the sentences or paragraphs numbered and labeled. Good dataful examples are often the most valuable part of your report.

You may have to double underline, or set off in some way, the part of the example you are focusing on. Or you may add an explanation after the example, telling the reader what he should see in the above example. Such an explanation is especially valuable if the example is hard to interpret or contains something new.

5. In all of this write-up of syntagmemes, we must stress the importance of all the 'be-kind-to-the-reader' paragraphs. You are an expert on your material, and you must assume the reader is off on some other topic. So you must convey all the information you have to help the reader understand and become excited about your material. Remember, be kind to your reader!

6. When you have written up and have illustrated each syntagmeme, you organize them in some logical order, write suitable introductions and transitions, add a table of contents, a list of abbreviations, and a title page, and you have a first draft of your grammar paper.

Here is a sample of a tentative write-up of the Binukid description noun phrase.

The description noun phrase in Binukid (data courtesy Ursula Post)

The description noun phrase is the most commonly used noun phrase in Binukid. It expounds various clause tagmemes and various phrase tagmemes. When it is not last in a clause, it is usually relatively short, but when it is final in a clause, it can be very long.

In its basic form, it comprises a determiner and a noun head. The determiner is expounded by focus and nonfocus particles. The noun head is expounded by nouns and other noun phrases. The full descriptive noun phrase comprises an initial deictic tagmeme, which is expounded by demonstrative pronouns, and premodifiers and post modifiers, which are expounded by adjectives, possessive pronouns, noun phrases and relative clauses.

The exponent of the premodifier is usually short, seldom being more than one or two words long. The premodifier serves a more identificatory function than does the postmodifier. The exponents of the postmodifier can be quite long. The postmodifier usually encodes old information, serving to remind the hearers of what they already know, thus serving a cohesive function in discourse. However, when this phrase is expounding the subject tagmeme of an existential clause, the postmodifiers can be used to give new information about the person or thing being introduced.

Description noun phrase

± Deictic$^{n=2}$	± Determiner	+(+Premodifier	+ Ligature)
demonstrative pronoun	focus and nonfocus particles	possessive pronoun adjective adjective phrase relative clause	ha

± Plural	+ Noun head	+(+ Ligature	+ Postmodifier)$^{n=2}$
mɨŋɨ	noun other noun phrases	ha	possessor pronouns adjective relative clause description noun phrase

Rules
1. The ligature is absent when it would be contiguous to a determiner, and is obligatorily present when no determiner is present.

2. The exponents of the premodifier tend to be only one or two words long.

3. The determiner may be absent if there is a deictic before it in the phrase.

4. The deictic may permute to the end of the phrase.

Note that in the examples below, nonfocus particles and pronouns
   will be glossed with lower-case letters and focus particles
   will be glossed with upper-case letters. The ligature will
   be glossed with a hyphen, its closest English equivalent.

Examples of the description noun phrase

1.   det   noun head

   kada   dalɨman   dumu'un   sidan   hu   balay
   (every   night   went   THEY)   the   house

      postmodifier   lig   postmodifier

      hu   hari'   ha   amin   du'un   sayawan
      the   king   -   there.was   there   dance

   'Every night they went to the king's house where there was
      a dance.'

   In the example above, the first post modifier encodes a
possessor of the noun head. The second post modifier is expounded
a relative clause which is an existential clause.

2.   deictic   det   premodifier

   Bini'ak   din   gan   ha'i   sa   huda'   kabi'ak
   (chopped   he)   earlier   this   THE   not   chopped

      lig   noun head

      ha   kayu
      -      wood

   'He chopped some wood from the woodpile.' (literally: the
      earlier unchopped wood)

   In the example above the premodifier is expounded by a relative
clause. The woodpile is newly mentioned in the story, so the relative
clause is placed in the premodifier. The <u>gan</u> 'earlier' is believed to
be a part of the clause in the premodifier.

3.   det   premodifier   lig   noun head

   Naka'aha'   sidan   hu   madagway   tuŋkay   ha   bahi
   (saw   THEY)   the   beautiful   very   -   woman

   'They saw a very beautiful woman.'

   The premodifier in the example above is expounded by an
adjective phrase.

4.   det   premod   lig   noun head

   Napadpad   ta'i   ha   bata'   sa   timbaŋ   ha   sapatus
   (dropped   this   -   child)   THE   half   -   shoe

20

postmodifier

din
his
---
his

'The child dropped one of his shoes.'

5.

	deictic det	premod		lig	n head		deic
Na'aha'	dan hayan	sa	malabuŋ	ha	±b±l	()	du'un
(saw	they) THAT	THE	thick	=	smoke		there

	deictic	lig	n head	postmodifier		
	tayan	ha	pulu'	tayan	ha	kayu
	that	=	top	that	=	tree

'They saw a thick smoke in the top of a tree.'

In the example above, one description noun phrase serves as the goal (object) of the clause and another description noun clause serves as the location in the clause. The latter phrase has another description noun phrase in its postmodifier. Note that in the last two phrases, the ligature occurs with the deictic in the absence of any other premodifier.

Now, if we look at our examples and the array above, we find that we have illustrated almost everything except the plural, the possessive pronoun, the permutation of the deictic and the double post modifiers. So at this point, we should look for another one or two examples that will illustrate these last few items, so that our examples will be complete.

B. Conventions for displaying examples

In giving examples, the best format is a three- or four-line format. The first line is the vernacular example; the second line is a literal word-for-word or morpheme-for-morpheme gloss; the third line is a free translation in good English; and the fourth line is an overhead line above the vernacular line that gives the tagmeme function labels that are being illustrated.

1. In line one, it is good to separate each morpheme in a word by a single space and a hyphen. The hyphen follows a prefix, precedes a suffix, and is not used on roots at all.

mi- ñʌk -pa
you- go -will

Note the hyphen + space following the prefix, and the space + hyphen preceding the suffix. (Some people like the vernacular spaced out to match the gloss. I prefer to have each vernacular word written compactly, with enough space between words to accommodate the long glosses.)

In general, you should hyphenate at least every morpheme you are discussing. If you are discussing word level, hyphenate every affix. If you are at phrase level, hyphenate any clitics you are discussing. If you are at a higher level where morphology is irrelevant, do not hyphenate at all if it clutters your examples. On the other hand, readers often like to see all morphemes hyphenated in all examples; it reduces their memory load.

Use a number sign '#' or a slashed zero 'Ø' to indicate zero allotagmas when the absence of an affix is meaningful. Do not underline the '#' or 'Ø', or call for italic versions of these two symbols; it may result in delays in printing.

2. The second line contains the literal glosses. Every space and every hyphen in the gloss of a word should correspond exactly to the spaces and hyphens in the vernacular word. This correspondence helps the reader match morphemes and their glosses.

If a morpheme is meaningless, or you do not know its meaning, gloss it with three dots '...'; save the question mark for glossing an interrogative-marker morpheme.

And if it takes two or more English words to gloss a single vernacular morpheme, link the words together with periods(full stops), for example:

Ø- oy -gak
he- go.and.return -again

'He went and came back again.'

Note how the reader can match vernacular and gloss by matching hyphens and spaces. Note how the gloss of oy is three words linked together by periods, and note the zero sign 'Ø' for a zero allotagma of the subject marker tagmeme. (Zero morphemes are philosophically a no-no.)

Since we use periods to link compound glosses, we do not use periods on abbreviations in the gloss line.

Similarly, if two or more vernacular words go together to correspond to one English word, they can be joined by two dots without disrupting the appearance of the vernacular line too much.

tayon..ta
because

Since we use periods to link compound glosses, we do not use periods on abbreviations in the gloss line.

In the case of an infix if you are discussing it, put hyphens on both sides of the infix and gloss both parts of the root, for example: (hypothetical)

$$\frac{\text{soka -'- 1}}{\text{run -emphatic- run}}$$

(Use this method if you are discussing the infix.)

$$\frac{\text{soka'1}}{\text{run.emphatic}}$$

This is perhaps the best way to gloss the word
if you are not discussing the infix.

$$\frac{\text{soka -'- 1}}{\text{run -emphatic- ...}}$$

This is another way to gloss the root and infix
but is perhaps the least aesthetic way.

Some linguists print semantic glosses in lower case and function glosses in upper case, especially abbreviated function glosses. Using this convention, our example above would be:

$$\frac{\text{soka'1}}{\text{run.EMPH}}$$

3. The third line should contain an understandable English translation. Avoid field-English. People working on a field tend to adopt words and grammatical patterns into their English from the local languages. Thus you have New Guinea English, Amazon jungle English, and so on. Such variants of English are often the easiest translation. But people on the other side of the world will not understand such regionalisms. So be sure the free translations are good standard English or other national language.

You may have to add additional information (sometimes in parentheses) to make the translation intelligible. Such added information is very valuable to help a reader to get a feel for what is going on.

$$\frac{\text{soka'1}}{\text{run.EMPH}}$$

'He ran!'

(Note: the /'/ in soka'1 is the emphasis infix.)

If the example is complex, hard to see, or presents something new, add an explanatory sentence or two to help the reader see what you are illustrating.

(As a general practice, it is good to gloss all of your databook entries in the national language. You can put in the glosses yourself, or you can have your language helper put them in. Then you can make your field notes available to the government or to national scholars by simple photocopy when they ask for your materials, instead of having to do a tedious rush job of translation at the last minute. There is something suspect about having three hundred pages of native texts, all unglossed, and unavailable to others.)

4. The fourth line is an overhead line above the vernacular example that gives the tagmeme function labels that are being illustrated. This line is optional, but it is especially useful at phrase, clause, and sentence levels. Here is an example from Tacaná (from Guatemalan Maya Texts, Paul G. Townsend, ed.):

   2.   Subject   Transitive Predicate: Verb phrase

i	te	su'x	k'-	ok	-e		ten	ki'i -l
and	sub.foc	woman	she.fut-	enter	-fut		remain	grind-nmzr

           Object

xi	č'oč'
the	earth

'The woman will begin grinding the clay/earth.'

On paragraph and discourse levels, these tagmeme function labels are usually placed in a vertical column at the left of the cited portion (see chapters 13 and 14).

5. Improving illustrations

For the sake of the curious reader, the construction being illustrated should be given in the context of a larger construction. Thus, for example, it is good to illustrate a phrase by giving the whole clause or sentence that contains the phrase, or to illustrate a clause by giving the whole sentence that contains it.

When we give the larger example, we need some way to signal to the reader what subpart is under focus. One convenient and aesthetically simple way for us to do this is to parenthesize the parts of the second line, or 'gloss' line, that are not in focus. For example, if we are giving an example of an instrumental phrase in Isneg (data from Rudy Barlaan), we would do it as follows:

8.	sugkawitan	mi	ka	kiwid	ngam	di	mi	masugkawit
	(reach.for.it	we)	with	spoon	(but	not	we	able.to.reach)

'We reached for it with our cooking spoons, but we could not reach it.'

Some people prefer a larger bracketing, but these usually have to be drawn in by hand.

8.	sugkawitan	mi	ka	kiwid	ngam	di	mi	masugkawit
	reach.for.it	we	with	spoon	but	not	we	able.to.reach

'We reached for it with our cooking spoons, but we could not reach it.'

We can also use the overhead line to point up the part of the example that is in focus in any of three ways. We can give the overhead line for only the part in focus or we can give the full overhead line and then mark the focussed part by an asterisk or by underlining. Consider again the Isneg example of an instrumental tagmeme.

a) Partial overhead line:
8.   Instrument

$$\left(\frac{\text{sugkawitan}}{\text{reach.for.it}} \; \frac{\text{mi}}{\text{we}}\right) \frac{\text{ka}}{\text{with}} \; \frac{\text{kiwid}}{\text{spoon}} \left(\frac{\text{ngam}}{\text{but}} \; \frac{\text{di}}{\text{not}} \; \frac{\text{mi}}{\text{we}} \; \frac{\text{masugkawit}}{\text{able.to.reach}}\right)$$

'We reached for it with our cooking spoons, but we could not reach it.'

b) Full overhead line with asterisk to show focus:
8.   Predicate   Subj *Instrument   Link Neg Subj Predicate

$$\frac{\text{sugkawitan}}{\text{reach.for.it}} \quad \frac{\text{mi}}{\text{we}} \quad \frac{\text{ka}}{\text{with}} \quad \frac{\text{kiwid}}{\text{spoon}} \quad \frac{\text{ngam}}{\text{but}} \quad \frac{\text{di}}{\text{not}} \quad \frac{\text{mi}}{\text{we}} \quad \frac{\text{masugkawit}}{\text{able.to.reach}}$$

'We reached for it with our cooking spoons, but we could not reach it.'

c) Full overhead line with underlining to show focus:
8.   Predicate   Instrument   Link Neg Subj Predicate

$$\frac{\text{sugkawitan}}{\text{reach.for.it}} \quad \frac{\text{mi}}{\text{we}} \quad \frac{\text{ka}}{\text{with}} \quad \frac{\text{kiwid}}{\text{spoon}} \quad \frac{\text{ngam}}{\text{but}} \quad \frac{\text{di}}{\text{not}} \quad \frac{\text{mi}}{\text{we}} \quad \frac{\text{masugkawit}}{\text{able.to.reach}}$$

'We reached for it with our spoons, but we could not reach it.'

Bibliography

Elson, Benjamin. 1974. Problem 165, Sierra Popoluca, in Merrifield et al.

Engel, Theodor. Verbs in Western Pokomchí. MS.

Furby, E.S. and C.E. 1977. A preliminary analysis of Garawa phrases and clauses. Pacific Linguistics, Series B. No. 42. Canberra: The Australian National University.

Merrifield, William R., Constance M. Naish, Calvin R. Rensch and Gillian Story. 1974. Laboratory manual for morphology and syntax, Revised edition. Santa Ana: S.I.L.

Chapter 4

Constituent trees

A. The basic notion of constituent trees is that each line represents a tagmeme and each node represents a syntagmeme. The lines branching from a node are the tagmemes that compose that syntagmeme represented by the node. The actual branches are a result of a 'reading' and of a 'permutation' of that reading of the syntagmeme (see R. E. Longacre, Grammar Discovery Procedures, 'Introduction').

A syntagmeme comprises an ordered sequence of obligatory and optional tagmemes, the columns of a bidimensional array. When one takes a 'reading' of a syntagmeme, one takes all the obligatory tagmemes and none, some, or all of the optional tagmemes. The result is an ordered sequence of constituents or tagmemes. Then if there are permutation possibilities given for the syntagmeme (permutation rules under the bidimensional array), one must decide whether to leave the tagmemes unpermuted (zero permutation) or to apply one or more of the possible permutations. The result is a (re-)ordered sequence of constituent tagmemes.

Now, one can draw a node, labeled with the name of the syntagmeme, and an emanating branch line for each occurring tagmeme, in the order that the tagmemes occur.

Next, one must choose an exponent for each tagmeme. In the bidimensional array, each tagmeme has a column of possible exponent subclasses. One has to choose one of these possible exponents. This is called 'exponentiation'. Then one does the same for the next tagmeme, and then the next, and so on.

For each branch coming from the first node, place a node at its lower end and label that node with the name of the exponent chosen for the tagmeme represented by that branch.

Now repeat the process for every new node that is a syntagmeme. For every node that is labeled with a morpheme class name, choose one of the morphemes and terminate that branch and node.

B. For example, suppose we have the following syntagmatic bidimensional arrays (from a tentative analysis of the Binukid declarative description clause.)

Figure 1. Declarative description clause

+ Description	+ Topic
adjective adjective phrase	description noun phrase

Figure 2. Adjective phrase

+ Adjective head	+ Intensifier
adjective	tuŋkay

Figure 3. Noun phrase

± Deictic	+(+ Modi- fier	+ Liga- ture)	± Plural	+ Noun head
demon- strative pronoun	adjective adjective phrase	ha	mɨŋɨ	noun noun phrase

+(+ Liga- ture	+ Modi- fier)n=2
ha	adjective adjective phrase

Rule: The ligature is absent when a determiner would be contiguous to it, but is present otherwise.

Figure 4. Apposition noun phrase

+ Noun head	+ Ligature	+ Apposition noun head
noun noun phrase	ha	noun noun phrase
		phrase lacks determiner

Figure 5. Name phrase

+ Determiner	+ Name head
hi	name name phrase

2. Trees

To use these arrays to make a constituent tree we start with the declarative description clause syntagmeme. We must choose both tagmemes since both are obligatory. Our reading is simply Description and Topic.

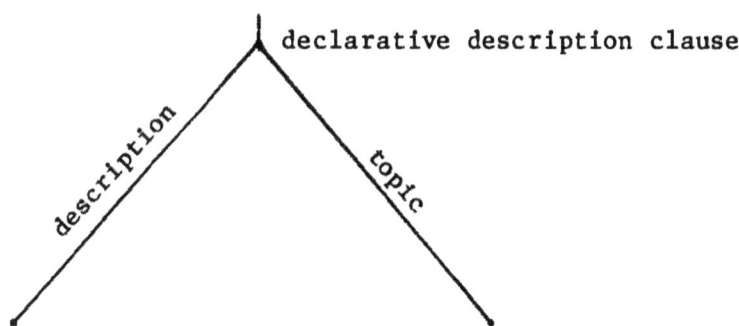

The declarative transitive clause array gives us a choice of exponents for each tagmeme. Let us choose: adjective phrase and apposition noun phrase. The tree now looks like:

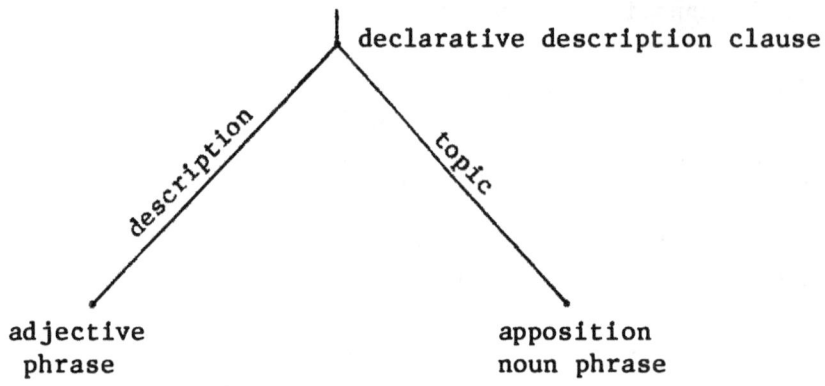

Now we expand the new nodes. First 'adjective phrase' is the name of a syntagmeme with two obligatory tagmemes, adjective head and intensifier. Also the apposition noun phrase has two obligatory tagmemes, noun head and apposition noun head.

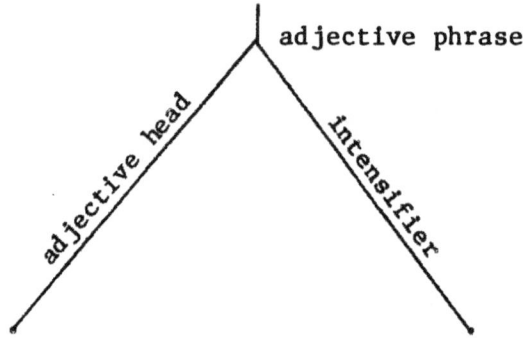

The array for the adjective phrase permits us to choose an adjective and tuŋkay. Let us choose the adjective uúmadagway 'beautiful.' The adjective phrase subtree is

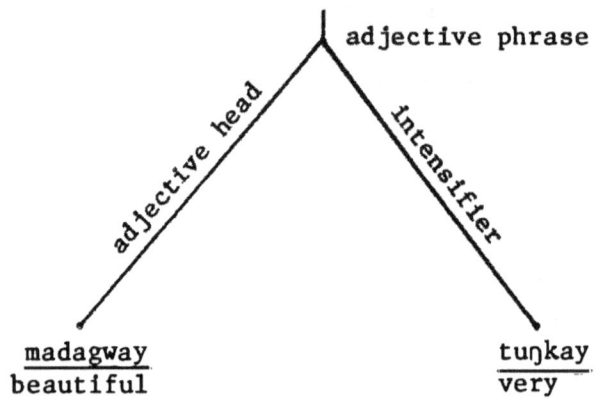

The appositional noun phrase also has two obligatory tagmemes, the noun head and the apposition noun head. Let us choose description noun phrases for both tagmemes.

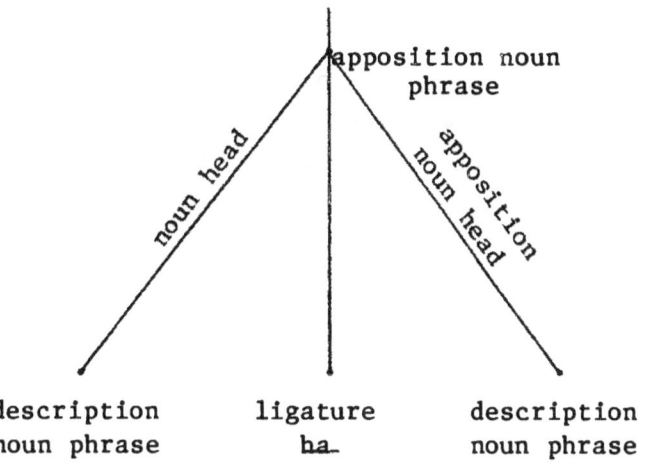

For the first description noun phrase, let us choose the determiner, the noun head and a postmodifier. And let us choose the exponents, too. For the determiner, we must choose the focus particle sa. For the noun head, let us choose the noun bata' 'child'. And for the modifier, let us choose a name phrase. The name phrase has a determiner so no ligature occurs in this phrase. The tree for the first description noun phrase is now:

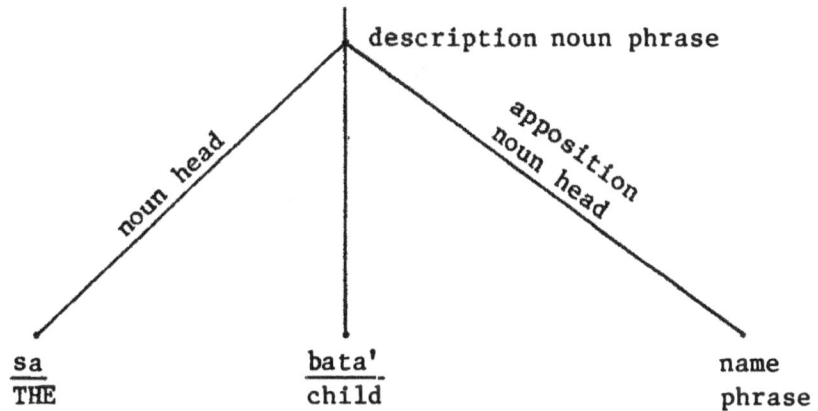

Now we can expand the name phrase. It has two obligatory tagmemes, and let us choose as exponents hi and a man's name Pedro. The tree for the name phrase is:
N14

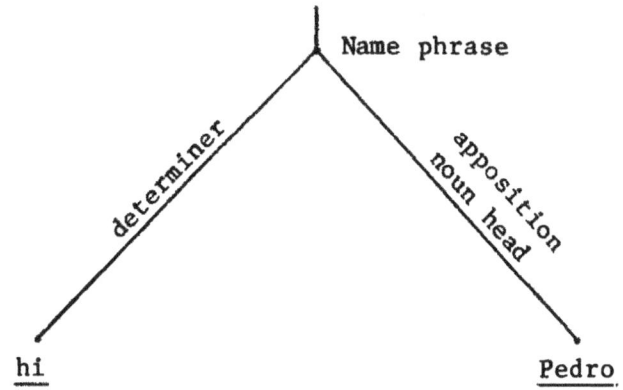

The description noun phrase in the apposition noun head still needs to be expanded in a tree. Let us choose the deictic tagmeme and the noun head. Note that we cannot choose the determiner because of the rule in the array.

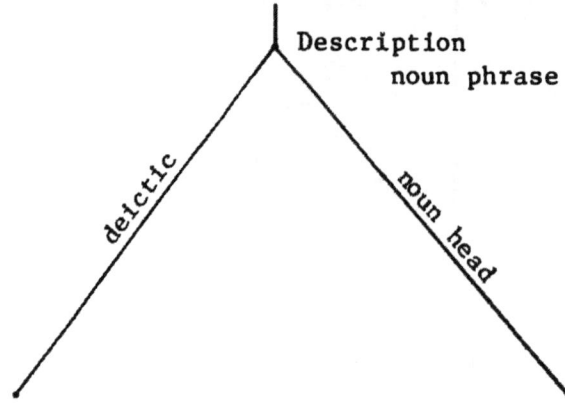

Now let us permute the deictic to the end of the phrase, and let us choose for exponents a demonstrative pronoun sa'ɨna 'that one out of sight' and bahi 'woman.' The tree for this description noun phrase is:

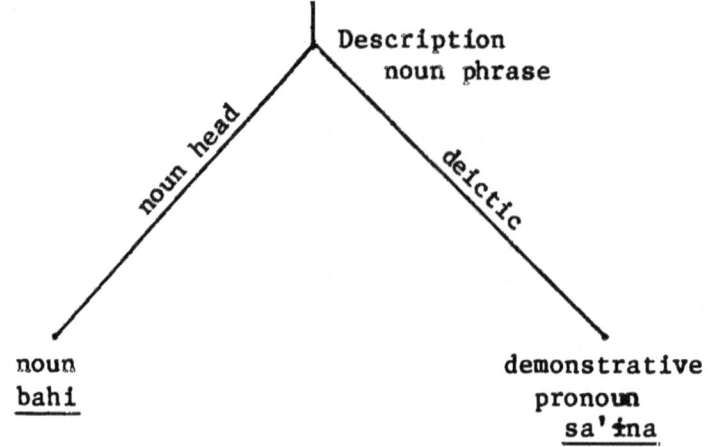

3. Final tree

Now that the branches have all been terminated, we can put them all together into one big tree (see the next page). Note how the various subtrees fit together in the derivation tree for a whole clause.

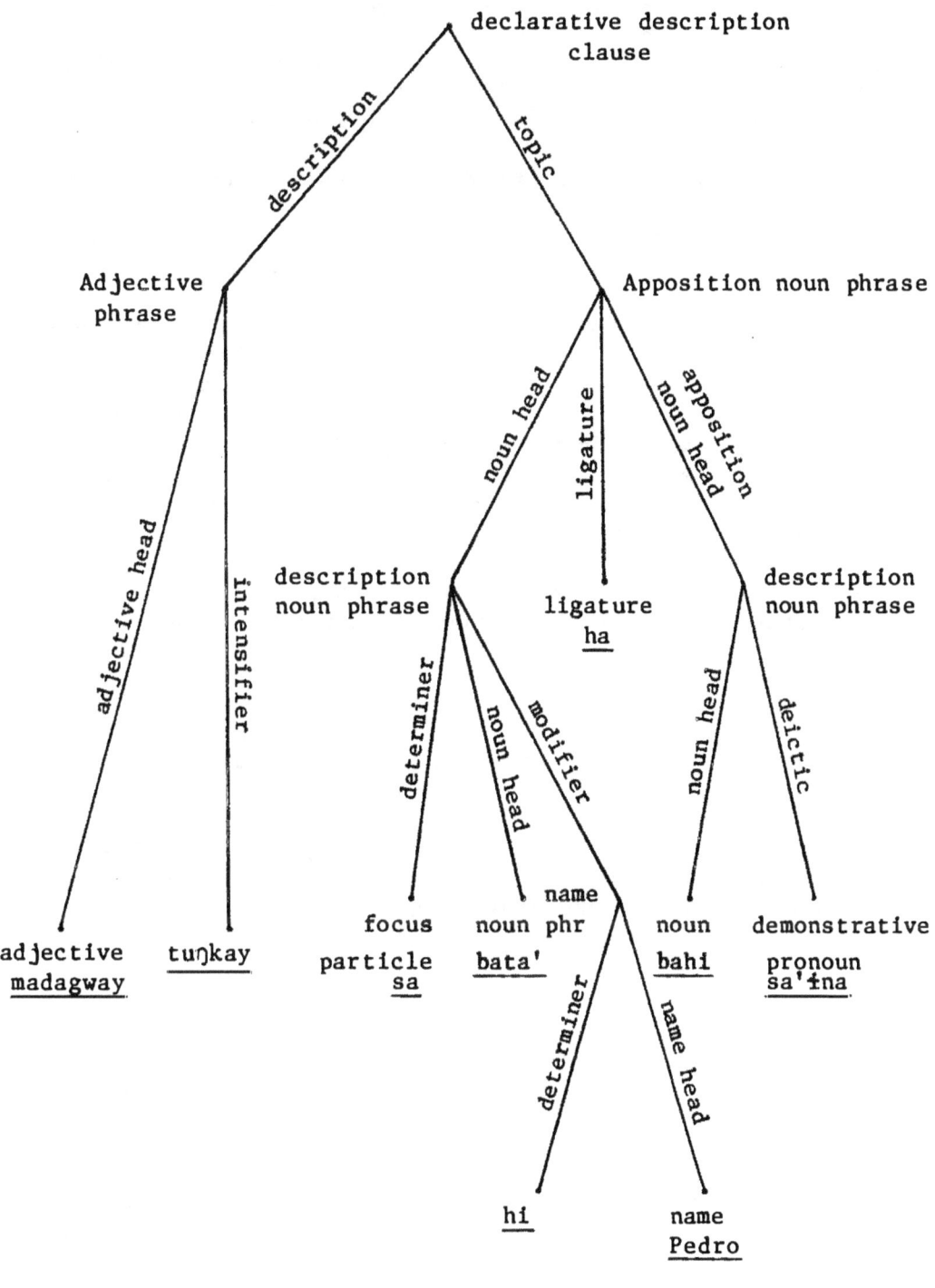

Complete derivation tree

madagway	tuŋkay	sa	bata'	hi	Pedro	ha	bahi	sa'ɨna
beautiful	very	THE	child	the	Pedro		woman	that

'That daughter of Pedro's is very beautiful.'

As you construct a tree, you may become aware of the different kinds of exponents. The normal exponents are syntagmemes from the next lower level of the hierarchy or from the 'zero' level of function morphemes such as conjunctions and prepositions. Longacre called these exponents 'primary' exponents. Trees with only 'primary' exponents come down through the various levels of the hierarchy quite neatly.

But often we get embedding, where the exponent is from the same level as its tagmeme, for example, a clause within a clause or a phrase within a phrase. Such nondescending exponents are called 'secondary' exponents.

All the other kinds of exponents are 'tertiary' exponents. They include exponents from a higher level than the tagmeme, which is called 'back-looping.' Examples are: a sentence within a clause or a clause embedded within a phrase. Tertiary exponents also include 'level-skipping' exponents; exponents from two or more levels down (but not from the zero level or single morphemes). Examples are: a phrase expounding a sentence-level tagmeme, or a word syntagmeme expounding a sentence-level or a clause-level tagmeme.

It is the secondary and tertiary exponents that give language its complexity and expressiveness. Without them, a language would be very simple.

4. Conclusion

Constituent trees have two useful purposes. One, they allow you to check your analysis.

Two, they are a beautiful way to show how syntagmemes of different levels (or of the same level) fit into each other. It allows you to show up to three or four levels on one chart, showing the constituents on each level.

Bill Leal adds the following comments.

Constituent trees can also be used transductively - for parsing. This tends to be a bottom-up kind of application, working with the data and deriving the tree backwards.

To apply this approach, we begin with a particular utterance. Then we identify the major construction type (clause, sentence, phrase, and so on) and identify its constituents (SPO, Head and margins, and so on). Each constituent is similarly analyzed and a tree is formed. With this approach, it is important to note that a prior analysis is assumed to which the parsing is related. This analysis is what gives us the labels we apply to the tree, and indeed provides us with the basic constituent analysis.

Transductive use of constituent trees is important for two reasons: (1) It gives you experience in making constituent cuts and helps you clarify your thinking about embeddings and such. (2) It is a very good check on your analysis - doing trees on data not considered specifically in your analysis forces you to verify that indeed the analysis is complete; and where it isn't, provides you with the specific items that need consideration (end of Leal's notes).

Bibliography

Longacre, Robert E. 1964. Grammar discovery procedures. Janua Linguarum, series minor nr. 33. The Hague: Mouton and Company. 'Introduction.'

_____. 1970. Introduction, Philippine languages: discourse, paragraph, and sentence. S.I.L. publications in linguistics and related fields, number 21. Santa Ana, California: S.I.L.

Merrifield, William R., Constance M. Naish, Calvin R. Rensch and Gillian Story. 1974. Laboratory manual for morphology and syntax, Revised edition. Santa Ana, California: S.I.L.

Pike, Kenneth L. and Evelyn G. Pike. 1977. Grammatical analysis. S.I.L. publications in linguistics, number 53. Dallas, Texas: S.I.L. and U.T.A.

Chapter 5

Stem-level structures

A stem is a cluster of two or more morphemes that functions in the same tagmemes as other single root morphemes do. A verb stem expounds a verb nucleus tagmeme just as verb roots do. A noun stem expounds a noun nucleus tagmeme just as noun roots do.

Stems are derived, compound, or reduplicated.

A. Derived stems have a (generally) class-changing affix attached to a root or another stem.

Stem-level affixes (derivationals) differ from word-level affixes (inflectionals) in their function and distribution. Most stem-level affixes change the class of the core morpheme; most word-level affixes do not change the class of the nuclear morpheme but add some dimension of meaning. Most stem-level affixes occur with only small, arbitrary classes of roots, most word-level affixes occur with whole classes of roots. Contrast -ize and the morphemes it occurs with and -s 'plural' with all the morphemes with which it occurs.

There are some exceptions, however. There are derivational affixes such as 'transitivizer' and 'causative' that may occur on whole classes of verb roots and change the class of the verb root. Consider the English -er 'nominalizer', which can be affixed to any verb to make a noun, for example: work -er; although it has the distribution of a word affix (occurs with a whole class of verbs), we still consider -er a stem-level affix (because it changes the class of the verb to that of a noun), and worker a derived noun stem.

Also there are some stem-level affixes with restricted distribution that do not change the class of the core morpheme, such as re- in replay, or un- in untie. How many verbs can take re- or un- and what difference do the prefixes make? And yet we count them as stem-level derivational affixes in English, because they do not fit well on word level.

   1. Derived verb stems have verbalizer affixes. Examples (in English) are:

       -ize   rubberize, winterize, Americanize, socialize, capitalize

               (-ize is the most productive verbalizer.)

      -ate   alienate, differentiate, validate

      -fy   simplify, vilify, liquefy, beautify

An array for one of these is:

Derived transitive verb stem

+ Derived transitive verb core	+ Verbalizer
noun root noun stem adjective root adjective stem	-ize

Note how the stem is a verb stem and its core is a verb core, even though the exponents of the verb core are noun and adjective roots and stems.

Note also that the array for a derived stem has only two tagmemes, no more.

2. Derived noun stems comprise a root or stem plus a nominalizer affix.

a. Derived noun stems based upon verb roots and stems

Noun stems derived from verb roots or stems may focus on the action of the verb, on the doer of the verb, on the receiver of the action of the verb, on the result of the action, on the instrument used in the action, or on the customary place for the action.

Some noun stems in English that focus on the action are those derived by adding the nominalizer -th, such as death, stealth, and tilth, or by adding -ing, such as writing, coughing, and harvesting (when used as a noun), or by adding -ment, as in retirement, employment, and advancement.

Derived noun stem-action

+ Derived noun core	+ Nominalizer
verb root or stem	-th

Derived noun stem-action

+ Derived noun core	+ Nominalizer
verb root or stem	-ing

Some derived noun stems focus on the doer of the action of the verb. In English, we have -er which gives us sender, teacher, listener, employer, director, and painter, and we have -ee, as in referee, and lessee.

Derived noun stem-actor	
+ Derived noun core	+ Nominalizer
verb root or stem	-er

Derived noun stem-actor	
+ Derived noun core	+ Nominalizer
verb root or stem	-ee

Other noun stems derived from verb roots or stems focus on the receiver of the action. In English we have -ee as in payee and retiree, and we have -ed as in disadvantaged and handicapped (when these are used as nouns).

Derived noun stem-receiver	
+ Derived noun core	+ Nominalizer
verb root or stem	-ee

Derived noun stem-receiver	
+ Derived noun core	+ Nominalizer
verb root or stem	-ed

A few derived noun stems focus on the result of the verb. In English we have -ing as in shavings and parings, and we have -tion as in construction, extrusion, impression, indentation, and correction.

Derived noun stem-result	
+ Derived noun core	+ Nominalizer
verb root or stem	-ing

Derived noun stem-result	
+ Derived noun core	+ Nominalizer
verb root or stem	-tion

Some derived noun stems focus on the instrument used in the action of a verb. In English, we use -er, which gives us such stems as mixer, cultivator, and typewriter.

Derived noun stem-instrument	
+ Derived noun core	+ Nominalizer
verb root or stem	-er

And some derived noun stems focus on the customary place for an action. In English we have very few such stems. We have pizzeria, washateria, and perhaps a few more. Other languages have more stems such as 'swimming place,' 'bathing place,' 'cooking place,' 'burying place,' and 'selling place.'

Derived noun stem-place

+ Derived noun core	+ Nominal- izer
verb root or stem	-eria

b. Derived noun stems based upon other roots and stems

Some derived noun stems are based upon adjective roots and stems. These may focus on the quality of the adjective, as happiness, cleanliness, truthfulness, and friendliness; or warmth, depth, length, or falsehood, childhood, or maturity, complexity, honesty, and opportunity.

Derived noun stem-quality

+ Derived noun core	+ Nominal- izer
adjective root or stem	-ness

Derived noun stem-quality

+ Derived noun core	+ Nominal- izer
adjective root or stem	-ity

Other derived noun stems based upon adjectives focus on the person who has that quality, such as stranger and foreigner.

Derived noun stem-person

+ Derived noun core	+ Nominal- izer
adjective root or stem	-er

Then there are the derived noun stems based upon place names, such as American, Russian, Peruvian, or Chinese, Bhutanese, or Dallasite, New Zealander, Africaner.

Derived noun stem-person	
+ Derived noun core	+ Nominalizer
place name	-ian

Derived noun stem-person	
+ Derived noun core	+ Nominalizer
place name	-ese

And there are those derived noun stems that refer to people who hold certain philosophies, such as communist, capitalist, traditionalist, and beatnik.

Derived noun stem-person	
+ Derived noun core	+ Nominalizer
noun root or stem	-ist

Derived noun stem-person	
+ Derived noun core	+ Nominalizer
noun root or stem	-nik

And there are the corresponding derived noun stems for the philosophies themselves, as communism, capitalism, and traditionalism.

Derived noun stem-philosophy	
+ Derived noun core	+ Nominalizer
noun root or stem	-ism

In English, as in some other languages, some nominalizers do not have just one function. On some roots or stems they do one thing and on other roots or stems they do something else. For example, -er usually indicates the doer of an action, but it can indicate the instrument used in an action and it can indicate the origin or place of residence. And -ee which denotes the doer of certain verb roots or stems, also denotes the receiver on certain verb roots and stems. Your language may or may not have such spillover.

3. There are also derived adjective stems. Some of these are:

-ish   boyish, childish, mannish, reddish, greenish

-(t)ic   Nordic, Asiatic

-al   normal, personal, causal, habitual, regional

-y   speedy, rocky, sandy, windy, sunny, cloudy, catty

-ful truthful, careful, doubtful, awful, wonderful

-able reliable, conceivable, receivable
~ -ible compressible, collapsible

-ive decisive, restive

-less thriftless, selfless, baseless, lifeless

The representative syntagmatic arrays are:

Derived adjective stem-a

+ Derived adjective core	+ Adjectivizer-a
noun root	-ish
adj root	
noun stem	

Derived adjective stem-b

+ Derived adjective core	+ Adjectivizer-b
verb root	-able
verb stem	

4. We have one derived adverb stem, made by adding -ly to an adjective.

 -ly speedily, readily, softly, widely

Derived adverb stem

+ Derived adverb core	+ Adverbializer
adjective root	-ly
adjective stem	

We have another adverb stem that is formed by adding -wise.

```
              Derived adverb stem
         _____
        | + Derived      | + Adverbializer |
        |   adverb core  |                 |
        |_____|_____|
        |  noun root     |  -wise          |
        |                |                 |
        |  noun stem     |                 |
        |_____|_____|
```

Some examples of this adverb stem are: clockwise, militarywise, disgracewise, dolarwise, and edgewise.

5. Derived stems, in English, can be embedded in derived stems. Consider the following:

      true   adjective root
      truth   derived noun stem
      truthful   derived adjective stem
      truthfully   derived adverb stem
      truthfulness   derived noun stem

      boy   noun root
      boyish   derived adjective stem
      boyishly   derived adverb stem

      compress   verb root
      compressible   derived adjective stem
      compressibility derived noun stem

B. Compound stems comprise two roots which are joined together to make the equivalent of a new root. The basic class of the roots used is quite variable. In English, the problem is blurred by the phenomenon that many roots can be either a verb root or a noun root, depending upon their usage. Consider such an example as 'smokestack'; both roots involved can be either a verb root or a noun root.

    Here are some more examples where at least one of the roots is clearly a noun root or a verb root.

      bedroom   paperback   playground
      doorway   cheeseburger driveway
      hallway   bookcase   blackbird
      stairwell   hubcap   supermarket
      songbird   football   broadcast
      tablecloth   blowpipe   footpath

Compound noun stem

+ Compound noun core-1	+ Compound noun core-2
noun root	noun root
verb root	noun stem
adjective root	

For <u>footsore</u>, <u>crestfallen</u>, <u>fireproof</u>, and so on, the array is:

Compound adjective stem

+ Compound adjective core-1	+ Compound adjective core-2
noun root	adjective root
	adjective stem

English has many compound noun and adjective stems in which one of the members is an adverbial particle:

noun	adjective
uptake	upstream
offset	downstream
upkeep	openair
putdown	openended
upstart	uptight
takeover	overdone
setup	
cutout	

Compound noun stem

+ Compound noun core-1	+ Compound noun core-2
adverbial particle	verb root / noun root
verb root / noun root	adverbial particle

Note how the reversal of order can be handled in the array.

43

English also has another set of compound verb/noun stems in which the first member is a bound particle. These bound particles are: mono-, bi-, di-, tri-, un-, re-, neo-, a-, anti-, dis-, and others.

Examples are:

monoplane	bistable	ditransitive
tricycle	tripartite	uncouple
undo	redo	reestablish
neonazi	amoral	anticommunism
disengage		

Some of these are noun stems, some are verb stems, and some are adjective stems. Here is an array for the above noun stems:

Compound noun stem

+ Compound noun core-1	+ Compound noun core-2
bound particle mono- tri- neo- anti-	noun root noun stem

C. The third group of stems is the class of reduplicated stems. Here, the two roots are phonologically similar. Often the second is almost meaningless.

zigzag	nitty-gritty	nono
willy-nilly	dumbdumb	wishy-washy
boo-boo	shilly-shally	hodgepodge
mishmash	flimflam	kowtow
helter-skelter	crisscross	

Most of these are reduplicated noun stems, but some are reduplicated adjective stems and reduplicated verb stems.

Reduplicated noun stem

+ Reduplicated noun core-1	+ Reduplicated noun core-2
noun root noun stem nonsense root	noun root noun stem nonsense root
	second member is phonologically related to the first member

Kaje (data by Carol McKinney) has reduplicated verb stems. Here are two examples:

ə- ni- swa- swat
he- will- dwell- dwell

'He will just dwell (there).'

ə- hywa   srwan- srwan
he- said   sit- sit

'He said, "Sit down."'

The reduplication of the verb root gives an exclusive emphasis to the verb in Kaje.

D. There is a special class of reduplicated stems in which the members are onomatopoeic roots. English has only a few such as: choochoo and ticktock. Other languages may have a large number of these onomatopoeic reduplicated noun or verb stems.

E. We can make a matrix of stem-level constructions that may help show the crisscrossing of vectors:

	noun	verb	adjective	other
derived				
compound				
reduplicated				

F. In English, there is only a fine line separating attributive noun phrases and compound noun stems. The rule is that if the second member is destressed, the two noun roots or stems are a compound noun stem. If the second member retains its stress, the pair is an attributive noun phrase. Technical terms start out as attributive noun phrases, and if they become common enough, they become compound noun stems. If they lose popularity, they revert to becoming attributive noun phrases. An example is 'walkie-talkie', which is now a reduplicative attributive noun phrase, because both parts retain their stress. Undoubtedly during combat, among troops using the instrument, it became a reduplicative compound noun stem, with 'talkie' being destressed. Other examples are: sportscar, rumbleseat, doubletree, nuclear fuel rods, and so on.

G. Conclusion

In this chapter, we have been describing clusters of two or more morphemes that act as single morphemes. Often, stem structures are a way to change nouns into verbs and vice-versa. Sometimes stems are combinations of morphemes to name some new item or action.

Some languages have a rich stem level, as English does, and others may have a sparse, small stem level. If a language has a small stem level, it probably has enrichment at word or phrase level to compensate.

Bibliography

Elson, Benjamin and Velma Pickett. 1962. An introduction to morphology and syntax. Santa Ana: S.I.L.

Gleason, H. A. 1961. An introduction to descriptive linguistics. Revised edition. New York: Holt, Rinehart, and Winston.

Harris, Zellig. 1951. Methods in structural linguistics. Chicago: The University of Chicago Press.

Hockett, Charles F. 1958. A course in modern linguistics. New York: The Macmillan Company.

McKinney, Carol. 1980. Kaje serial verb constructions. MS.

Nida, Eugene A. 1948. Morphology: the descriptive analysis of words, 2nd edition. Ann Arbor: University of Michigan Press.

Young, Richard E., Alton L. Becker and Kenneth L. Pike. 1970. Rhetoric: discovery and change. New York: Harcourt, Brace and World, Inc.

Weber, David. 1976. Suffix as operator analysis and the grammar of successive encoding Llacón (Huánuco) Quechua. Documento de trabajo núm. 13. Yarinacocha, Perú: Instituto Lingüístico de Verano.

Chapter 6

Word-level structures

A word, in general, is a root belonging to an open class surrounded by affixes from closed classes. Sometimes the root is replaced by a stem, and sometimes it is not a member of an open class, but these are the exceptions.

The ordering of the root and affixes is usually quite fixed and uninterruptible. Words tend to be quite inflexible in their internal structuring.

A word is usually a minimal utterance, found in answers to questions and in context. If a person stammers or gets confused, he will usually go back to the beginning of a word to begin anew.

It sometimes happens that what is grammatically a single large word is written as two or more words in practical orthography. This mismatch is all right, so long as it is consciously recognized. You don't have to change either one.

A. Nonverbs

1. Nouns

Noun words may have number affixes, such as singular, dual, and plural. In Kiowa, nouns are inherently singular, dual, or plural, and take affixes to achieve the other numbers.

Noun words and names often take diminutive affixes. In English, most childhood names have a -y suffix, for example: Billy, Jacky, Chrissy, Chucky, and Tommy, and so on. In Spanish, nouns take a diminutive -(c)ito/-(c)ita, for example: cas -ita 'house -little,' gat -ito 'cat -small.masculine', puebl -ito 'town -small', pobre -cita 'poor little girl'.

Diminutive name (English)

+ Name nucleus	+ Diminutive
name root	-y

Diminutive noun (Spanish)

+ Noun nucleus	+ Diminutive
noun root	-(c)ito
name root	-(c)ita

Nouns are marked for gender in some languages. The classics in this area are Latin and its daughter languages, such as Spanish. Most gender systems include feminine, masculine, and often, neuter. Some gender systems may add other semantic components and end up with from four to ten genders.

In Spanish most nouns and adjectives are marked for masculine or feminine.

Adjective

+ Adjective nucleus	+ Gender marker
adjective pronoun root	-o 'masc' -a 'fem'

Noun

+ Noun nucleus	+ Gender marker
noun	-o 'masc' -a 'fem'

Examples:

una niña pequeña
a   girl small

'a small girl'

un niño pequeño
a   boy small

'a small boy'

In some languages, nouns are marked for case, such as 'nominative', 'accusative', 'genitive', 'dative', and so on. Case markers are more relational than modificational, and as such, are more like relators on phrase level. They tell how the noun is used in context.

It may be all right to treat case on word level, in which case the array would be:

Noun (word)

+ Noun nucleus	+ Case marker
noun root	<-o>
noun stem	<-a>

But it might be better to put 'case' on phrase level (see Prepositional phrases in the next chapter):

49

Case-marked noun phrase

+ Noun axis	+ Case relator
noun	⟨-o⟩
noun phrase	⟨-a⟩

Rule: The case marking clitic is suffixed to all the adjectives and nouns in the exponent of the axis.

And, lastly, nouns may be marked as possessor or as possessed. Mayan languages mark possessed nouns with a possessed marker prefix: (Pokomchí data from Ted Engel)

<u>u-</u> <u>axaw</u> Juan   <u>ki-</u> <u>so'</u> <u>winaq</u>
his- father John   their- clothes man

'John's father'   'the men's clothes'

<u>w-</u> <u>axaw</u>   <u>qa-</u> <u>so'</u>
my- father   our clothes

'my father'   'our clothes'

Possessed noun

+ Possession marker	+ Noun nucleus
Class II person prefixes	noun

In many languages, nouns are divided between obligatorily possessed nouns and optionally possessed nouns (and, sometimes, obligatorily nonpossessed nouns). These possession differences may be reflected by affixes on the nouns.

2. Kinship terms

Closely related to nouns are the kinship terms, which may be inflected for possession, respect, age, and so on. Kinship nouns often participate in different phrase types than regular nouns.

Here are some kinship words from Golin (Papua New Guinea), reported by Gordon Bunn:

Kinship word (Golin)

+ Kinship nucleus	+ Possessor marker	+ Honorific
kinship root	possessor suffix	-bi(a)
		the honorific is used only for kin same age as ego or older.

Examples:

ebin -an -bi
wife -my -respect

'my wife'

nen -in -bi
father -your -respect

'your father'

3. Pronouns

Pronouns may be simple morphemes as in English, or there may be special pronoun roots that are inflected for person, number, and case. Their analysis is especially difficult when roots and affixes are phonologically fused.

Here are the regular pronouns of the Selepet language (K. A. McElhanon. Pacific Linguistics, Series A, no. 26, Papers in New Guinea Linguistics no. 13, 1970.)

	Singular	Dual	Plural
1st person	nak	net	nen
2nd person	gak	yet	yen
3rd person	yak	(yak)yet	(yak)yen

Pronouns-a (Selepet)

+ Person marker	+ Pronoun nucleus
n- 'first'	ak 'singular'
g- ~ y- 'second'	et 'dual'
y- 'third'	en 'plural'

g- 'second person' is used in the singular, y- is used in dual and plural.

Third person dual and plural is distinguished from second person dual and plural by a complementary yak 'third person singular'.

4. Adjectives

Adjectives may be affixed with emphasizers such as comparative and superlative, for example: in English we have big, bigg -er, bigg -est, tall, tall -er, tall -est. Few languages have both comparative and superlative.

Adjective

+ Adjective nucleus	± Augmenter
adjective root	-er 'comparative'
adjective	-est

5. Prepositions and conjunctions

And, finally, prepositions and subordinating conjunctions are, in some languages, inflected for the person of their object. Mayan languages have inflected prepositions.

Uspantec (as reported by Margot McMillen) has several different inflected prepositions. One type has person prefixes:

Prepositions-a (in Uspantec)

+ Preposition marker	+ Person marker	+ Preposition nucleus
č<u>i</u>- 'toward' p<u>i</u>- 'for' and others	person prefixes set II	<u>e</u> benefactive

Example:

<u>či</u>- w- <u>e</u>
toward- me- benefactive

'to me'

<u>pi</u>- w- <u>e</u>
for- me- benefactive

'for me'

Some Melanesian languages have inflected subordinating conjunctions, my-because, your-since, his-reason, our-purpose, and so on.

B. Verbs

The most highly inflected words around the world are verbs. In some languages, verbs are so highly inflected that it takes a fairly large clause to translate them into English.

Affixes on verbs can be classified as person markers, tenses, aspects, voices, moods, and relationals. We will treat them in this order.

1. Person markers

Person marker affixes are either subject person markers or object person markers or indirect object or benefactee or referent person markers.

Person markers usually have first, second and third person distinctions. Singular and plural may be distinguished, as well. Some languages add a fourth person, and some add a dual number. Fourth person is an additional third person that is further away or less in focus than third person.

Sometimes it is difficult to tell whether pronouns are free pronouns or are pronominal affixes. There are three criteria that may help in the decision.

1. Separability: Can other clause-level tagmemes come between the pronoun and the verb? If they can, the pronoun is probably free.

2. Complementary distribution: Is the pronoun in complementary distribution with a noun or noun phrase having the same function, or, stated another way, do the pronoun and noun or noun phrase occur together with the same function? If they do, the pronoun is probably an affix. If one or the other, but not both, occurs, the pronoun is probably a free pronoun.

3. Phonology: Does the pronoun have an accent or other features of free words? If it does, it is probably a free pronoun.

Person marker affixes often comprise several sets of marker affixes. Often one set will occur contiguous to a root or stem initial consonant, another set with vowel-initial roots or stems. Sometimes one set will occur with present-tense markers and another set will occur with past-tense markers, or one set will occur with continuous aspect and another set will occur with all the other aspect markers. There may be other distinctions, too.

One phenomenon that occurs frequently is 'ergativity'. First, the 'nominative-accusative' system has one set of subject-person markers (nominative) that serves on both transitive and intransitive verbs; and another set (objective) for object-person markers. This is the system that we are most familiar with as speakers of English.

Another possible system is an 'ergative' system in which there is one set of marker affixes, called 'absolutive' that serve as subject-person marker affixes on intransitive verbs and as object-person markers on transitive verbs; and another set called 'ergative' that serves as subject-person markers on transitive verbs. We can diagram the differences as follows:

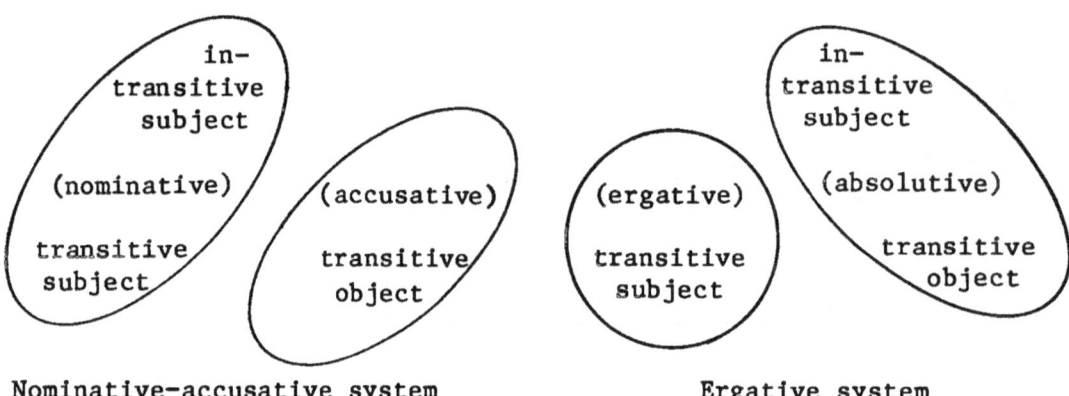

Nominative-accusative system   Ergative system

A language with an 'ergative' system often also has other verbal forms such as 'antipassive'.

Another pattern of person marker usage is the so called 'active' pattern, in which active verbs of both transitive and intransitive types take one subject marker affix, called 'agent', and nonactive verbs take the same affix that marks transitive object for their subject marker. The chart for the active pattern is as follows:

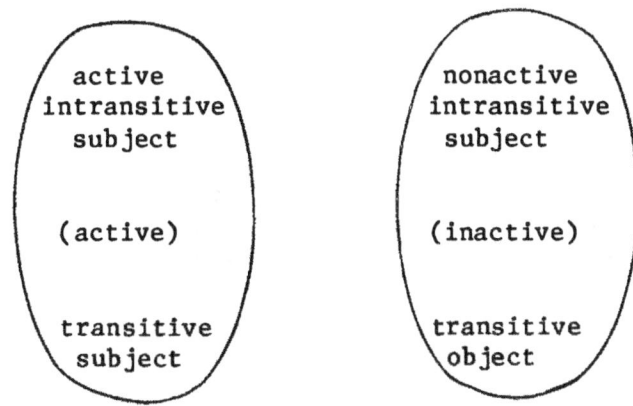

Examples of an active intransitive are:

    Henry ran away.   Henry coughed. (on purpose)

And examples of a nonactive intransitive verb are:

    Henry died.   Henry coughed. (involuntarily)

(See Fillmore, 1968, pp. 53, 54.)

2. Tense

Tenses mark the time of the action of the clause. The time may be relative to the time of telling, or, in some languages, it is relative to the time set at the beginning of a paragraph or chapter. In the latter case, a future tense on a verb is future to the story line but may be past relative to the hearer.

Tenses are basically past, present, and future, but there can be elaborations of these, such as remote past, immediate past, immediate future, and remote future, or historical past, narrative past, and impending future. In a few languages, a distinction is made between night and day, especially in the near past, present, and near future tenses. (Night and day distinctions might also show up as aspect markers.) Some languages have 'earlier today' and 'later today' tenses.

Sometimes a tense will have a basic meaning and some metaphorical extensions. For example, a speaker may use a recent past tense for an action that should have far past tense because he wants to imply its relative recentness compared to something else.

Temporal aspects include such tenselike meanings as completed and incompleted, or completive, present continuous and impending future. Some temporal aspects may involve punctiliar versus continuous.

3. Aspects

Some aspects add increments of meaning to the action of the verb root or stem.

Some aspects refer to the duration of the action of the verb. These include inceptive or inchoative (begin to), cessative (stop), terminal (stop), habitual (used to, keeps on), and durative (still, yet).

Still other aspects deal with the emotions of the agent, such as desiderative (want to), volitional (intend to), optative (hope to), phobic (afraid to, reluctant to), abilitative aspect (able to), potential (might), and possibility aspect (be possible that or possibly or be impossible).

Other aspects deal with location, such as nearness aspect, farness aspect, accompanying motion aspect (coming or going or returning), and awareness aspect (action is visible or action is invisible, secret).

Other aspects have to do with manner and with importance, such as stative (have done or had done), emphatic aspect (really), diminutive aspect (a little bit or unimportantly), augmentive aspect (a lot or strongly or forcefully), expected aspect (as expected or characteristically), unexpected aspect (unexpectedly or suddenly), accidental, avolitional, unwittingly, inadvertently, or unintentional aspect, potential aspect (might happen or could happen), and relevance or relative action aspect (this action leads to the next or this action is the result or outcome of the previous action).

Some languages have a distinction between sort of a specific versus general aspects of action. The specific is a bit more emphatic and certain. The general is less specific and less emphatic.

And you may find aspects not mentioned above. Aspects are the 'open' class of affixes in the languages of the world. It is not at all rare to hear of a new kind of an aspectual affix in some newly analyzed language. Just remember that aspect affixes add meaning to the verb. Other affixes relate the verb to participants, time, and context.

Here is an example, the Golin independent verb:

Declarative independent verb in Golin

+ Verb nucleus	± Negative	+ Tense	+ Subject person marker	+ Accomp	+ Aspect	+ Mood
verb root	⟨-ki⟩ 'not'	-∅ non-future	-bin 'I, we'	-i 'also'	⟨-u⟩ unrestricted	-e info interr
		⟨-na⟩ future	-n ~ -∅ 'you'		⟨-g⟩ restricted	-o vocative
		-nala near future	⟨-m⟩ 'he, she, they'		⟨-i⟩ specific	-a narrative
			-bil two			-e indicative
			⟨-1⟩ 'I'			-i definitive
						-iray emphatic 'of course'
					⟨-u⟩ with -o, -a, -e.	
					⟨-g⟩ with -o, -a, -e, -i, -iray.	
					⟨-i⟩ with -o, -a,	

⟨-u⟩ unrestricted aspect is continuative, customary, habitual, process

⟨-g⟩ restricted aspect is complete in itself without reference to any other specific action or time.

⟨-i⟩ specific aspect refers to a specific event and time.

The aspects in the array above are probably significant to discourse structure.

The Uspantec declarative transitive verb has the following array:

Declarative transitive active verb in Uspantec

± Tense	+ Object marker	+ Subject marker	+Trans verb nucleus
š- past	in- 'me'	in- 'I'	trans verb
ø- nonpast	at- 'you'	a- 'you'	trans verb stem
	t(i)- 'him / her'	x- 'he / she'	
	o:x- 'us'	qa- 'we'	
	at- 'you.pl'	a- 'you.pl'	
	t(i)- 'them'	x- 'they'	

± Pl mkr	± Oblig asp	± Rep asp	± Dir asp
-taq plural (2nd 3rd person)	-na 'have to'	-čik 'again'	-bi(k) 'away'
		-qe 'only'	-ɫ 'toward'

58

4. Voice

Voice affixes deal with how the participants in a clause are emphasized and deemphasized. Passive voice is the most frequent voice affix. It brings the recipient of the action or the undergoer into prominence and deemphasizes the agent or actor of the verb. Of all the voices, passive voice is most likely to have important uses in discourse, being used to keep principal participants in focus, even when they are the recipient or undergoer of an action.

Ergative languages often have an antipassive voice which puts extra emphasis on the actor or agent and deemphasizes the recipient or undergoer, and marks the verb as intransitive. In some languages, the recipient or undergoer is even elided from the clause. In Mayan languages, the antipassive is used to emphasize somebody who does something, without upsetting the story line and the focuses on the thematic participants. The actor of the antipassive may be the thematic participant or someone else, but the antipassive clause is seen as almost parenthetical emphasis as far as the story line goes.

The antipassive is also used in questions asking 'who' did the action, and in answers to such questions, 'X did it'. The antipassive is also used in actor-nominalized clauses, 'the one who did or does' (see Butler and Peck).

In other languages, the antipassive means 'incomplete' or 'partial' accomplishment of the action. (See Hopper and Thompson.)

An absolutive voice stativizes the action of a verb or breaks up the action on the verb in various ways. In some languages, it ascribes the action as a characteristic of the actor or agent, such as 'you are sneezer,' that is, that is your characteristic.

Another voice is object-incorporation voice, in which the object noun is incorporated into the verb phrase, making the clause otherwise objectless. The effect of this is to make the clause sort of a generic statement that is used in recapitulation, amplification, and repetition of some of the preceding sentence.

Some languages also have instrument promotion voice, in which the verb is marked with an instrument marker, and then the instrument is permuted to the front, or near-front, of the clause. All this gives special prominence to the instrument.

More common affixes that should be classed as voice affixes are causative, reflexive, and reciprocal markers, since these all affect how participants are related to the verb.

Often, however, causative is a stem-level derivational affix, and the reflexive and reciprocal meanings are conveyed by pronouns in the object tagmeme. Some languages, however, have reflexive and reciprocal markers in the verb.

A reflexive clause is: <u>He painted himself.</u>

A reciprocal clause is: <u>They painted each other.</u>

5. Moods

Mood markers include the usual declarative, imperative, and interrogative markers. Some languages add polite imperative, prohibitive, hortatory, and jussive markers. In languages with medial verb and final verb distinction, mood markers occur only on sentence-final verbs.

Mood markers tell the hearer how the verb and clause relate to him. Is he to take it in and enjoy it; is he supposed to do something; is he supposed to reply?

For example, the Golin declarative independent verb given earlier is converted to an interrogative verb by expounding the mood tagmeme with -o 'yes or no interrogative' or with -e 'information interrogative' (also used for alternative questions). It can also be made into an imperative verb by expounding the mood tagmeme with <-o> 'simple imperative', -a 'abrupt imperative' or -ga 'imperative request.'

Closely related to the mood markers are the disclaimer markers that convey the speaker's certitude. Such markers can mean: 'I know what I say is true because I saw it happen'; 'I was told this'; 'I deduce this', or 'I suppose or guess this.'

Disclaimers give trouble to Bible translators where languages require 'I was told this' marker throughout the book of Luke, for example. The translator would like to add more certainty.

6. Relationals

In languages with medial and final verbs, the medial verbs have relational markers. The simplest relational marker tells whether to keep the same actor or not for the next clause.

Some highland New Guinea languages even have look-ahead person markers on a medial verb. Such markers tell who is going to be the actor in the next clause, if he is to be different from the actor of this clause.

Some relational markers also tell how closely the present action and the next action are related in time. They can indicate that the next clause follows closely in time or follows some time later.

Some languages place 'subordinating conjunction' relational affixes on verbs. Such relational affixes mark their verb and clause as the reason for another verb or action, as the result, as the time, as the condition, and so on. Often one has the feeling that these affixes belong not so much to the verb as to the clause as a whole and should be treated as clause-level clitics.

The Kobon medial verb has the following array: (Note the relationals)

Medial verb in Kobon

+ Verb nucleus	+ Medial marker
verb root	⟨-em⟩ anticipated action same subject
	⟨-nê⟩ anticipated action different subject
	-el simultaneous action same subject
	-ningk purpose action same subject

In some languages, nominalized and adjectivized clauses have special affixes on the verbs. These affixes are a kind of relational affix that tell how this clause is related to its context, whether the clause is acting as a noun or as a modifier to a noun.

Bibliography

Bunn, Gordon. 1974. Golin grammar. Workpapers in Papua New Guinea languages vol. 5. Ukarumpa: S.I.L.

Butler, James and Charles Peck. 1980. The uses of the passive, antipassive, and absolutive verbs in Tzutujil. Journal of Mayan Linguistics, vol. 2, no. 1.

Dawson, Marcus and May. 1974. Kobon phrases. Workpapers in Papua New Guinea languages, vol. 6. Ukarumpa: S.I.L.

Engel, Theodor. Verbs in Western Pokomchí. MS.

Fillmore, Charles J. 1968. The case for case. Universals in linguistic theory, ed. by Emmon Bach and Robert T. Harms, pp. 1-88. New York: Holt, Rinehart, and Winston.

Hopper, Paul J. and Sandra A. Thompson. 1980. Transitivity in grammar and discourse. Language 56:2.251-99.

McMillen, Margot. The substantive phrase of Uspantec. MS.

McMillen, Stanley. How action is expressed in Uspantec. MS.

Chapter 7

Allomorphs

Grammatical analysis presupposes that the data are spelled emically, usually in a phonemic alphabet and spelling, but, sometimes, in popular orthography. (Rarely are the phonemic orthography and practical orthography the same.) Allophones of phonemes are irrelevant to grammar; they belong in a phonological description and in a pedagogical grammar. In grammar, we have allomorphs that differ from each other in terms of full phonemes, and it is our purpose here to review how to describe such phonemic changes.

The most common phonologically conditioned allomorphs are those that can be described by a rule in terms of the environment. There are several such rules: assimilation, deletion, metathesis, fusion, harmony, and epenthesis.

A. Assimilation

Assimilation describes the process in which a sound becomes more like its environment. The change can be in manner of articulation or in place of articulation. Frequently a sound becomes voiced or unvoiced to become more like its neighbor(s).

The form of the rule for such a change is:

> The phoneme /x/ of morpheme 'meaning' assimilates
> to its voiced (or voiceless) counterpart /y/ when
> it is contiguous to (or precedes or follows) a voiced
> (or voiceless) consonant (or vowel)

where /x/ and /y/ are phonemes differing only in voicing, and /x/ is (usually) the initial or final phoneme of the morpheme under discussion.

If this is a general rule for the whole language, you would replace the "of morpheme 'meaning'" with 'always'.

A sound may change its place of articulation. A common example of this is a nasal assuming the place of articulation of a following consonant, or a stop assuming the place of articulation of a preceding contiguous stop.

The rule for such alteration is:

> The phoneme /x/ of zyyx 'meaning' assimilates
> (fully) to the place of articulation of a contig-
> uous (or preceding or following) phoneme (class)
> being replaced by /w/

where /x/ and /w/ differ only in place of articulation and /x/ is (usually) an initial or a final phoneme in the morpheme zyyx.

For example, in English, the /n/ of in- 'not' assimilates fully to the place of a contiguous stop, becoming /m/ or /ŋ/.

> Examples: in- eligible
> in- terminable
> im- proper
> iŋ- capable

Another way to handle the above problem is to use a morphophonemic symbol for the phoneme that gets changed. We could write the phoneme as /N/ and the morpheme as iN- 'not'. The rules would have to be the same, replacing /n/ with /N/, but writing the capital /N/ alerts the reader to look for allomorphic changes. When describing such processes as assimilation, harmony, fusion, and deletion, you should consider using capital-letter morphophonemic symbols as a way to alert your readers to the allomorphic changes. (These morphophonemic symbols may conflict with the use of capital letters to symbolize voiceless phones.)

The opposite of assimilation is dissimilation, but it is rare. Its rules would be similar in form.

B. Deletion, reduction or elision

Another common allomorphic change is deletion, reduction or elision, the loss of an initial or final phoneme in certain contexts. The rule looks something like this:

> 'The phoneme /x/ of morpheme 'meaning' is deleted when it is contiguous to (or precedes or follows) a consonant (or vowel or affix).'

Or a general rule might be:

> 'The final vowels of verb stems are deleted when they are followed by a suffix beginning with a vowel.'

As a general rule, it is better to use deletion than addition. Choose the longest allomorph of a morpheme for the canonical form, and then delete parts of it. If you choose a shorter allomorph and then add things to it in certain contexts, the rules become more confusing and ad-hoc looking.

For example, Mayan verb roots end with a consonant most of the time. But in the presence of some suffixes, a vowel appears between the root and the suffix. The vowel quality is not predictable. So some people set up root classes of verb roots, each class taking a certain 'thematic' vowel. A far more elegant solution is to write the verb root ending with a vowel. The rule is much simpler. You delete the final vowel in certain (most) environments.

So choose deletion over addition, if you can.

Deletion may involve initial or final phonemes, sequences of phonemes or syllable patterns. In many languages, when two identical phonemes come together, one is deleted because reduplicated phonemes do not occur. Sometimes when two phonemes that are similar in some way come together, the first or second is deleted.

And in some languages with long sequences of affixes, there may be deletion and metathesis to rearrange the phonemes to make prettier syllable patterns that are easier to pronounce.

Note, however, that when an affix (or root) is wholly deleted, its function still remains. Consider the plural and possessive affixes in English, as in the following example:

'the girls' club'

(= 'the girl -s -'s club')

Even though either -s or -'s is completely deleted, its function is still present (see Stemberger).

C. Metathesis

A process that helps make words easier to pronounce is the process called metathesis, in which two phonemes trade places, or one skips over to the other side of the other phoneme.

For example, the sequence /yt/ may become /ty/. So the
rule would be:
'When /y/ is contiguous to a following
stop, it metathesizes with that stop.'

Or, if it metathesizes only in certain cases, the environments would need to be added to the rule.

D. Fusion

Another process that helps make words easier to pronounce is the process called fusion, in which two phonemes are replaced by a third. Often the sequence /au/ is replaced with /o/.

Consider the sequence:

got you -> goča

where the /ty/ is fused into /č/.

The rule looks like this:

'When the /x/ of morpheme-a 'meaning-a'
and the /y/ of morpheme-b 'meaning-b'
become contiguous, they fuse and become /z/.'

E. Harmony

Phonemic harmony is important in some languages. Vowel harmony is important in some southwest Asia (Asia Minor) languages, and tongue-root harmony plays a part in some southeast Asia languages and in some African languages. What usually happens is that roots have certain vowels and consonants, and affixes have some vowels or consonants that agree with some parts of the root.

There may be full harmony, where the vowels or consonants of the affix agree completely with some part of the root. There may be partial harmony, where the affix phonemes are adjusted toward a part of the root, but the agreement is not complete.

For example, Mayan languages have an affix which we write -Vn 'passive' in which the vowel /V/ harmonizes with the vowel in the last syllable of the root. (/V/ is a /u/ for /u/ in the root, /o/ for /o/ in the root and /a/ for all other vowels in the root. (/V/ is a morphophonemic cover symbol.)

Harmony may include nasalization. In Amarakaeri of Peru, oral and nasalized vowels contrast in root morphemes and are phonemically distinct, while vowels in affixes are conditioned by the root phonemes and may be either oral or nasal depending upon their contexts. Affixual vowels are nasalized when they are contiguous to nasal vowels or consonants. It is a kind of harmony of nasalization. Some have called this phenomenon 'spreading nasalization' (see David Payne's 1975, U.T.A. thesis: Nasality in Aguaruna).

F. Replacement

Sometimes a phoneme or phoneme cluster is replaced by another very different phoneme, where the process cannot be described as assimilation, dissimilation, or fusion, or other process. We simply say that one phoneme or phoneme cluster is replaced by another phoneme in certain contexts, without assigning any other process.

G. Epenthesis

Epenthesis is the insertion of a glottal stop, a semivowel, or a centralized vowel to aid pronunciation in certain contexts. It should be used with caution. It is usually better to posit a longer form for a morpheme and then delete the extra part than it is to add it by epenthesis.

But in some languages, there are rules that insert a /y/ between /i/ and another vowel, and /w/ between /u/ and/or /o/ and another vowel. Or there may be a rule to insert a glottal stop between two vowels that become contiguous at morpheme boundaries. And some languages add an epenthetic schwa or barred /ɨ/ between consonants that come together. If the epenthetic rule is simple and general, you can use it.

H. The three parts of an allomorph description

All the rules given so far have three parts. The first part is the phoneme involved and what morpheme(s) it is a part of. The second part of the rule is the process involved and the resultant phoneme. The third part is the environment in which the change occurs. If the rule applies throughout the language, the part three can sometimes be omitted or shortened.

There are various ways of arranging these three parts. They can be 1, 2, 3, or 1, 3, 2, and there are various arrangements of independent and dependent clauses. But be sure all three parts are given.

There is a standard shorthand formula that looks like:

$$x \longrightarrow y \:/\: z\underline{}$$

or $\quad x \longrightarrow y \:/\: \underline{} z$

where $\underline{} z$ means preceding z, and $z \underline{}$ means following z.

Notice that each rule has its three parts, the initial phoneme, the resultant phoneme, and the environment. These formulas do not name the process going on, and are deficient to that extent.

In this course, we prefer the full English prose statement.

I. Grammatically conditioned allomorphs

Sometimes no reasonable environment or reason for allomorphic changes can be found. The changes seem to be arbitrary. In this case, we can set up grammatically conditioned allomorphs. We divide the environmental class of morphemes into subclasses, and say that each subclass occurs with a different allomorph of the morpheme that is changing.

Thus we set up subclasses of verb roots that cooccur with different allomorphs of an affix. Often it is useful to make a matrix display of two dimensions, the allomorphs in one dimension and the subclasses in another. A matrix is easy to see and helps reinforce your rules.

The rules are of the form:

'The allomorph x-a of x 'meaning' occurs with subclass-a of verb roots,

The allomorph x-b of x 'meaning' occurs with subclass-b of verb roots,'

and so on.

J. The place of allomorph statements in a grammar paper

The allomorph rules should be given beneath the bidimensional array where the morpheme sequences in question are described. Then if you need to refer to them again, put in a reference to where they are found, or else restate the rules.

Since the examples follow the bidimensional array, the reader needs your allomorph rules just above the examples and below the array in order to follow your examples.

Bibliography

Nida, Eugene A. 1948. Morphology: the description of words. Second edition. Ann Arbor: University of Michigan Press.

Payne, David Lawrence. 1974. Nasality in Aguaruna. Thesis presented to the University of Texas at Arlington for the Master of Arts degree.

Stemberger, Joseph Paul. 1981. Morphological haplology. Language 57:4. 791-817.

Chapter 8

Phrase-level structures

On phrase level, there are generally three broad classifications of phrases: A) noun phrases and modifier phrases, B) prepositional phrases, and C) verb phrases. The phrases in group A) usually consist of one of more heads with various modifiers and qualifiers. The phrases in group B) always have only a relator and an axis. The relator is expounded by a preposition, a postposition or a case marker, and the axis is expounded by a group A) phrase. The phrases in group C) have one or more main verbs and various auxiliary verbs, adverb modifiers, and various particle modifiers.

A. Noun phrases

1. Description noun phrase

We will discuss the tagmemes in the description noun phrase first:

a. Noun head

The main tagmeme in a description noun phrase is the noun head. It is typically expounded by nouns, attributive noun phrases (see sec. 3.), certain pronouns, nominalized verbs, and, in some languages, possessed noun phrases.

Nouns may be count nouns such as house, man, rock, mountain, cup; or mass nouns such as air, water, sand, wheat, and wind; which cannot quantified (that is, *one air, *two wheats).

Some languages make a distinction between innately possessed nouns (obligatorily possessed) such as body parts, clothing, and kinship terms, such as arm, face, skirt, sandal, brother, mother, cousin, and innately unpossessed nouns (optionally possessed) such as tree, stone, cloud, machete, chair, and others. Just which nouns are innately possessed differs from language to language, and cannot be predicted in advance.

Some languages can use pronouns in the noun head of a description noun phrase and some cannot. English, for example, allows only numbers, for example, 'the last complete one,' 'the big three.'

Nominalized verbs typically include actor-nominalized verbs such as work+er, sing+er, employ+er, sometimes goal-nominalized verbs such as employ+ee, and often action-nominalized verbs such as sing+ing, hunt+ing, die+ing (dying), die+th (death).

b. Modifiers

Modifier tagmemes follow or precede the noun head and are expounded, usually, by adjectives. In some languages, the ordering of adjectives is fixed, so that the modifier tagmemes can be differentiated as size modifer, color modifier, quality modifier, quantity modifier, evaluation modifier, and so on. In other languages, including English, the ordering of the adjectives is variable, controlled by other factors, such that it seems best to set up a single modifier tagmeme and let it recur as many times as needed. In this case such a modifier has the whole class of adjectives and numerals as exponents (see Vendler).

Size adjectives include big, small, tall, short, and others. Color adjectives include black, white, red, mottled, speckled, striped, and others. Quality adjectives include rough, smooth, hard, soft, old, young, round, strong, weak, sweet, sour, and others. Quantity adjectives include some, few, many, and others. (Numbers and number phrases also expound a quantity modifier.) Evaluation adjectives include good, bad, dear, darling, awful, and others.

c. Limiter

The limiter tagmeme is expounded by particles such as just, or only, and usually occurs near the beginning or the end of the phrase.

d. Deictic or Determiner

Deictic or determiner tagmemes are expounded by definite articles, the, indefinite articles, a, an, demonstrative pronouns, this, that, these, those, quantity words, any, every, all, and, in some languages by focus markers or discourse-level or paragraph-level topic or nontopic marker particles that mean something like 'our hero,' 'the person we were talking about earlier,' 'this new participant,' and others.

The word 'deictic' and its related form 'deixis' are derived from the Greek word for 'pointing'. In linguistic theory, anything that helps the hearer to pin down the exact persons, times, and places being talked about is called 'deictic' (see Fillmore). Since the word deictic does have other uses in linguistic theory, some people prefer to call the deictic tagmeme in a noun phrase a 'determiner' tagmeme.

In some languages, a deictic-like tagmeme called 'focus' is posited. It is expounded by focus-marker particles that also function on paragraph or discourse level. It is useful to posit such a tagmeme if such focus markers occur in the same phrase with demonstrative pronouns or articles. The tagmeme expounded by the pronouns and articles can be called a 'determiner,' and the one expounded by the focus particles can be called 'focus,' or 'emphasis.'

The order of tagmemes in a noun phrase varies from language to language. Some languages place the noun head at the end of the phrase, some at the beginning, some somewhere in the middle. English and some Mayan languages do the latter, placing the simpler modifiers ahead of the noun head and placing the more complicated modifiers after the noun head, for example: the old red barn on the farm on Highway 81, a middle-aged man too drunk to walk, a man for all seasons, and others. Some languages, such as Spanish, prefer one order and give special meaning to a different order, for example: un hombre grande (a large man) contrasts with un gran hombre (a great man).

Summary of description noun phrases

Description noun phrases are related transformationally to descriptive clauses which also consist of a noun and an adjective, and in some languages they are homophonous, in which case whether an adjective + noun or noun + adjective pair is a description noun phrase or is a descriptive clause depends entirely upon its usage: is it a name of something, or is it a statement about an item? In other languages, the order of tagmemes and the presence of determiners may make the difference between a clause and a noun phrase.

Here is an example, adapted from Joyce Huckett's 'Notes on Iduna Grammar,' in Workpapers in Papua New Guinea Languages, Volume 3. (She called this phrase the 'basic noun phrase'.)

Description noun phrase in Iduna

+ Referent	+ Deictic	+Premodifier^n	+ Descrip noun head	+Premodifier-1
free pronoun (demonstrative pronoun)	demonstrative pronoun	adjective	noun possessed noun phrase	adjective phrase adverb substantive modifier modifying clause
may permute to end of phrase		may permute to post-head position		

	+Postmodifier $n=2$	+ Quantifier	± Limiter	± Emphatic
	adjective coordinate adjective phrase	numeral quantity adjective enumerative pronoun coordinate numeral phrase	-gagana 'only' mo'a 'only'	emphatic pronoun
	may occur twice	may permute to elsewhere in clause	choice is probably controlled by context	

Rules:

1. Various changes in order are possible but the order in the display is the preferred order.

2. The description noun head is usually to the fore of a phrase.

3. Usually, a description noun phrase is only two or three tagmemes long. Long description noun phrases are rare.

4. The quantifier tagmeme may permute to other places in the matrix clause, thus becoming discontinuous with the noun phrase of which it is a part.

5. The referent tagmeme may permute to the end of the phrase, and only then may the demonstrative pronoun expound it.

For a discussion of the very complicated description noun phrase in English, see Peter Fries, 1970.

Relative clauses

One reason the noun phrase is complicated in English is that we use a lot of embedded clauses in our noun phrases. Such clauses are either nominalized clauses or (modifying) relative clauses.

Here are some examples of relative clauses:

'The man who sold you that car sold you a lemon.'

'The girl (that) you told me about yesterday came again today.'

'The idea that we could win was preposterous.'

'These instructions for filling out these tax forms aren't very clear to me.'

We handle these relative clauses as exponents of a post (noun head) modifier, for example:

+ Description noun head	+ Post- modifier
noun	relative clause
noun phrase	qualifying prep phr
	location prep phr
	possessor prep phr-b
and others	and others

In English and in related languages, we have 'restrictive' and 'nonrestrictive' relative clauses. 'Restrictive' relative clauses are essential to the identification of the person or thing referred to by the noun phrase. A 'nonrestrictive' relative clause merely adds more information. In 'The man who sold you that car is a scoundrel,' we need the relative clause to tell who the man was, so it is a restrictive relative clause. But in 'Sam Scott, who sold you that car, is a known scoundrel,' we do not need the relative clause to tell who is meant. So it is a nonrestrictive clause.

In languages without relative clauses, the same information can be handled by clause pairs, for example: 'The man sold you that car, therefore he is a scoundrel,' (restrictive); 'Sam Scott is a known scoundrel, and he sold you that car,' (nonrestrictive).

2. Possession phrases in English

The status of possessor and possessed noun phrases differs from language to language. Often the possessor constructions expound a tagmeme within the description noun phrase, as it does in English, and other languages make the possessed+possessor a separate phrase type.

In English, we have two ways to express possession. One is to expound the determiner tagmeme of the description noun phrase with a phrase that has the clitic relator -'s.

This possessor phrase has the following array:

Possessor phrase-a in English

+ Possessor axis	+ Possessor relator-a
name description noun phrase (possessor pronoun)	-'s

Rule: The axis cannot be expounded by a pronoun when the phrase is expounding a determiner tagmeme.

Examples:

'John's old blue car' (compare with 'an/the old blue car')

'the company's new president'

'the robin's nest'

In English, when a possessor phrase-a or a possessor pronoun is expounding the determiner tagmeme, a possession intensifier own may expound a following modifier tagmeme. For example:

'John's own car'   'his own car'

'the sailing club's own new president'

'my own red pencil'

Intensified possessor phrase-a in English

+ Possessor Head	± Intensifier
possessor phrase-a possessor pronoun	own

Possession may also be expressed by expounding the first postmodifier tagmeme of a description noun phrase with a possessor preposition phrase.

Possessor phrase-b in English

+ Possessor relator-b	+ Possessor axis
of	description noun phrase
	possessor phrase-a
	possessor pronoun

Rule: The possessor phrase-a must have its axis expounded by a pronoun, a name, or a kinship word or phrase.

Examples:

'the history of my family' is paraphrasable as 'my family's history'

'the new home of the insurance company'

'the mayor of the city'

'that new car of Henry's'

'that book of yours'

'that chair of your father's'

(Note that the demonstrative pronoun seems to be obligatory in the last three examples. Note too, that possessor phrase-b can be paraphrased by a possessor phrase-a.)

3. Possessed noun phrase in other languages

Unlike English, some other languages have a separate possessed noun phrase, in which they embed description noun phrases.

Possessed noun phrase

+ Possessor	+ Possessed head
possessor prepositional phrase	noun description noun phrase other noun phrases

The order of the tagmemes may be different, and it may be the possessed head that would be expounded by a case-marked phrase instead of the exponent of the possessor, or both may have case-marked (prepositional) phrases.

4. Qualifying prepositional phrase

The possessor phrase-b is homophonous with another prepositional phrase in English, which might best be called a 'qualifying prepositional phrase.'

Qualifying prepositional phrase in English

+ Qualifying relator	+ Qualifying axis
of	description noun phrase

Examples:

'a heart of gold'

'the magnitude of the deficit'

'a clear demonstration of wishful thinking'

'a bottle of root beer'

Clearly, none of the above can be paraphrased by a possessor phrase-a, so they cannot be possessor phrase-b's. However, one will often encounter examples on the borderline between possessor phrase-b and the qualifying prepositional phrase. (In the case of bottle of root beer, the bottle of may be reanalyzed as a quantifier in the noun phrase; see Fries.) The qualifying prepositional phrase is used in many different ways.

Other languages also often have a certain general-purpose prepositional phrase. Some of the Mayan languages have a phrase with the preposition ri or či that can be used in almost any marginal tagmeme, where it seems to take attention away from that tagmeme. If a speaker wants to give more emphasis to a marginal tagmeme, he uses the prepositional phrase more appropriate to that tagmeme.

5. Attributive noun phrase

An attributive noun phrase consists of a noun head tagmeme and an attributive tagmeme. The two tagmemes may come in either order, depending upon the language. In English, the attributive precedes the noun head. Both tagmemes are expounded by nouns, with the attributive noun modifying the head noun. Examples are: kitchen counter, airport noise, grade school principal, influenza vaccine, highway signs, brick house, apple pie, space vehicle, and kidney beans.

Attributive noun phrases may be embedded in the attributive and noun head tagmemes, as in ball+point-pen, crank+case-oil, top+speed-jet+planes, canary+yellow-sports+car.

Attributive noun phrases are closely related to compound noun stems which also consist of two noun roots. In English, there is a tendency to make often-used attributive noun phrases into compound noun stems, and to reduce little-used compound noun stems to attributive noun phrases. For example, sports car was a compound noun stem for some of us of the older generation; it was pronounced as one word with stress on the first syllable only. But for the younger generation, it has reverted back to two words, each stressable in an attributive noun phrase. Icecream probably began as an attributive noun phrase ice cream, and is now a compound noun stem with stress on the first syllable only, at least for some people.

Attributive noun phrase

+ Noun attributive	+ Noun head
noun root	noun root
noun word	noun word
attributive noun phrase	attributive noun phrase

6. Coordinate noun phrase

Coordinate noun phrases consist of two or more coordinate noun heads with one or more coordinate links expounded by and, with, or -with (that is, the conjunction may be a phonologically bound clitic). In some languages, the coordinate noun phrase is limited to only two noun heads, sometimes to three heads.

Some English examples are: <u>apples, oranges and plums; men and women; scientists, artists, politicians and businessmen.</u>

The formula for the syntagmeme is +(Coordinate Head-1)n +Coordinate Link +Coordinate Head-2. This formula gives an indefinite number of items with an <u>and</u> between the last two. Other languages may use a conjunction between each pair. The formula, then, is +Coordinate head-1 +(+Coordinate link +Coordinate head-2)n or (Coordinate head-1 +Coordinate link)n An example of the latter formula might be <u>apples-with, pears-with, plums-with, oranges-with.</u> Some languages have other patterns; some are very flexible in their use of coordinate conjunctions.

Coordinate noun phrase

+ Coordinate^n noun head-1	+ Coordinate link	+ Coordinate noun head-2
noun	and	noun
description noun phrase	with	description noun phrase
attributive noun phrase		attributive noun phrase

Perhaps we should distinguish between coordinate noun phrases and coordinate description noun phrases, because the former can occur in places where the second cannot.

If we do distinguish them, we would have two arrays:

Coordinate noun phrase

+ Coordinate^n noun head-1	+ Coordinate link	+ Coordinate noun head-2
noun	and	noun
attributive noun phrase	with	attributive noun phrase

Coordinate description noun phrase

+ Coordinate^n noun head-1	+ Coordinate link	+ Coordinate noun head-2
description noun phrase	and with	description noun phrase

The coordinate noun phrase, then, can expound the noun head tagmeme of the description noun phrase, for example:

'Those old, tumbledown stores and office buildings are scheduled for demolition.'

The coordinate description noun phrase would be:

'Those old, tumbledown stores and those unused office buildings will be torn down soon,'

or 'They bought Smith's grocery store and Brown's book store.'

7. Serial noun phrase

The serial noun phrase is similar to the coordinate noun phrase, except that it lacks the link tagmemes and, instead, has an additional appositional summary tagmeme which is expounded usually by a brief noun phrase. Examples are:

white willow, yellow gum, green gum, those three trees;

Davey, Jim, Bob, Andy, you four; boys, girls, everyone.

The syntagmeme formula is +(Serial noun head)^n +Appositional summary.

Languages that have both the coordinate noun phrase and the serial noun phrase usually limit the coordinate phrase to two or three items, and use the serial noun phrase to list a greater number of items.

Serial noun phrase

+ Serial noun head-1	+ Serial noun head-2	+ Serial^n noun head-3	+ Appositional summary
noun	noun	noun	pronoun
name	name	name	noun phrase
descriptive noun phrase	descriptive noun phrase	descriptive noun phrase	pronoun phrase
		May occur several times	Usually includes a quantifier

Some languages, however, blend the coordinate noun phrase and the serial noun phrase into a single syntagmeme with both links and an (optional) appositional summary. English is in this class of languages, for example: boys and girls, everyone; the old and the young, whole families; Andy, Jim and Bob, you three.

8. Alternative noun phrase

Alternative phrases are composed of two or more alternative heads separated by an alternative link expounded by the conjunctions or and nor. The alternative head tagmemes are expounded by almost any kind of pronoun, noun, or noun phrase. An alternative introducer expounded by either and neither may introduce the phrase: either if or is used; neither if nor is used.

The syntagmeme formula is ±Alt intro +Alt noun Head-1n + Alt Link +Alt noun head-2 which gives an or or nor only between the last two heads, for example: pronouns, nouns or noun phrases; nails or screws; neither pronouns, nouns nor noun phrases.

The syntagmeme formula may be +Alt Intro +Alt noun Head-1 +(+Alt Link +Alt noun Head-2)n with a rule that the +Alt Link is taken as always + or always -, that is, it is always absent or is always present, except that the last one is always present. Relaxing this rule permits the conjunction to occur or not to occur between any pair of Heads. If we encounter such a phrase in English, we see it as containing embedded alternative phrases, for example: apples or bananas, plums or prunes or pineapples (apples or bananas is one phrase, plums or prunes or pineapples is another; or perhaps plums or prunes is one phrase and pineapples is a third alternative).

Alternative noun phrase for English

+ Alternative intro	+(+ Alternative noun head-1^n	+ Alternative link)^n	+ Alternative noun head-2
either	noun	or	noun
neither	noun phrase	nor	noun phrase
May occur only if only one alternative noun head-1 is present.		This link is obligatory between the last two heads. It is either present between all other heads or is absent between all other heads.	

Perhaps we should distinguish between alternative noun phrases and alternative description noun phrase.

Alternative noun phrase

+ Alternative intro	+(+ Alternative noun head-1	+ Alternative link)^n	+ Alternative noun head-2
either	noun	or	noun
neither	attributive noun phrase	nor	attributive noun phrase

Example: 'Please get me some small red <u>pencils</u> <u>or</u> ball-point <u>pens</u>.'

(where the alternative noun phrase expounds a description noun head.)

Alternative description noun phrase

+ Alter- native intro	+ (+ Alter- native noun head-1	+ Alter- native link)^n	+ Alter- native noun head-2
either	description noun phrase	or	description noun phrase
neither		nor	

Example: 'Please get me either some red pencils or some red ball-point pens!'

9. Appositional noun phrase

An appositional noun phrase consists of noun head and apposition tagmemes. Both are expounded by nouns or noun phrases that refer to the same entity. The order of the two tagmemes depends upon the language. Generally, the apposition nominal is more specific than the head nominal, or is as generic as the head nominal but the two together are more specific than either one individually.

In English, the noun head comes first and is followed by the apposition. Examples are:

my uncle, the mayor;   my cousin, your uncle;

my brother, John;

a metal table, the kind they sell at Sears;

smallpox, the scourge of developing nations;

two main divisions: the New World monkeys on the one hand
   and the Old World monkeys and hominoids on the other
   (with a coordinate NP in the apposition);

things that no other 35mm SLR camera can do, things that
   make picture-taking easier.

Appositional noun phrase

+ Noun head	+ Noun apposition
noun	noun
noun phrase	noun phrase
name	name
name phrase	name phrase

10. Reduplicated noun phrase

Many languages use reduplicated phrases to express grammatical categories such as plural, intensification, reduction, or distribution. For instance, <u>dog dog</u> could be 'dogs', 'many dogs', 'a dog here and a dog there and another one over there'. <u>Red, red rose</u> can mean 'red roses', 'a very red rose' (English?), or 'a reddish rose'.

In English, reduplicating a noun or adjective seems to be more poetic than common.

Reduplicated noun phrase

+ Noun head	+ Reduplicating noun head
noun-i noun phrase-i	noun-i noun phrase-i
	This exponent must be the same as the exponent of the first tagmeme.

A language may permit reduplicating whole phrases, for example: <u>a big green snake, a big green snake,</u> and the meaning of the reduplication can be any of those mentioned above.

11. Replacive noun phrases

Replacive phrases are rare among the world's languages. English has three varieties, but their usage is rare; in fact, they are often viewed as reduced antithetical sentences because of their obligatory phonological break.

Examples of replacive noun phrases are:

  John, not Peter;   sand, not dirt;

  milk, not water;   men, not boys;

and not John but Peter; not dirt but sand;

  not punch but milk;   not boys but men.

English can also use _instead of_ and _rather than_ as links in the replacive phrase.

 'I want three cans of paint, instead of four (cans of paint).'

 'He bought a four-door car rather than a two-door one.'

The fact that a language lacks replacive phrases is no great handicap. The same ideas can be expressed in antithetical sentences.

 'I want a blue, not a red, tie.'

can be said as:

 'I don't want a red tie, but (instead) I want a blue one.'

Replacive noun phrase-1

+ Replacing noun head	+ Negative link	+ Replaced noun head
noun noun phrase	, not , instead of , rather than	noun noun phrase
	The comma intonation break is obligatory with not	The head of the noun phrase may be elided if same as in first noun phrase

84

Replacive noun phrase-2

+ Negative intro	+ Replaced noun head	+ Replacive link	+ Replacing noun head
not	noun noun phrase	, but	noun noun phrase
		comma intonation break is obligatory	some elision of repeated items

12. Compound noun phrase

Compound phrases are usually idiomatic combinations of nouns (or adjectives or verbs) whose meanings are more than or different from the sums of the meanings of the individual parts. For example, in some Mayan languages, 'my-older.brother my-younger.brother' means 'all my brothers' or even 'all my siblings'; 'my-grandfather my-grandmother' means 'my ancestors'; 'my-chickens my-ducks' means 'all my little domesticated animals'.

Compound noun phrase

+ Compound noun head-1	+ Compound noun head-2
noun noun phrase	noun noun phrase
The choice of exponents is limited to certain idiomatic pairs	

B. Other phrases

1. Phrase search matrix

Many of the complex structures that we have been discussing for noun phrases also apply to other types of phrases. They can be arranged in an etic search matrix as follows, with the construction types on one axis and the types of exponents of the head tagmemes on the other axis:

Matrix of phrase types

	Attributive	Coordinate	Serial	Alternative	Appositive	Reduplicative	Replacive	Compound
Noun								
Noun phrase								
Kinship								
Pronoun								
Name								
Name phrase								
Possessed noun phrase								
Possessor noun phrase								
Number								
Number phrase								
Adjective								
Adjective phrase								
Adverb								
Adverb phrase								
Time word								
Time phrase								
Location word								
Location phrase								
Time prepositional phrase								
Location prepositional phrase								
Referent prepositional phrase								
Instrumental prepos. phrase								
Dative prepositional phrase								
and so on								

2. Kinship phrases

A kinship phrase may consist of a determiner, an honorific, a possessor, and a kinship head tagmemes, but it usually cannot take all the modifiers that are found in the description noun phrase. The determiner is expounded by demonstrative pronouns, the honorific by adjectives such as <u>dear</u>, <u>dear-deceased</u>, honorable, beloved. The possessor is expounded by possessive pronouns and possessive phrases, and the kinship head is expounded by nouns denoting kinship. Examples are: <u>my</u> dear aunt; that dear-deceased grandfather of <u>mine</u>; <u>my</u> honorable cousin.

Again, not all languages would have the kinship phrase separate from the description noun phrase. It is doubtful that it would be a separate phrase in English. However, for another language, the kinship phrase should be set up at the preliminary stage of analysis and retained until it is shown to be a subtype of some other phrase, or not.

Kinship phrase

+ Determiner	± Honorific	+ Kinship head
demonstrative pronoun	dear	kinship word
	beloved	name
possessor pronouns	younger	name phrase
possessor phrase	honorable	
	American	
article		
not used in vocative		

Attributive kinship phrases are possible. We do not have them in English except as <u>cross cousin, country cousins, city cousins</u>.

Attributive kinship phrase

+ Kinship attributive	+ Kinship head
noun	kinship word
kinship word	
Only certain combinations are possible.	

Coordinate kinship phrases are: <u>my uncles and my aunts</u> (<u>my uncles and aunts</u> could be a possessed noun phrase with a coordinate kinship phrase expounding the possessed item), <u>your sisters, and your cousins, and your aunts</u>.

Coordinate kinship phrase

+ Coordinate^n kinship head-1	+ Coordinate link	+ Coordinate kinship head-2
kinship word	and	kinship word
kinship phrase		kinship phrase

Alternative kinship phrases include: <u>my</u> <u>brother or my father</u>; <u>my</u> <u>mother or your mother,</u> and others.

Alternative kinship phrase

+ Alternative intro	+ Alternative kinship head-1	+ Alternative link	+ Alternative kinship head-2
either	kinship word	or	kinship word
neither	kinship phrase	nor	kinship phrase

Appositional kinship phrases are <u>my mother, your aunt</u>; <u>my first</u> <u>cousin, my closest relative</u>; and so on.

Appositional kinship phrase

+ Kinship head	+ Kinship apposition
kinship word	kinship word
kinship phrase	kinship phrase

3. Pronoun phrases

Pronoun phrases are not common. They consist of an emphasizer and a pronoun plus, perhaps, an emphatic pronoun: <u>just you</u>; <u>only you yourself</u>; <u>just I myself,</u> etc.

Pronoun phrase

± Emphatic deictic	+ Pronoun head	± Emphatic head
just only	pronoun	emphatic pronoun

Coordinate pronoun phrases are: you and I, you and him.

Coordinate pronoun phrase

+ Coordinate pronoun head-1	+ Coordinate link	+ Coordinate pronoun head-2
pronoun	and	pronoun

Alternative pronoun phrases include us or them, you or me, I or he.

Alternative pronoun phrase

± Alternative intro	+ (Alternative pronoun head-1	+ Alternative link)^n	+ Alternative pronoun head-2
either	pronoun	or	pronoun
neither		nor	

4. Name phrases

Name phrases may consist of a determiner, one or more honorifics, and one or more name heads. In some Mayan languages, one type of name phrase is used for calendar and geographical deities, another type for older people who have gained certain ranks in the community, another for relatives. In English, our name phrases have an honorific, expounded by mister, miss, missus, miz, doctor, judge, and so on; then a first-name head and a last-name head, with optional middle-name heads between the latter two, for example: Judge Raymond B. Smith; Ms. Mary Jane Adams.

The specific name phrases will certainly vary from culture to culture, as social customs vary. Very often they will be greatly influenced by dominant cultures, giving an assortment of indigenous name phrases and dominant-culture name phrases, (for example, Amerindian). Also, the name phrases used in vocative tagmemes may be more complex, or different in some way, from the name phrases used in subject and object tagmemes or in possessor tagmemes. The name phrases used in vocative tagmemes in prayers may be even more complex.

Name phrase

± Deter- miner	± Honorific	+ First name head	± Second name head	± Family name head
article demon- strative	mister missus sir madam judge and others	name	name	name
not used in vocative	not used with determiner		not often present	

Names enter into larger phrases much the same as nouns do. We can have attributive, coordinate, serial, alternative, appositional and replacive name phrases. You might decide in your language that the name phrases are not emically distinct from noun phrases and would hence combine them.

Attributive name phrases are common for place names. We have <u>Ohio State</u>, <u>Smith Street</u>, <u>Mississippi River</u>, <u>Texas City</u>, <u>Iowa State University</u>, <u>Smith Street Library</u>, <u>Smith Street service station</u>.

Attributive name phrase

+ Name attributive	+ Name head
name attributive name phrase	name attributive name phrase

Coordinate name phrases are common: <u>Bob</u> <u>and</u> <u>Bill</u>; <u>Mr. Birdwhistle and Mr. Blackburn</u>; <u>Mrs. Johnson, Mrs. Hunter, Mrs. Smith and Mrs. Adams</u>; <u>Jane and Rosie</u>.

Coordinate name phrase

+ Coordinate^n name head-1	+ Coordinate link	+ Coordinate name head-2
name attributive name phrase	and	name attributive name phrase

Serial name phrases are also possible: '<u>Rori, Berny, Eddy, you three,</u> come with me.'

Serial name phrase

+ Serial name head^n	+ Appositional summary
name attributive name phrase	noun phrase pronoun phrase
must occur at least twice	

Alternative name phrases include: <u>Mary</u> <u>or</u> <u>Sally</u>; <u>Henry, Alan</u> <u>or</u> <u>Harlan</u>.

Alternative name phrase

+ Alternative intro	+ Alternative name head-1	+ Alternative link	+ Alternative name head-2
either	name	or	name
either	name phrase	nor	name phrase
may occur only if only one alt. name head-1 occurs.			

Appositional name phrases often involve a name and a pronoun or kinship (phrase). Some examples are: <u>you, Hank</u>; <u>Sally, my cousin</u>; <u>my cousin, Sally</u>; <u>'Berny, Bernard Thomas Hawkins,</u> you come here this minute!'

Appositional name phrase

+ Name head	+ Name apposition
name	name
name phrase	name phrase
pronoun	pronoun
kinship word	kinship word
kinship phrase	kinship phrase

Replacive name phrases are also possible. They can be: <u>Hank, not Wes</u>; <u>not Wes but Hank</u>; <u>Hank, instead of Wes</u>; <u>Hank, rather than Wes</u>.

Replacive name phrase-1

+ Replacing name head	+ Replacive link-1	+ Replaced name head
name name phrase	, <u>not</u> , <u>instead of</u> , <u>rather than</u>	name name phrase

Replacive name phrase-2

+ Replacive intro	+ Replaced name head	+ Replacive link-2	+ Replacing name head
<u>not</u>	name name phrase	, <u>but</u>	name name phrase

5. Number phrases

Number words may be cardinal numbers: <u>one</u>, <u>two</u>, <u>three</u>, and so on; or ordinal numbers: <u>first</u>, <u>second</u>, <u>third</u>, and so on; or distributive: <u>by ones</u>, <u>by twos</u>, <u>by threes</u>; or <u>one by one</u>, <u>two by two</u>, <u>three by three</u>, and so on; or quantifiers: <u>a single</u>, <u>a pair</u>, <u>a triple</u>, and so on. In general, the cardinal numbers enter into phrases more than the others, but sometimes ordinal numbers enter into phrases, also.

In many minority language groups, there are two or three ways of counting. The industrial world's decimal system is quite common, but a native scores system (built on twenty instead of ten) is also quite common. Rarely, some other ceremonial system of counting may be found. We will treat the number phrase built on twenty, here.

Almost every language has the digits from one to four, some have them for one to nine. For those with only one to four, there is a phrase such as: <u>one hand only</u> (five), <u>one hand one</u> (six), <u>one hand four</u> (nine).

Digits number phrase-1

+ Hand multiplier	+ Hand head	+ Added digit
number	hand (or other morpheme)	number
one two	foot	

In the array above, we have included two systems. One system has: one hand (only) (five), two hand(only) (ten), and three hand (only) (fifteen). Other systems use: one hand (only) (five), two hand(only) (ten), one foot only (fifteen) or, possibly, two hand one foot (only) (fifteen).

However one gets to nineteen, twenty equals one person's total digits. And the system above twenty is:

one man one   (21)

one man one hand two   (27)

two man two hand two   (52)

one hand man (and) one hand one   (106)

three hand four man (and) three hand four   (399)

Scores number phrase

+(+ Number multiplier	+ Score) head	+ Addition head
number	person	number
digits number phrase	man	digits number phrase

The above is a very simple, regular system, which few languages have. They usually have some irregularities that will require several more arrays (constructions). Elizabeth Murane (1974) found that it took seven arrays to describe the Daga (Papua New Guinea) number system.

Number phrases also enter into alternative and replacive phrases.

Alternative number phrases are common: two or three, one or two hundred.

Alternative number phrase

+ Alternative intro	+ Alternative number head-1	+ Alternative link	+ Alternative number head-2
either	number	or	number
neither	number phrase	nor	number phrase
	Elision of repeated elements in the exponents of subsequent heads is common.		

Replacive number phrases are possible also. They are: six, not seven; not seven but six; six instead of seven; six rather than seven. The arrays are much the same as previously described replacive phrases and will not be reproduced here.

6. Adjective phrases

a. There may be two varieties of adjective phrases: a shorter one that occurs in modifiers in noun phrases, and a longer one that occurs in the description tagmeme of descriptive clauses.

The shorter adjective phrase usually consists of at most three tagmemes: negative, intensifier, and adjective head. The negative is expounded by not. The intensifier is expounded by very, somewhat, and rather. The adjective head is expounded by adjectives. Examples are: 'a very small needle', 'a not very old car' (English does not use the negative very much and only with very, as the preceding example shows), 'a somewhat tattered sail'.

The longer adjective phrase is similar to the shorter one but has a post-modifier which is expounded by a benefactive prepositional phrase or an infinitive verb phrase. English may need too in the intensifier tagmeme. Examples are:

    too big to fit into the box,

    too purple for my kitchen,

    very good for canning,

    too cold to work outside,

<u>very</u> <u>cold</u> <u>for</u> <u>working</u> <u>outside</u>,

<u>beneficial</u> <u>to</u> <u>many</u> <u>people</u>.

In most languages, the longer adjective phrase expounds the description tagmeme of descriptive clauses, while the shorter adjective phrases expound post-modifiers in noun phrases, for example:

'a <u>very</u> <u>straight</u> chair <u>too</u> <u>hard</u> <u>to</u>
    <u>be</u> <u>comfortable</u>'
(obviously, such an involved noun phrase has
limited usage as a modifier in a noun phrase).

Adjective phrase-1

± Negative intro	± Intensifier-1	+ Adjective head-1
<u>not</u>	<u>very</u>	adjective root
	<u>somewhat</u>	adjective stem
	(<u>rather</u>)	adjective word

The larger adjective phrase is:

Adjective phrase-2

± Negative intro	±Intensifier	+ Adjective head-2	+ Post modifier
<u>not</u>	<u>too</u>	adjective root	infinitival clause
	<u>very</u>	adjective stem	for-nominalized clause
		adjective word	benefactive preposi- tional phrase
		adjective phrase	

b. Attributive adjective phrases are rare, but English has
   <u>sky</u> <u>blue</u>, <u>brick</u> <u>red</u>, <u>mammoth</u> <u>big</u>.

Attributive adjective phrase

+ Adjective attributive	+ Adjective head
adjective root noun root	adjective root

c. Coordinate adjective phrases are: <u>red, white, and blue;
big and wide; old and wrinkled.</u>

Coordinate adjective phrase

+ Coordinate^n adjective head-1	+ Coordinate link	+ Coordinate adjective head-2
adjective root adjective stem adjective attributive adj phr	and	adjective root adjective stem adjective attributive adj phr

d. Some alternative adjective phrases are: <u>red or blue;
full or half-full; old or young; soft or mushy.</u>

Their syntagmeme formulas are (in English):

$$+\text{Alt Adj Head-1}^n \quad +\text{Alt Link} \quad +\text{Alt Adj Head-2}$$

$$+\text{Alt Adj Head-1} +(+\text{Alt Link} +\text{Alt Adj Head 2})^n$$

Alternative adjective phrase

± Alternative^n intro	+ Alternative adjective head-1	+ Alternative link	+ Alternative adjective head-2
either	adjective root	or	adjective root
neither	adjective stem	nor	adjective stem
	attributive adj phr		attributive adj phr

e. Reduplicated adjective phrases are quite common in some languages. They are rare in English, but examples are: a red, red rose; a big, big elephant; an old, old man; a fierce, fierce lion.

Reduplicated adjective phrase

+ Reduplicated adjective head	+ Reduplicating adjective head^n
adjective root-i	adjective root-i
adjective stem-i	adjective stem-i
adjective-i	adjective-i
	exponent must be same as in previous tagmeme

f. Examples of replacive adjective phrases are: big, not little; old, not young, blue not green; soft, not hard; and not little but big; not young but old; not green but blue; and not hard but soft.

98

Replacive adjective phrase-1

+ Replacing adjective head	+ Negative link	+ Replaced adjective head
adjective root adjective stem adjective attributive adj phr	, <u>not</u> , <u>instead of</u> , <u>rather than</u>	adjective root adjective stem adjective attributive adj phr

Replacive adjective phrase-2

+ Negative intro	+ Replaced adjective head	+ Replacive link	+ Replacing adjective head
<u>not</u>	adjective root adjective stem adjective attributive adj phr	, <u>but</u>	adjective root adjective stem adjective attributive adj phr

7. Time phrases

a. Modified time phrase

Modified time phrases are similar to modified noun phrases, but are usually simpler. Examples of the modified time phrase are: <u>next Tuesday</u>; <u>last year</u>; <u>the next ten minutes</u>; <u>the present decade</u>; <u>the first three Saturdays in July</u>.

Modified time phrase

+ Deictic	+ Time modifier	+ Number modifier	+ Time head	+ Time modifier
article demonstrative pronoun	next present past ordinal number	number word number phrase	time word date name	location prep phrase possessor phrase-2

b. Date phrases

Date phrases are an important time phrase. Americans usually give the month first, then the day second. Others place the day first, for example: 1 July, 1950.

Date phrase-1

+ Month head	+ Day head	+ Year head
month name	ordinal number	number phrase

Date phrase-2

+ Determiner	+ Day head	+ Day link	+ Month head	+ Year head
the any every this that	ordinal number ------ cardinal number	of	month name	number phrase

c. Complex time phrases

Attributive time phrases are common: Monday morning, Thursday afternoon, tomorrow night, Christmas day, July sixteenth.

Attributive time phrase

+ Time attributive	+ Time head
time word	time word

Coordinate time phrases include: Wednesday, Thursday, and Friday; this month and next (note the elision of the noun month in the second noun phrase; such elision of repeated words is common).

Coordinate time phrase

+ Coordinate^n time head-1	+ Coordinate link	+ Coordinate time head-2
time word	and	time word
time phrase		time phrase
date phrase		date phrase

Alternative time phrases are: tomorrow or the next day; Monday, Tuesday, or Wednesday; now or later; sooner or later.

Alternative time phrase

± Alternative intro	+ Alternative time head-1^n	+ Alternative link	+ Alternative time head-2
either	time word	or	time word
	time phrase		time phrase
neither	date phrase	nor	date phrase
	time particle		time particle

An appositional time phrase would be: tomorrow, Friday; next Monday, the twentieth; noon, when the sun is directly overhead. It comprises time head and appositional time tagmemes.

Appositional time phrase

+ Time head	+ Time apposition
time word	time word
time phrase	time phrase
date phrase	date phrase
	time subordinate clause

Examples of replacive time phrase are:

now, not tomorrow   or   not tomorrow but now.

Replacive time phrase

+ Replacing time head	+ Replacive link	+ Replaced time head
time word	, not	time word
time phrase	, instead of	time phrase
date phrase	, rather than	date phrase
time particle		time particle
time subordinate clause		time subordinate clause

(We leave the other array for the reader to construct. See earlier replacive phrases.)

8. Location phrases

There are only a few modified or attributive location phrases, such as: right here; over there; over here. There are so few that an array is not justified. Many locations are encoded in descriptive noun phrases and in name phrases, but these occur in the time-axis tagmemes of time preposition phrases.

Some examples of coordinate location phrases are: here and there and everywhere; near and far; Chicago and St. Louis.

Coordinate location phrase

+ Coordinate^n location head-1	+ Coordinate link	+ Coordinate location head-2
location word location prep phr	and	location word location prep phr

Alternative location phrases are: here or there; New York or Washington or Boston.

Alternative location phrase

± Alternative intro	+ Alternative location head-1^n	+ Alternative link	+ Alternative location head-2
either	location word	or	location word
neither	location prep phr	nor	location prep phr

Appositional location phrases usually have clearly a generic-specific relationship. Examples are: there, behind the sofa; over there, to the market; to Salinas, to the market; in Tecpan, in the hospital.

Appositional location phrase

+ Location head	+ Location apposition
location word location prep phr	location word location prep phr

Examples of replace location phrase are: <u>here</u>, <u>not there</u>; <u>not there but here.</u> The arrays are left to the reader to construct.

C. Prepositional phrases

Another morpheme is added to a noun phrase to make a prepositional phrase. That morpheme marks the case of the noun phrase or relates the noun phrase to the rest of the clause. Such an added morpheme may precede the noun phrase, or may follow it, or may occur within it. It may be phonologically a free word or a phonologically bound affix, called a clitic.

English has several free pre-positional prepositions, such as: <u>in</u>, <u>on</u>, <u>at</u>, <u>besides,</u> and others; and one bound post-positional clitic preposition, the -<u>'s</u> possessive, as in 'the queen of England<u>'s</u> crown.' In some languages, there may be morpheme clusters that act as single prepositions. In English, for example, there are such forms as: <u>in relation to, on top of,</u> that function as single prepositions.

The essential characteristic of a preposition is that it does not modify the noun of a noun phrase; it does not limit or expand the meaning of the noun phrase; it only relates the noun phrase to its surrounding structure.

Prepositions may have a clear overt meaning, as do such prepositions as: <u>in, on, over, under;</u> or they may have only a signaling function, such as case markers, in, for example, Latin.

The formula for a prepositional phrase is either:

+ ... Relator + ... Axis

or + ... Axis + ... Relator

where the '...' is replaced with 'subject', 'object', 'possessive', 'time', 'location', 'instrument'.

There may need to be rules added to tell exactly where the 'relator: preposition' occurs, if it is not initial or final, or gets permuted into the noun phrase.

The relator is expounded by a preposition, and the axis by a noun or noun phrase. (The term 'relator' is appropriate, but the term 'axis' leaves something to be desired and some people object to its use. We haven't yet found a better term. It is for this reason that we speak of 'prepositional phrases' and not *'relator-axis phrases'.)

A prepositional phrase always has two and only two tagmemes: the relator and the axis. Any modifiers or deictics are a part of the exponent of the axis.

The two tagmemes are both obligatory, unless the preposition is inflected for person, in which case the axis is conditionally optional; see the discussion at the end of this section.

1. Location prepositional phrases

Location and direction prepositional phrases are characterized by a location or direction preposition such as: in, on, over, under, at, toward, away from, beside, behind, and before, plus a locatable noun. Examples are: in the air; on the ground; behind the sofa; at home.

In some languages, it is worthwhile to posit several location or direction prepositional phrases, such as allative (toward), ablative (away from), locative (at, in, on), translocative (past, beyond), route (by), and tactile (by, as in 'hold a lizard by his/the tail'). In other languages, these are only semantic variants of a single location prepositional phrase.

Location prepositional phrase

+ Location relator	+ Location axis
in at by under over behind in front of	noun phrase (locatable)
	The axis exponent must be locatable.

Direction prepositional phrase

+ Direction relator	+ Direction axis
toward away from past up down away	noun phrase (locatable)

2. Time prepositional phrases

   Time prepositional phrases often have many of the prepositions that location prepositional phrases have, such as: in, at, before, after, and specific time prepositions such as: during, until. Examples are: at noon; in three days; after Tuesday; for three hours; before noon. There are two semantic variants of time prepositional phrases: one variant refers to a point in time (at three o'clock); the other refers to a duration of time (for three hours). In some languages these might be emically distinct phrases.

Time prepositional phrase

+ Time relator	+ Time axis
at	time word
before	
after	time phrase
in	

Duration prepositional phrase

+ Duration relator	+ Duration axis
during	time word
for	
until	time phrase

3. Instrument prepositional phrases

   Instrument prepositional phrases have a preposition (bound or free) meaning with, or by, or using. Examples in English all use with or, sometimes, by, for example:

   'She peels the manioc with a machete.'

   'He manufactures hose with/by a new process.'

Instrument prepositional phrase

+ Instrument relator	+ Instrument axis
with by using	noun noun phrase (concrete)
	The exponent of the the axis must refer to an entity that can be used as an instrument.

4. Accompaniment prepositonal phrases

Accompaniment prepositional phrases may expound a clause-level tagmeme called 'accompaniment', or they may expound the coordinate noun heads of a coordinate noun phrase, or they may expound a post modifier in a description noun phrase.

The accompaniment preposition in English is with.

'Holly went to school with Sally.'

'Sally, with Anne and Helen, went to the ball game.'

Accompaniment prepositional phrase

+ Accompaniment relator	+ Accompaniment axis
with	noun noun phrase name name phrase

5. Manner prepositional phrases

Manner prepositional phrases in English have prepositions in...(manner) and with...(manner).

'Jerry worked <u>with lots of energy</u>.'

'Jerry worked <u>in</u> <u>an energetic way</u>.'

Manner prepositional phrase

+ Manner relator	+ Manner axis
<u>with</u> <u>in</u> and others	noun noun phrase

6. Benefactive prepositional phrases

The benefactive preposition in English is <u>for</u>. Other languages may distinguish the different kinds of benefactive.

'Anita bought a shirt <u>for</u> <u>Harry</u> to surprise him.'

'Anita bought a shirt <u>for Harry</u> because he told her to.'

'Anita washed Harry's shirt <u>for</u> <u>him</u>.'

Benefactive prepositional phrase

+ Benefative relator	+ Benefactive axis
<u>for</u>	noun noun phrase name name phrase

7. Object prepositional phrases

Some languages mark the object of a transitive or bitransitive clause with a prepositional or postpositional case marker. In general, such a phrase should be analyzed as a +axis+relator or +relator+axis structure. Here, an example from Latin will be useful.

Object prepositional phrase in Latin

+ Object axis	+ Object relator (or Object case marker)
noun	-um (male singular)
noun phrase	
name	-am (female singular)
name phrase	plus others

Rule:
1. The object case marker must agree with the gender and number of the exponent of the axis.

2. The object case marker must be suffixed to every word in the exponent of the axis.

8. Subject prepositional phrases

Some languages require a case marker on the word or phrase expounding the subject of a clause. These, also, would have a +relator+axis or +axis+relator structure. There is no English example of this structure.

9. Complex prepositional phrases

Prepositional phrases can be combined in appositional, coordinate, series, alternative, reduplicated and replacive combinations. The important distinction is that each phrase retains its relator.

In the following example, the two locative phrases are in a coordinate locative phrase: 'Julia works at the shop and at home.'

But in the following examples, we have two nouns in a coordinate noun phrase expounding the axis of a single simple locative phrase: 'Jason worked at home and the shop.' or 'Mary has lived in Chicago and St. Louis.' We will run through some examples of complex English phrases:

1. appositional time phrase
    'We go swimming a lot in the summertime, when the weather is warm.'

2. series instrumental phrase
    'Harry built his house with a square, with a saw, with a hammer, with only those hand tools.'

3. alternative benefactive phrase
   'I'll make a cake for you or for your friends.'

4. reduplicated time phrase
   'I'll come to see you at two o'clock, at two o'clock!'

5. replacive location phrase
   'Put your toys in the box, not on the floor!'
   or
   'Put your toys not on the floor, but in the box.'

The reader can supply other examples. As a language, English is exceptionally rich in its phrase level, and examples are easy to come by. Most other languages do not have as rich a phrase level. They may transfer that load of communication to word level, to clause level, or to sentence level.

10. Prepositional phrases with inflected prepositions

In some languages, the prepositions are inflected for person. Here is an example from the Uspantec language of Guatemala (data from Margot McMillen). Uspantec has nearly a dozen different sets of prepositions, but here are two fairly regular ones.

pi -w -e	'for me'	č -in -wič	'in front of me'
pi -aw -e	'for you'	č -a -wič	'in front of you'
pi -r -e	'for her, him, it'	(č -i) -wič	'in front of her, him, it'
pi -q -e	'for us'	či -qa -wič	'in front of us'
pi -aw -e -čaq	'for you all'	č -a -wič -aq	'in front of you all'
pi -r -e -čaq	'for them'	č -i -wič -aq	'in front of them'

And here is one of the prepositional phrases:

Location prepositional phrase in Uspantec

+ Location relator	+ Location axis
locative inflected prepositions other non-inflected locational prepositions, for example: ax 'from'	noun phrase pronoun dependent clause plus others
Inflectional affixes must agree with the person and number of the exponent of the axis.	

Rule:

1. When the preposition is inflected for first and second person the axis must either be elided or be expounded by a corresponding pronoun for emphasis.

2. When the preposition is inflected for third person, the axis may be deleted only if the inflection on the preposition is semantically sufficient.

11. Distribution matrix

Earlier in this chapter we gave a construction search matrix that showed what kinds of complex phrases are possible. It is important to know also where they can be used, in what tagmemes. So we can make a matrix with the types of complexity on one axis, and all the tagmemes that can be expounded by phrases on the other axis. The filled-in cells then will indicate what phrases can occur in what tagmeme. It may be necessary, too, to give additional rules to supplement the matrix.

Distribution of complex phrases:

	Phrase types							
Tagmemes	Modified	Attributive	Coordinate	Serial	Alternative	Appositional	Reduplicated	Replacive	Compound
Transitive subject									
Intransitive subject									
Object									
Time									
Location									
Instrument									
Referent									
Indirect object									
Accompaniment									
Noun head									
Pronoun head									
Time head									
Location head									
-plus other tagmemes									
Time axis									
Location axis									
Instrument axis									
Referent axis									
Accompaniment axis									
-plus other tagmemes									

For your own matrix, include only the complexities you have found, and all the tagmemes you have found. The chief value of this matrix is to suggest new things to look for. You may find some interesting restrictions. For instance, Susan Garland, (Koiari, Papua New Guinea) found that coordinate and alternate noun phrases could expound a subject tagmeme but could not expound an object. Nor could complex phrases expound time or location tagmemes.

D. Verb phrases

Verb phrases are clusters of verbs and auxiliaries that go together to make a syntagmeme that expounds the predicate of a clause.

When the verb phrase consists of a single verb head and one or more auxiliary tagmemes expounded by closed-class words and particles, it is easily identified as a verb phrase. When it consists of two or more verb heads expounded by open-class verbs, the identification is a bit more complex. Do the verbs make up a verb phrase or are they verbs of separate clauses in a close-knit clause cluster? The main criterion for determining their status is separability. If the verb cluster can be expanded by adding other clause-level constituents between any pair of verbs, then there is probably a clause-break at that point and the verbs belong to different clauses.

Another cohesive factor is the distribution of verb affixes. In some languages, some of the verb affixes go on the first verb and some on the last verb of a verb phrase. If this happens, the verb cluster is clearly a verb phrase.

The inventory of verb phrases around the world is quite a varied lot, and an etic classification has not yet been made. We will describe some broad categories of verb phrases and hope it helps you approach the verb phrases you are analyzing.

1. The English verb phrase

The English verb phrase involves a main verb head and several auxiliaries. Perhaps the best account of the English verb phrase was given by Chomsky (in <u>Syntactic Structures</u>). He set up several rules to generate a string such as the following. (I have changed his notation.)

Active verb phrase in English

+ Tense	+ Mood	+Perfective auxiliary	+Continuous auxiliary	+ Verb head
-∅ ~ -s present -ed past -en past-past	will can may shall must	have + en	be + ing	verb

113

Then he made a rule that any suffix preceding a non-suffix is moved to a position following the non-suffix. So all the tense suffixes, the -en and the -ing, all jump over the following root.

There are rules such as:

> will + -s -> will   can + -s -> can
>
> will + -ed -> would   can + -ed -> could
>
> want + -en -> wanted   may + -ed -> might
>
>   plus others.

Later there is a rule that introduces a dummy verb do to carry the tense suffixes when there is no other auxiliary and the tense has to be fronted for interrogative constructions. (See also Pike and Pike, p. 230 for another treatment of the English verb phrase.)

Other languages, especially those with limited verb affixation (such as English or Asian languages), usually have verb phrases having modal auxiliaries.

The Mopan Mayan language of Guatemala has several verb phrases involving modal auxiliaries (see Ulrich and Peck).

2. Manner modifiers

Many languages incorporate manner adverbs into the verb phrase. For example, the Mixe language of Mexico (data from J. D. and W. Van Haitsma) has the following verb phrase:

Auxiliary predicate phrase in Mixe

± Auxiliary		+ Main verb head
cač	'strongly'	any verb
coʰk	'hurriedly'	
ha:	'in vain'	
ha:k	'more'	
ka	'not'	
ʼok	'doubt/politeness'	

Daga of Papua New Guinea (Elizabeth Murane) has a verb phrase in which the manner is verbalized and inflected:

Qualified verb phrase in Daga

+ Verb head	+ Qualifying auxiliary

any verb stem
 	
various VPs
   all uninflected
	any verb based on a
	   verbalized adjective
	   or noun

Some examples are:

ta   otu   -m   -ivin
do   little -verbalizer -I.present.continuous

'I am making it smaller.'

tunu amun -am -ivin
cook warm -verbalizer -I.present.continuous

'I am heating (it) (in a pot).'

wa   taman -am -eton
say straight -verbalizer -we.past

'We corrected the speech.'

3. Motion auxiliaries

A common verb phrase is a phrase in which one verb is an auxiliary of motion, such as, go or come. The formula would be +motion auxiliary +main verb head.

Mixe (data from Van Haitsma)

wen   nikš   mo:kma:kpɨ
optative she.go   corn.wash

'Let her go wash corn.' or 'May she go wash corn.'

Daga (data from Murane)

barao barao on   -iwand -in
put   put   come -it.continuous -it.past

'It was being handed down.'

4. Desiderative auxiliaries

Another similar verb phrase, the desiderative verb phrase, uses a verb of <u>want</u> and an infinitival verb. In English we have:

Desiderative verb phrase

+ Desiderative auxiliary	+ Activity head
<u>want</u> <u>seek</u> <u>try</u> plus others	Infinitive verb phrase

Example:

'I <u>want</u> <u>to</u> see it.'

In English, we would probably combine this phrase with some others, or count it as a merged sentence (see chapter 12). In Daga (data from E. Murane), the phrase is:

Desiderative verb phrase in Daga

+ Activity head	+ Desiderative auxiliary
nominalized verb	any inflected form of <u>anu</u> 'want'

Example:

<u>ma</u> <u>-t</u>   <u>anu</u> <u>-ivin</u>
eat -nominalizer   want -I.present.continuous

'I want to eat!'

5. Do+infinitive verb phrase

A verb phrase may consist of the verb <u>do</u> plus an infinitival or nominalized form of an activity verb. In <u>Mayan</u> languages, this verb phrase is a common way to include borrowed Spanish verbs into vernacular speech.

Do+infinitive verb phrase in Mayan

+ Auxiliary	+ Verb head
any inflected form of the verb ban 'do'	any vernacular infinitive verb any Spanish infinitive verb

Example:

<u>š-</u> <u>ø-</u> <u>a-</u> <u>ban</u> <u>-on</u>   <u>pensar</u>
past- it- you- do -have   to.think (Spanish)

'You have thought.' = 'You have taken thought.'

Other languages may reverse the order of these tagmemes.

6. <u>Give</u> verb phrase

Some languages have a verb phrase involving the verb <u>give</u> plus a generic noun or verb.

Examples might be:

<u>blow give-he-present his brother stick</u>
'He is hitting his brother with a stick.'

or <u>food give-he-present his son meat</u>
'He is feeding his son meat.'

or (Daga) <u>pan wa- n -an</u>
           tie him- give -they
           'They tied it on him.'

7. Aspectual auxiliaries

There are a number of other possible auxiliary verbs that can enter into verb phrases. Such verbs are: <u>be, be necessary, be able, try, begin, stop, know, and say</u>, and negatives of these. Many of these verbs have an aspectual meaning that in other languages is carried by verb affixes in highly inflected verbs. So these phrases are usually named various aspectual names.

117

Aspectual verb phrase

+ Main verb head	+ Aspectual head
noun root verb root	inflected form of: be be necessary be able try begin stop plus others
Only certain roots occur here.	

In another language, the order of tagmemes may be different.

For English, Longacre analyzed many of these aspectual structures as merged sentences (see his 'Sentence structure as a statement calculus'). According to Longacre, one must make the decision anew for each language as to whether a combination of an aspectual verb plus a main verb is a verb phrase or is parts of two clauses in a merged sentence.

8. Idiomatic compound verb phrase

Verb phrases consisting of an idiomatic combination of verbs are quite common. One such idiomatic pair from Papua New Guinea is 'cut drop' meaning to 'cut a limb off a tree.' Verb clusters describing a single event or action are usually compound verb phrases.

In Vietnamese languages the verbs are often nearly synonymous, and the pairing of verbs is used for poetic eloquence. Sometimes a nonsense rhyming word is inserted between the verbs to add beauty.

Here are some examples from Jeh (data from Dwight Gradin):

ěn	pĭ	kŏng	au
he	hit	beat	me

'He beat me.'

ěn	chŏng	cha
he	eat.rice	eat.meat

'He is eating a meal.'

ěn	patou	patoh	tanoh	wal
he	teach	...	relate	say

'He instructs.'

ěn	răk	rìng	trìng	jăng	hay
he	guard	....	shield	block	us

'He guards and protects us.'

ěn	chǒk	bùh	cha	ka
he	take	roast	eat	fish

'He takes, roasts, and eats a fish.'

au	chiều	chǒk	mahěk
I	go	get	stuff

'I will go and get the stuff.'

Some African languages have large compound verb phrases: several verbs in a sequence that expound a single predicate. Carol McKinney reports that the Kaje language of Nigeria has a frequently-used compound verb phrase. Here are some of her examples:

ba-	cat	drok	-a	ba'
they-	want	leave	-nominative	not

'They do not want to leave.'

ə-	srwa	wa	bvom
he-	sit	begin	sing

'He sits down to sing.'

ə-	wa	kai	hywei
he-	enter	take	bee

'He begins to take bees.'

a-	ni	nat	wan	kinya
you-	will	go	cook	food

'You will go to cook food.'

McKinney also reports that the most common first verbs are:
nat	'go'
ši	'be'
cat	'want'
wa	'enter', 'begin'

Bibliography

Dawson, Marcus and May. 1974. Kobon phrases. Workpapers in Papua New Guinea languages, volume 6. Ukarumpa: S.I.L.

Fillmore, Charles J. 1975. Santa Cruz lectures on deixis. Bloomington, Indiana: Indiana University Linguistics Club.

Fries, Peter H. 1970. Tagmeme sequences in the English noun phrase. Norman: S.I.L. and the University of Oklahoma.

Gradin, Dwight. 1976. The verb in Jeh. Mon Khmer studies V, ed. by. Kenneth J. Gregerson and David Thomas. Manila: S.I.L.

Huckett, Joyce. 1974. Notes on Iduna grammar. Workpapers in Papua New Guinea languages, volume 3. Ukarumpa: S.I.L.

McKinney, Carol. 1980. Kaje serial verb constructions. MS.

Murane, Elizabeth. 1974. Daga grammar from morpheme to discourse. S.I.L. Publications in Linguistics and Related Fields Number 43. Norman: S.I.L. and the University of Oklahoma.

Pike, Kenneth L. and Evelyn G. Pike. 1977. Grammatical analysis. S.I.L. publications in linguistics, number 53. Dallas, Texas: S.I.L. and U.T.A.

Pride, Kitty. 1965. Chatino syntax. S.I.L. Publications in Linguistics and Related Fields Number 12. Norman: S.I.L. and The University of Oklahoma.

Ulrich, Matthew and Charles Peck. Mopan Mayan verbs. MS.

Van Haitsma, Julia Dieterman and Willard. 1976. A hierarchical sketch of Mixe as spoken in San Jose El Paraíso. S.I.L. Publications in Linguistics and Related Fields Number 44. Norman: S.I.L. and the University of Oklahoma.

Vendler, Zeno. 1968. Adjectives and nominalizations. The Hague: Mouton and Co.

Chapter 9

Clause-level structures

A clause usually involves a verb and the nominals related to it, or involves a noun to which some property is attributed. It is the threshold of speech communication, a minimal utterance that is not the answer to a question. None of the definitions of clauses is completely adequate, but we will proceed anyway.

It is good to get clause data from conversations and different kinds of texts, because clauses in some texts, such as legendary narratives, are often very abbreviated and not very useful for analysis. Fuller and longer clauses will usually be found in conversations, sermons, political speeches, arguments, and debates. In the beginning of language work, elicited clauses may be most useful, but an analysis based on them should be checked against unelicited clauses later on.

Clauses, in general, are built around a verb or verb phrase or are built around a nominal. We will call the first group 'verbal' clauses and the second group 'verbless' clauses.

Verbal clauses are of four general types: bitransitive, transitive, intransitive, and ambient. Verbless clauses include: descriptive, equational, possession, location, name, and existential, and possibly others. In English, the verbless clauses have a dummy verb 'be'.

A. Verbal clauses

1. Bitransitive or ditransitive

A bitransitive or ditransitive clause involves three participants, one of which is usually inanimate. In English, the verbs for exchange of property, such as give, sell, buy, rob, steal, donate, bequeath, and perhaps some others, are bitransitive verbs. In general, the class of bitransitive verbs is not a large class. Examples in English are:

Jared gave a pencil to Susie.

I sold my copy of the book to another student.

Declarative active bitransitive clause

± Subject	+ Decl.act. bitr.pred	± Object	± Indirect object
subject pronouns	decl.act. bitr.verb	object pronouns	indirect object preposition phrase
proper nouns	decl.act. bitr.verb phrase	proper nouns	
noun phrases		noun phrases	
agent		objective	goal

± Time	± Location	± Manner	and any others
time word	location word	manner adverb	
time phrase	location phrase	manner phrase	
time	location	verb modifier	

In English, we have another array with the object and indirect object transposed, and with the indirect object expounded by pronouns, proper nouns and noun phrases. The array is left to the reader.

In some languages where there are two objects marked only by the animateness of the two entities referred to by the two object nominals, the array is:

Declarative active bitransitive clause

± Subject	+ Decl.act bitr.pred	+ Inanimate object	+ Animate object
subject pronoun	decl.act bitr.verb	inanimate pronoun	animate pronoun
proper noun	decl.act bitr.verb phrase	inanimate noun	animate noun
noun phrase		inanimate noun phrase	animate noun phrase

± Time	± Location	± Manner	and any others
time word	location word	manner adverb	
time phrase	location phrase	manner phrase	

The order of tagmemes may be different for any particular language. Note that the two objects may be distinguished by their animateness more than by any case markings.

Todd Ireland (private communication) suggests that for Latin, we could set up the following clause types:

    Bitransitive, with a dative and an accusative object,

    Ditransitive, with two accusative objects,

    Semitransitive, with a genitive, a dative, or an ablative, or a combination of these as objects,

    Transitive, with one accusative object.

For your language, these terms are available for whatever complications you find in this area.

2. Transitive

A transitive clause has two participants. Examples are:

Allen watched Monica.

Lucy cut the cake.

The water washed away the soil.

Declarative active transitive clause

+ Subject	+ Decl.act tr.pred	+ Object	+ Time	+ Loc.	+ Manner
subject pronoun	decl.act tr.verb	object pronoun	time word	location word	manner word
proper noun	decl.act tr.verb phrase	proper noun	time phrase	location phrase	manner phrase
noun phrase		noun phrase			

The array above gives the English tagmeme order. Other languages may put the tagmemes in quite different orders.

In English, some transitive clauses cannot be made passive. Consider the pair:

Jason has a girl friend.

*A girl friend is had by Jason.

Also, in English and in other languages, there are transitive clauses without overt objects, for example:

Roger is driving today.

Jimmy doesn't smoke.

You are always eating.

But notice that it is not a foolish question to ask:

What is Roger driving today?

What is it that Jimmy doesn't smoke?

What are you always eating?

124

Such questions would be foolish if the clauses were intransitive.

*What are you smiling?
(Don't confuse the intransitive 'smile' with the transitive 'smile at.')

*What are you sleeping?

Some motion verbs are transitive, even in English, such as enter, leave, approach. The passives of these clauses are possible, but sometimes with special meanings. Consider the following:

Thieves entered the building last night.

The building was entered by thieves last night.

The mob approached the building.

Harry was approached by a friend.

Because motion verbs can be transitive, they should never be taken automatically to be intransitive.

Certain causative-motion verbs are transitive and require a locative or destination in the clause, for example:

Randall put the book in a box.

Terry placed the book on the table.

Willy withdrew his money from the bank.
(withdraw also has an intransitive case frame.)

Lucy took her brother home.

Notice how these clauses would be defective without their locative phrases.

Declarative active transitive clause with location

+ Subject	+ Decl.act tr.pred w.loc	+ Object	+ Location	+ Time	+ Manner
	(caus. motion verb)		loc word loc phr		
agent		objective	goal source	time	manner

125

There is another small class of transitive verbs that take both an object and a designation complement. These verbs are <u>elect, appoint, make, name, call, classify,</u> and perhaps a few others.

<u>They elected Sally Williams president of the union.</u>

<u>The committee appointed Al chairman of the sub-committee.</u>

<u>We named our son James.</u>

<u>The city council made Mr. Smith mayor pro tem.</u>

Some of these verbs allow, some require, a link between the object and the complement, such as <u>as, to, to be</u>; and sometimes the complement is expounded by a prepositional phrase or an infinitival clause.

<u>They appointed Al as chairman.</u>

<u>They appointed Al to the chairmanship.</u>

<u>They elected Al to be mayor.</u>

<u>They classified Jim as a class-one athlete.</u>

<u>The chairman named Sarah to serve as a committee of one to collect public response to the proposition.</u>

Transitive clause with a designation complement

± Subj	± Decl tr act pred with desig compl	± Object	± Designation link	±Designation complement	± Time	± Loc
noun	desig tr vb	noun	as	noun		
noun ph		noun ph	to	noun ph		
name		name	to be	name		
name phr		name phr		infinitival clause		
pronoun		pronoun				

In another language these verbs may function more as quotation verbs or as entering into some kind of a merged sentence (see ch. 11). For example:

<u>They elected Rori that he will be leader.</u>

In some languages, some of these verbs are replaced with the verb 'say' in a quotation sentence:

They all said that Rori will be the new chief.

3. Intransitive

An intransitive clause has a single participant. Clauses involving body motions and functions make up the bulk of intransitive clauses. Beryl coughed / slept / fell / stumbled / leaned / got up / dreamed / urinated / belched / aged, and others. These clauses never have an object (some can be made transitive by the addition of a particle to the verb) and never have a passive counterpart.

Declarative intransitive clause

± Subject	+ Decl.intr pred	± Time	± Loc.	± Manner
subject pronoun	decl.intr verb	time word	loc. word	manner adverb
name phrase	decl.intr verb phrase	time phrase	loc. phrase	
noun phrase				

Some motion verbs are intransitive and require a locative or destination phrase, for example:

Mary came to school.

Mary came from England.

Mary went to school.

Mary went to England.

Other such verbs are walk, run, race, and fall.

Declarative intransitive clause with destination

± Subject	± Decl.intr motion pred	± Destination	± Time	± Manner
	decl.intr motion verb	location word		
	decl.intr motion verb phrase	destination phrase		

Also, there is a set of intransitive verbs that require adjectival complements. Such verbs are: <u>grow, turn, become, turn out, taste, smell, get to be,</u> and possibly others. In traditional linguistics these verbs are classed with the copula verb <u>be,</u> and their clauses have been classed as 'descriptive clauses', which we will cover later. Here are some examples of clauses with intransitive verbs with adjectival complements:

<u>My dog finally grew old on me.</u>

'<u>The milk turned sour</u> before it should have.'

'<u>Marie has become more friendly</u> than she used to be.'

<u>Henry's job got to be too taxing for him.</u>

Declarative intransitive descriptive clause

± Subject	± Decl.intr descr.pred	± Descriptive complement	± Benefactive	± Location
noun	decl.intr descr.verb	adjective word	dative prep.phr	location word
noun phrase	decl.intr descr.vb phrase	adjective phrase	location prep.phr	location phrase

Another variant of this clause in English is the perceived description clause. It involves verbs such as <u>look, feel, taste,</u> and <u>seem.</u>

<u>This coat looks new.</u>

<u>His ideas seem odd to me.</u>

This soup tastes too salty.

I feel fine, today.

The array for this clause would be very similar to the array above. Only the verbs expounding the predicate would be different. These same verbs enter into the perceived description sentence described later in chapter 11.

4. Ambient

Ambient clauses have no participants. They usually refer to the weather or to the environment. English requires a subject, so a dummy 'it' is used as subject. Most speakers are at a loss, however, to say what 'it' refers to.

Examples are:

It is raining.	It was cold.
It is thundering.	It will be hot.
It is snowing.	It has been cold.
It must have been raining.	It is calm.

Other languages may leave out the subject altogether, except as a pronominal affix on a verb. For example, here are a couple of examples from Amarakaeri of Peru:

o-   wi   -nde
3rd-   rain -daytime

'It is raining.'

nda-   wa-   huhu   -nda
emphasis-   adjective.marker- cold.wind -stative

'It's cold and windy.'

Some ambient verbs act as intransitive verbs, receiving a subject marker, aspects, tense, and mood markers. Other ambient verbs act as adjectives in a description-like clause. The first class includes 'rain', 'snow', 'hail', 'thunder', and so on. The other class includes 'hot', 'warm', 'cool', 'cold', 'calm', 'windy', 'dark', plus others.

Declarative ambient verbal clause

± Dummy subject	+ Ambient pred	± Time	± Loc
it	inflected ambient verb or verb phrase		

Note: Omit the dummy subject if it is not used in your language.

Declarative ambient description clause

± Dummy subject	± Copula	+ Ambient description	± Time	± Loc
it	inflected form of be	ambient adj ambient adj phr		

Note: Omit the dummy subject and/or the copula if they are not used in your language.

B. Verbless clauses

The 'verbless' clauses all use a dummy verb be in English, but in other languages, no verb is used at all. These clauses all involve a nominal to which some characteristic is attributed.

1. Descriptive clause

A descriptive or topic-comment clause attributes an adjective to the noun, for example:

This book is new.   That mountain is high.

Eggs are expensive.   Elisa is ill.

Lettuce is good for you.

Declarative descriptive clause

± Subject	+ Copula	+ Description	± Time	± Loc
pronoun noun noun phr name name phr	inflected form of <u>be</u>	adjective adjective phrase		

Note: Omit the copula if it is not used in your language.

If the description precedes the subject or the topic, the array would have a different order.

2. Equational clause

An equational clause attributes some nominal to the subject, for example:

<u>Jerry is a senator.</u>

<u>My brother is a factory worker in St. Louis.</u>

Declarative equational clause

± Subject	+ Copula	+ Equivalent	± Time	± Loc
pronoun noun noun phr name name phr	inflected form of <u>be</u>	noun noun phrase name name phrase		

Note: Omit the copula if it is not used in your language.

3. Possession

A possession clause attributes a possessor to the subject. The following examples are English translations of such clauses. The possessor may be in a possession phrase or in a dative phrase, for example:

> that horse, Henry's
>
> Henry's, that horse
>
> that horse to Henry
>
> to Henry, that horse

Normal English possession clauses have the copula.

> This coat is Susan's.
>
> That brick house on the corner is ours.

English can also use the transitive verbs have and own to express ownership.

Declarative possession clause

± Subject	± Copula	± Possessor	± Time	± Loc
pronoun noun noun phr	inflected form of be	dative prep. phrase possessor prep phr-a		

Note: Omit the copula if it is not used in your language.

4. Location clause

A location clause attributes a location to the subject, for example: (in English translation),

> My horse in pasture.
>
> In-pasture my-horse.

More normal English examples are:

> My car is in the repair shop.
>
> The main offices are in St. Louis.

Declarative location clause

+ Subject	+ Copula	+ Location	± Time
pronoun noun noun phr	inflected form of <u>be</u>	location word location phrase	time word time phr

Note: Omit the copula if it is not used in your language.

5. Name clause

A name clause attributes a name to the subject, as in the following examples:

<u>Roger</u>, <u>his-name</u> <u>my-brother</u>.

<u>His</u> <u>name</u> <u>Roger</u>.

<u>Merlin</u> <u>his</u> <u>name</u>.

Declarative name clause

+ Name	+ Copula	+ Subject
proper noun name name phrase	inflected form of <u>be</u>	pronoun noun phrase kinship phrase possessed phrase

Omit the copula if it is not present in your language.
In many languages the subject precedes the name.

6. Existential clause

An existential clause attributes existence to the subject. Very often, this clause uses some uninflected particle for its 'predicate.' Some examples, in English translation, are:

<u>Exist</u> <u>a</u> <u>man</u> <u>in</u> <u>the</u> <u>country</u>.

<u>Exist</u> <u>one</u> <u>his-son</u>.

In Mayan languages, such clauses are used to introduce characters into a story. In fact, all the nonverbal clauses serve more as background material in discourse. We will cover this later in this course.

Some more normal English examples are:

<u>There</u> <u>was</u> <u>once</u> <u>a</u> <u>king</u> in <u>a</u> <u>foreign land.</u>

<u>There</u> <u>are</u> <u>some</u> Cuban soldiers in <u>Ethiopia.</u>

Declarative existential clause in Mayan

+ Existential Pred	+ Subject	± Location	± Time
wi' 'there is/was'	noun noun phrase	location word location phrase	time word time phrase

C. Clause constituents

Until now, we have been using the more typical clause tagmemes in the arrays. Now we will look at the whole list of possible clause constituents or tagmemes.

1. Predicate tagmeme

Nuclear to all 'verbal' clauses is the predicate tagmeme, which is expounded by a verb or a verb phrase. In many languages, the predicate may be the only constituent of most clauses in narrative discourse.

Since the predicate is nuclear to a clause, predicates should be contrastively labeled, for example: declarative active transitive predicate, yes-no interrogative passive transitive predicate.

2. Subject tagmeme

Subject is usually nuclear to a clause. In English the subject is almost always obligatory. In other languages it is quite optional and is used only when a different participant begins to act or speak, or when one wishes to emphasize the subject participant.

The exponent of the subject often must agree with the pronominal affix expounding the subject marker tagmeme of the verb. The two should not be confused, however. A subject-marker tagmeme can have only pronominal affix exponents of first, second, and third person. Clause-level subject has all kinds of free pronouns, demonstrative pronouns, names, nouns and all kinds of noun phrases for its exponents. The subject tagmeme can have far more explicit exponents than the subject-marker tagmeme. However, if the clause-level subject and the subject marker on the verb never cooccur, that is, they are in complementary distribution, they may both be counted as the clause-level subject.

Recent studies have pointed out that a 'subject tagmeme' has at least two major functions. First, it is related to the predicate of its clause by certain role relationships and often by surface structure agreement with affixes on the verb of the predicate. Secondly, it serves as the topic or theme of the clause, the entity that 'is being talked about,' and is used to tie a clause into its context to make a coherent stretch of speech. Thus a subject has an inside-the-clause function and an outside-the-clause function. Some languages seem to divorce these two functions. Tagalog of the Philippines can have an 'actor' in a clause but have some other constituent marked as 'topic.'

You may find it difficult to posit a 'subject' in certain clause type(s); in which case, you may have to resort to more case-oriented terms such as 'actor', 'patient' and so on. (See various papers in Li's book, Subject and Topic, and see also Foley and Van Valin.)

3. Object tagmeme

In transitive and bitransitive clauses, there is an object tagmeme. The object tagmeme is often optional, being absent when the exponent of the object is obvious from the context or from the verb.

In many languages, the exponent of the clause-level object must agree in person, gender, or number with the pronominal affix expounding the object-marker tagmeme of the verb. Like the clause-level subject, the clause-level object can have many kinds of nominal exponents.

4. Indirect object tagmeme

Closely related to the object is the indirect object. In English, the indirect object is expounded by a prepositional phrase with to as its preposition, for example:

'Billy gave his lunch to Betty.'

There is often confusion between the (direct) object and the indirect object, because of our English bias. In English, we put the 'things' in the direct object and the people in the 'indirect object' for our most often used verbs, such as give, teach, steal, sell, buy, and say. Some other languages always put the personal participant in the direct object tagmeme and put the inanimate item in the indirect object, or, sometimes, in a tagmeme called 'referent'. Consider, for example, the English word teach, which takes the material taught as a direct object and the learner as an indirect object, for example:

Stewart taught the intricacies of algebra to many
    successive large classes of freshmen at Lincoln
    Junior College.

But, in other languages, 'teach' requires the learner in the direct object and the material in the referent tagmeme, somewhat as the English verbs train, school, drill, and tutor do:

> William trained many successive large classes of freshmen at Lincoln Junior College in the intricacies of algebra.

In English, the verb give takes the thing given as a direct object and the recipient as indirect object, as seen in the following:

> 'Mr. Smith gave a new house to his daughter when she got married.'

In other languages, the verb give acts more like the English verb enrich, which takes the recipient as direct object and the gift as an instrumental:

> 'Mr. Smith enriched his daughter with a new house when she got married.'

Our bias toward the indirect object is one bias we English speakers have to guard against.

5. Benefactive

The benefactive tagmeme is related to the indirect object tagmeme. In English, it is expounded by a for prepositional phrase:

'Allen fixed a clock for Mary.'

'My mother bought a new shirt for me.'

'Alice drew a picture for me.'

6. Time and location

Time and location tagmemes are more peripheral to a clause but are important to discourse structure. Clauses early in a paragraph may be more likely to have time and location tagmemes than those in the body of a paragraph.

Time tagmemes may be divided into two types, durational and punctiliar:

> 'Judy studied for an hour.'

> 'Judy went to bed at eleven o'clock.'

Location tagmemes may be divided into several types:

> location: 'Howie worked at home.'
>
> direction: 'Jerry walked toward the intersection.'
>
> allative: 'Thomas walked to the store.'

ablative:	'Helen walked <u>from the store</u> to school.'
translocative:	'Mary walked <u>past the school</u>.'
tactile:	'Roger caught his dog <u>by its tail</u>.'
	'Johnson held his dogs up <u>by their ears</u>.'

In many languages these are not emically different. In Australian Aborigine languages, they are quite distinct and important.

7. Manner tagmeme

Manner is one tagmeme that may be a clause-level or a verb-phrase level tagmeme. Manner is a modifier of the predicate verb. It may be expounded by adverbs and by prepositional phrases in English:

'Watson <u>skillfully</u> mended the clock.'

'Watson mended the clock <u>with great skill</u>.'

The main criterion for deciding the status of the manner is its separability from the predicate. In the example above, the manner is separate from the predicate, so it is a clause-level tagmeme. In other languages, the manner may be inseparable from the predicate and thus should be included in a verb phrase expounding the predicate.

8. Negative

Negative is another tagmeme that may be on the clause level or may be on a verb-phrase level. In English, it is probably in the verb phrase, since it always has to be close to the verb, if it is negating the verb.

9. Instrument tagmeme

Instrument tagmeme may occur in transitive and bitransitive clauses, very rarely in intransitive and other types of clauses, for example:

'Rolao mended the clock <u>with a screwdriver and a knife</u>.'

'Rolao mended the clock <u>by the new methods he learned in school</u>.'

Some languages express instrument in a separate clause which uses a verb <u>take</u> or <u>use</u>, such as:

'Sammy <u>took a knife</u> and cut the meat.'

'Sammy <u>used a shovel</u> and dug a ditch.'

'Sammy <u>had a can of paint</u> and painted his bookcase.'

10. Purpose tagmeme

    Some clauses can have a purpose tagmeme:

    'Susie went to the store for milk.'

11. Reason tagmeme

    Some clauses can have a reason tagmeme:

    'Ralu got sick because of the heat.'

12. Accompaniment tagmeme

    Accompaniment is another clause constituent that can occur with verbs of activity and motion, for example:

    'Sulo rides to work with Reza.'

    'She plays tennis with Tanya.'

13. Summary of clause syntagmemes

    The full bidimensional array of a clause can have eight or ten tagmemes when all possible constituents are included. In a description of the clauses of a language, it is most convenient to draw out the whole bidimensional array for the longest clause and discuss all the marginal tagmemes there. Then subsequent clause discussions can refer back only briefly to the earlier discussion of the marginal tagmemes.

    Note that we are not using Pike and Pike's ideas of clauses and clause roots. A clause has nuclear and marginal tagmemes, but they are all a part of the clause; nothing is gained by dividing them between different levels. An array of a full bitransitive clause might look like the following:

Delarative Active Bitransitive clause

+ Subject	+ Decl.bitr Predicate	+ Direct object	+ Indirect object	+ Manner
subject pronoun	decl bitr act verb or verb phrase	object pronoun	indir obj pronoun	manner word
name		name	indir obj phrase	manner phrase
noun		noun		
subject noun		object noun		

± Negative	± Instrument	± Purpose	± Reason	± Accompaniment
not	Instrument phrase	Purpose phrase	Reason phrase	Accompaniment phrase

Rules:
1. No more than one or two peripheral margins may occur in any one clause.

2. The margin tagmemes are permutable among themselves.

3. The negative tagmeme may permute to any part of the clause.

D. Voice

Transitive and bitransitive clauses may have different 'voices'. Voice describes how a verb in a clause is related to the other clause constituents.

1. Accusative versus ergative languages

Most languages are either nominative-accusative or are ergative-absolutive in clause structure. English is a nominative-accusative language; we treat the subjects of intransitive and transitive clauses alike and treat the transitive object differently, that is, we have one set of pronouns for subjects and another for objects. An ergative-absolutive language has one set of pronouns, case markers, or pronominal affixes (called absolutive) that it uses for intransitive subjects and transitive objects. It then has another set (called ergative) that it uses for the transitive subject. The voices that follow may apply to both types of languages or to only one or the other.

2. Passive voice and object advancement

The best known alternative voice is 'passive' in which the object of the verb becomes the subject and the previous subject is relegated to a less important constituent. Passive clauses have important roles in discourse structure.

Bitransitive clauses have two passive paraphrases, for example:

A pencil was given to Susie by Terry.

Susie was given a pencil by Terry.

Transitive clauses usually have only one passive counterpart.

<u>Sally</u> <u>was</u> <u>watched</u> <u>by</u> <u>Billy</u>.

<u>The</u> <u>cake</u> <u>was</u> <u>cut</u> <u>by</u> <u>Lucy</u>.

<u>The</u> <u>soil</u> <u>was</u> <u>washed</u> <u>away</u> <u>by</u> <u>the</u> <u>water</u>.

Declarative passive transitive clause

± Passive subject	± Decl. pass.tr. pred.	± Agent	± Time	± Loc
	decl.pass tr.verb	agentive prep. phrase		
	decl.pass tr.verb phrase			
objective		agentive		

Some languages have a process of 'object advancement' that resembles the passive voice. Object advancement may move the object to the front of the clause without demoting the subject or changing its form or position. There may be some change in the verb inflection.

3. Antipassive and subject enhancement

Another voice that occurs in ergative languages is the 'antipassive'. The passive emphasizes the recipient of the action of the verb, so the antipassive emphasizes the agent of the verb. It is a subject emphasis clause. Here is an example from Tzutujil (data from Butler and Butler):

<u>atat</u>   <u>eq.qas</u>   <u>n- at- tix -ow -i</u>
you   surprise   continuous- you- eat -antipassive -intransitive

<u>xa</u>   <u>n- sandia</u>
the   my- watermelon

'So it is you who is eating my watermelon.'

Note how the verb is marked as intransitive in the antipassive voice.

The usual transitive form of the same clause is:

n-	ø-	a-	ti(x)	-x	xa	n-	sandia
continuous-	it-	you-	eat	-transitive	the	my-	watermelon

'You are eating my watermelon.'

The antipassive puts much more emphasis on the subject.

And here is an example from Tongan (data by Ross Clark, quoted by Hopper and Thompson):

Ordinary transitive:

na'e	kai	-i	'a	e	ika
past	eat	-transitive	absolutive	definite	fish

'e	he	tamasi'i
ergative	the	boy

'The boy ate the fish.'

Antipassive:

na'e	kai	'a	e	tamasi'i	'i	he	ika
past	eat	absolutive	definite	boy	oblique	the	fish

'The boy ate some of the fish.'

Here the antipassive means that the boy did not eat all the fish, only some of it. The action on the object is only partial, so in that sense the object has been demoted a bit.

Other languages may have other ways to demote the object to an adjunct prepositional phrase.

4. Object incorporation and object demotion

The process of object incorporation is closely related to the antipassive process. Here, the object is somehow included in the verb phrase so that only an activity involving an object is in focus, the specific object is not mentioned. The Mopan Maya language, for one, has such a process of object incorporation:

Ordinary transitive clause:

walak	u-	ć'ok	-s	-ik	a	t'an	-a
habit	he-	believe	-cause	- continuous	the	word	-juncture

'He obeys the words.'

Object-incorporated clause:

    walak   u- ƛ'ok -s -ah -t'an
    habit   he- believe -cause -intransitive -word

'He is obedient.'

Notice how in the transitive clause the verb is transitive and the object noun phrase has an article preceding the noun. In the object-incorporated clause, the verb is marked as intransitive and the noun lacks an article. The noun is a part of the predicate verb phrase. See Frantz 1971 p. 72, for a discussion of object incorporation in Blackfoot.

In English, we have some object incorporation, especially with -ing verbs. Some examples are:

We went bird-watching yesterday.

We bird-watched all day.

This is the salmon-fishing season.

Is today bread-baking day?

He is a penny-pincher.

He penny-pinches all the time.

He is always penny-pinching.

Sally babysat the Johnson children all last week.

She will babysit them again next week.

The questionable examples above show that object incorporation is an arbitrary process in English.

5. Instrument advancement

Some languages have clauses in which the instrument is promoted to the status of topic of the clause. The verb may have a special inflection and the instrument itself may be moved to the front of the clause. An example from Tzutujil will illustrate it.

    xun mačĕt š- ∅- in- kam -s -be -x
    one machete completive- it- I- die -cause -instr -trans

'With a machete I killed it!'

Such a clause gives prominence to the instrument, and one of the chief uses of the instrument-promoted clause is as a relativized or nominalized clause focusing on the instrument, 'the machete <u>with which I killed it</u>.'

6. Other advancements

Other advancements are possible in some languages, such as location promotion, time promotion, and so on. Again, such clauses may be used in appropriate contexts to emphasize the location or time and in nominalized and relativized clauses that focus on the location or time. In English, we use different subordinating conjunctions to change the focus of relativized clauses, such as: <u>when</u>, and <u>where</u>.

'The year <u>when we moved here</u> was a good year.'

'The migrants moved to a place <u>where they could make a living</u>.'

E. Moods

Clauses not only may be declarative, but are also interrogative, imperative, nominalized and dependent.

1. Declarative clauses

a. Indicative and subjunctive clauses

In some languages, there are two varieties of declarative clauses, often called indicative and subjunctive, realis and irrealis, or perfect and imperfect. The subjunctive, irrealis, or imperfect, is used in clauses that express hypothetical activities, such as future events, conditional events, events that have not happened yet. The indicative, realis, and perfect is used for present and past events that have actually taken place.

The distinction between the indicative and subjunctive is usually marked in the morphology of the verb, but in some languages they may have a slightly differing clause structure. We have no examples here, but if you need these terms to describe a language, they are here.

b. Final and medial clauses

Also, in many languages, there is a distinction between medial and final clauses. Medial clauses end with relational markers that signal such things as same or different subject in following clause and as close time linkage or delayed time linkage. Final clauses have regular mood markers.

c. Active and stative clauses

There may also be a difference between active and stative clauses. An active clause describes an action as actually occurring or actually having occurred. A stative clause describes the subject of that clause as in the condition of having done or suffered the event. In English, the perfective aspects translate stative clauses quite well. 'William has / had eaten.' Active clauses occur in the backbone of a narrative discourse, and stative clauses occur in setting and background of narrative discourse. Here are examples of active and stative clauses in Tzutujil:

Active:

<u>n-</u>　　<u>e-</u>　　<u>ki-</u>　<u>čaxi</u>　<u>-x</u>　　　　　　　　　　<u>či</u>　<u>üȼ</u>
continuous- them- they- care.for -transitive　　re　good

<u>xa</u>　　<u>täq</u>　　<u>ki-</u>　<u>karnelo</u>
the　plural　their- sheep

'They take very good care of their sheep.'

Stative:

<u>xa</u>　　<u>Dios</u>　<u>in-</u>　<u>r-</u>　<u>čaxi</u>　<u>-n</u>　　　　　<u>či</u>　<u>üȼ</u>
the　God　me-　he- care.for -stative　　re　good

'God has taken good care of me.'

Note that the stative verb obligatorily lacks any aspectual prefix. (See Butler and Butler.)

2. Interrogative clauses

There are three kinds of interrogative clauses. One type demands an answer of 'yes' or 'no'. The second demands a choice between two or more alternatives. The third demands an answer that gives information.

a. Yes-no questions

The yes-no interrogative is usually minimally different from a declarative clause. In English, we can give an interrogative intonation to a declarative clause and have a yes-no question, for example:

<u>Mary came yesterday?</u>

Or we can promote the tense and an auxiliary verb to the fore, for example:

<u>Did Mary come yesterday?</u>

<u>Does</u> / <u>will</u> Rulon <u>want</u> <u>to</u> <u>come</u>, <u>too</u>?

In other languages, an interrogative affix on the verb or an interrogative particle somewhere in the clause will signal a yes-no question.

b. Alternative questions

Alternative interrogatives are often related to the yes-no interrogatives in the way they are formed. The difference is that one of the tagmemes of the clause is expounded by an alternative phrase, or two clauses with some shared elements are collapsed into an alternative structure. The answer is expected to be one of the alternatives:

<u>Did Mary come yesterday or the day before?</u>

<u>Would you like apple pie or mince pie?</u>

<u>Did Hiram, or Seymour, tell you that?</u>

<u>Will the country go into a recession or be able to recover reasonably soon?</u>

(This last example might better be analyzed as a sentence-level structure.)

c. Information questions or queries

Information interrogatives usually involve substituting an interrogative pronoun for some clause constituent and then permuting the interrogative pronoun to the front of the clause, for example:

<u>Who came yesterday?</u>

<u>What did he do yesterday?</u>

<u>Where did he go yesterday?</u>

<u>When did he go?</u>

<u>Why did he go yesterday?</u>

<u>Whom did he see yesterday?</u>

Notice that English also requires the fronting of an auxiliary verb with the tense for all questions except those beginning with <u>who</u>.

A few languages do not front the interrogative pronoun. This is also acceptable in English. for example:

<u>Mary saw what yesterday?</u>

<u>Mary saw Jerry when/where?</u>

3. Command clauses

There may be two or three variants of command clauses. The most basic and most common is the second-person imperative:

  Come here!

  Give me that!

  Don't break that plate!

Another common type of command clause is the hortatory clause involving first person plural:

  Let's go out tonight!

  Let's eat!

A rare but useful type of command involves a third person actor. This command may be called 'jussive'. In English, we have to use an optative here, for example:

  Let them play this afternoon!

  Let the light shine on your book!

Other languages have true third-person imperatives.

4. Optative and desiderative clause expresses a hope and a wish. English has three types of optative clause:

  a. Let the rain come!

   Let the wind blow through the house!

  b. Oh, that it would rain.

   Oh, that the wind would blow.

  c. Would that it would rain.

   Would that I were strong enough to do it.

All of these optative clauses sound a bit archaic or academic. They are not in common use. A more common way to express the same wishes or hopes is with an indirect quotation sentence:

  I hope it will rain.

  I wish it would rain.

(We are going through these English examples not so much to teach English grammar but to teach the names and what they refer to, so that they can be applied to another language.)

F. Nominalized clauses

1. Clauses can be nominalized to focus on the predicate, subject, object, or any clause-level tagmeme. In English, we nominalize a clause to focus on its predicate by using a nominalized verb:

'<u>Harley's</u> <u>sudden</u> <u>change</u> <u>of</u> <u>attitude</u> surprised us.'

'<u>Lara's</u> <u>objections</u> caused <u>our</u> <u>reconsideration</u> <u>of</u> <u>our</u> <u>plans</u>.'

Note how the subject exponent is changed to a possessor phrase and the verb is nominalized. We might treat the clause as a noun phrase, also.

Nominalized clause - focusing on predicate - A

± Nominalized subject	+ Nominalized predicate-A	± Nominalized object	+ other tagmemes
possessor phrase-A (-'s)	nominalized verb	possessor phrase-B (of...)	

We can also nominalize a clause to focus on its predicate by using a participial -ing verb.

'<u>Driving</u> <u>on</u> <u>the</u> <u>wrong</u> <u>side</u> <u>of</u> <u>the</u> <u>road</u> is against the law.'

'<u>Passing</u> <u>that</u> <u>test</u> was no easy task.'

Nominalized clause - focusing on predicate - B

± Nominalized subject	+ Nominalized predicate-B	+ Object	+ other tagmemes
possessor phrase-A	verb nominalized with -ing 'participial'	noun phrase pronoun proper noun plus others	

We could also treat these as descriptive noun phrases.

2. Clauses can be nominalized to focus on their subjects if the exponent of the subject is indefinite (in English).

'<u>Anyone living in a glass house</u> should be careful about throwing stones.'

'<u>Whoever wins first prize</u> will receive a free trip for two to Hawaii.'

Nominalized clause - focusing on the subject

+ Nominalized subject	+ Nominalized predicate	+ Other tagmemes
<u>anyone</u>	verb nominalized with <u>-ing</u>	
<u>whoever</u>	verb (singular)	

3. We nominalize clauses to focus on their objects by using passive clauses, for example:

'<u>Anyone being seen out late</u> will be disciplined.'

'<u>Whoever is seen out late</u> will be disciplined.'

The arrays are the same as the two above but with passive verbs expounding the nominalized predicate.

4. In English we can nominalize a clause on both its subject and object by preposing a <u>that,</u> for example:

'<u>That Silas passed the exam</u> surprised no one.'

'<u>That the earth revolves around the sun</u> was a new idea in the sixteenth century.'

Nominalized clause - focusing on the whole clause

+ Nominalizing relator	+ Nominalized axis
<u>that</u>	any clause or sentence

5. In Mayan languages, a clause is nominalized on its subject by preposing an article:

   Nominalized clause: focusing on subject (Mayan)

+ Nominalizing relator	+ Nominalized axis
'the' 'the emphatic'	any declarative clause

   Here is an example of a nominalized clause in Chorti of Guatemala (data supplied by John Lubeck):

   tua'   war   che ke   tua'
   in.order.to continuous say that in.order.to

   u-   bahk   -se
   he- fear.passive -cause

   e
   the   (nominalizing article)

   tin   war   u-   šot -i   -ob   ut
   whoever   continuous he- stop -transitive -plural face

   e   hahar o   e   iyk'ar
   the rain   or the wind

   o   ah-   war   -kin
   or professional- stand -heaven

   o   en kontra   tua' e   hahar
   or in against of   the rain

   tua'   ma'chi uy- akt -ob   a-   k'aši e   hahar
   in.order.to not   he- stop -plural his- fall   the rain

   'He is doing this to frighten anyone who is trying to stop the rain or the wind or the rain makers or whoever is against the rain so that they won't stop it from falling.'

   (In other words, the rain god sends thunder to frighten any who would oppose him.) Note how the e nominalizes the following three clauses, which are conjoined by o 'or'. The nominalized cluster serves as the object of u- bahk -se.

In some languages, a clause is nominalized by a postclitic on the verb, or by special inflections on the verb.

G. Relativized clauses

Relative clauses are clauses that modify a noun. We might call them adjectivized clauses.

Relative clauses in English, and related languages, are called restrictive and nonrestrictive. Restrictive relative clauses are necessary to the identification of the referent of the noun. Nonrestrictive relative clauses only add further information. We set off the latter with commas, for example:

(Restrictive)

'The students who are in the anthropology class will meet today at 3 PM.'

'The person that took Longacre's book from the library should return it today.'

(Nonrestrictive)

'My father, who is an accountant, always has lots of work to do.'

'The president, who gets all the privileges, is to serve on all three committees.'

In English, both kinds of relative clauses are formed by the same changes.

Relative clause

+ Relative Relator	+ Relative Axis
who that	any clause minus its subject
whom that	any transitive passive clause minus its subject

In some languages, it is hard to say whether a relative clause is indeed a modifying clause or whether it is a nominalized clause in apposition to the noun preceding it. These languages have such structures as:

the man the he-me-sold corn ...

'The man who sold me the corn ...'

or 'The man, the one who sold me the corn ...'

H. Dependent clauses

Clauses are made dependent by adding a subordinating conjunction such as when, if, since, after, before, because, and several others. Usually, such clauses are of the same form as declarative clauses, but they are made dependent by the connectors attached to them, or they may have specially inflected verbs to mark dependency.

In English, the subordinating conjunctions are all preposed free words. In many languages, the conjunctions are clause-level clitics that look like verb suffixes. (A clitic is a bound affix that operates on phrase level or higher; ordinary affixes operate at word level.) For English the general form is:

Dependent temporal clause

+ Temporal relator	+ Temporal axis
when	any declarative clause

For other languages, the general form is:

Dependent temporal clause for other languages

+ Temporal axis	+ Temporal relator
any declarative clause, minus mood	-ke 'when'

Dependent clauses usually expound margin tagmemes on sentence level and clause level. Because each different one expounds a different tagmeme, we do not group them into one clause type. We have such clauses as: Dependent prior time clause, Dependent simultaneous time clause, Dependent conditional clause, Dependent reason clause, Dependent concession clause, and so on. Giving them all distinctive names simplifies referring to them in sentence formulas.

When giving examples of dependent clauses, be sure to give full-sentence examples to show how they are used, for example:

Dependent concession clause example:

> 'Although Rori worked on his garden, he couldn't keep ahead of the weeds.'

An example of a dependent condition clause (Inibaloi):

<u>talaka'n iamagkan</u>   <u>to</u>   no   <u>aman -ikdog</u>
(probably make.for   he)   if   laying -egg

'Probably he will make (a nest) for her if she is egg-laying.'

In some languages, the subordinating conjunctions are inflected for the person (and, possibly, number) of the person in the axis. Such a construction looks like:

'<u>my-because</u> I was sick, I didn't come to school'

or: 'I didn't come to school, <u>my-because</u> I was sick'

'<u>his-condition</u> he is able, he will work tomorrow'

or: 'he will work tomorrow, <u>his-if</u> he is able'

The syntagmeme array for the dependent clause would be the same as for a noninflected subordinating conjunction. But there would have to be a word-level syntagmeme to describe the inflected conjunction.

I. Other dependent, modifying clauses

In English we can have subordinate clauses modifying nouns and adjectives. Consider the following:

Subordinate clauses preceded by a subordinating conjunction as in the following examples:

1. 'a special form <u>for sending in your application</u>'

2. 'various methods <u>whereby we can achieve our goals</u>'

Also constructions involving an adjective and an infinitive clause:

1. 'too hot <u>to handle</u>'

2. 'too complicated <u>to solve in one evening</u>'

Similarly, a construction involving a noun or an adjective and an infinitive clause:

1. 'It is time <u>to apply for the scholarship.</u>'

2. 'He is willing / ready / able / bound <u>to</u> <u>apply</u> <u>for the scholarship.</u>'

In the above examples, the subordinate clauses in the first group have a relator-axis structure, the second two groups do not, but have infinitival verbs. All function as postmodifiers in a noun phrase or in an adjective phrase.

Matrix of clause types

	Declar	Interr	Command	Medial	Final	Yes-no	Alternative	Information	Imperative	Hortatory	Jussive	Optative	Nominalized	Relative	Dependent
Bitransitive active															
passive															
passive															
Transitive active															
passive															
Transitive+location															
Intransitive															
Intransitive+location															
Intransitive+complem.															
Ambient															
Descriptive															
Equative															
Possession															
Name															
Location															
Existential															

J. Clause-search matrix

The clause types we have discussed can be placed in an etic search matrix. The degrees of transitivity and verbless clauses are placed on one axis of the matrix and the moods and related things are placed on the other axis (see above).

Comments on the search matrix

First of all, this matrix is not a complete etic matrix. Some languages will have clause types not on this matrix, for example: semitransitive, pseudopassive. Second, no language will have all these clause types as emically separate constructions. For example, in English, the intransitives and ambient clauses do not contrast, the descriptive and equative do not contrast, and name, possession and kinship clauses fall into the regular transitive clauses or into the descriptive-equative pattern. For any particular language, the number of rows should be reduced or increased to the number needed for that language.

K. Cohesion in clauses

There are several methods of keeping relationships clear in a clause. They include: fixed word order, case markings, gender cross-referencing, and person hierarchy.

1. English has a fixed word order in which the subject precedes the predicate and the object follows the verb. Exceptions to this are possible but rare, and often poetic.

2. Latin had a full system of case markers. The words could come in any order, because one could always tell their function by their case markings.

English constituents, other than subject and object, have prepositions that serve as case markers. English prepositional phrases can come in almost any order, since their function is signaled by the preposition.

3. Some languages have an intricate system of genders and/or noun classes that are cross-referenced into the pronominal affixes on the verb. Some Arnhemland languages in Australia have such a system, with six genders or noun classes, and a complex system of verb prefixes. This crossreferencing is usually called 'agreement' or 'concord'.

4. Some American Indian languages use a hierarchy of persons, such as: first person, second person, third person definite, third person indefinite, and fourth person. Any verb with a subject whose person is of lower number than the person of the object has one form. If the person of the subject is of a higher number than that of the object, another form of the verb must be used. Here is an example that Don Frantz has given:

nit-   a-   ino -a   -oa   imitaoa
1- durative-   see -up.rank -3   dog.3

'I see the dog.'

nit-   a-   ino -k   -∅   imitaoa
1- durative-   see -down.rank -3   dog.3

'The dog sees me.'

Bibliography

Butler, James and Judy Garland Butler. 1977. Tzutujil verbs. Guatemala: The Summer Institute of Linguistics.

Foley, William A. and Robert D. Van Valin, Jr. 1977. On the viability of the notion of 'subject' in universal grammar. Proceedings of the 3rd annual meeting of the Berkeley Linguistics Society. Berkeley, California: Berkeley Linguistics Society, University of California.

Frantz, Donald G. 1966. Person indexing in Blackfoot. I.J.A.L. 32. 50-58.

_____. 1971. Toward a generative grammar of Blackfoot (with particular attention to selected stem formation processes). Norman, Oklahoma: Summer Institute of Linguistics and the University of Oklahoma.

Hopper, Paul J. and Sandra A. Thompson. 1980. Transitivity in grammar and discourse. Language 56:2.251-99.

Li, Charles N., ed. 1976. Subject and Topic. New York: Academic Press, Inc. (This book has several germinal articles.)

Sadock, Jerrold M. 1980. Noun incorporation in Greenlandic: a case of syntactic word formation. Language 56:2.300-319.

Ulrich, Matthew and Charles Peck. Mopan Mayan verbs. MS.

Van Haitsma, Julia Dieterman and Willard Van Haitsma. 1976. A hierarchical sketch of Mixe as spoken in San José El Paraíso. Norman, Oklahoma: Summer Institute of Linguistics and the University of Oklahoma.

Chapter 10

Case grammar

In this survey of grammatical constructions, it seems appropriate to discuss briefly the lexical studies that have been made on words and stems. Many people have been unhappy with the emphasis that has been placed on grammar and surface structures recently and have worked, instead, on the meaning of languages, which is a large science in itself. Here we will discuss the lexical decomposition of verbs.

A. Lexical decomposition of verbs

Some verbs describe complex actions. For example, Peter Landerman (Landerman and Frantz, Notes on Grammatical Theory, 1972) gives a Quechua verb:

    alli -ya -chi
    well -become -cause

    'to heal'

Even in English, the verb 'heal' means 'to cause someone to become well'. ('Heal' can also mean 'to become well' in an intransitive sense.)

Consider the verb 'persuade' in the sentences:

    Estelle persuaded Samuel to go to work.

    Samuel begins to intend to do something as a
        result of Estelle's action.

So 'persuade' means 'cause someone to begin to intend'. 'Persuade' also almost means that the persuaded person actually does the thing he intends, so 'persuade' may mean 'to cause someone to intend and to do something'. And if something intervenes to prevent the doing, we have to state that fact explicitly.

Now, let's look at the words we used in that last sentence, words like 'intervene' and 'prevent'. 'Intervene' involves 'causing' and 'negativelike' components. Perhaps we could break it down into 'to try to cause someone not to do' or 'to do something to cause someone to intend not to do'. 'Prevent' means 'to cause not to do'.

Certain religious terms such as 'forgive', 'believe', 'trust', 'sanctify', and 'redeem', are composite terms that can, and often must, be reduced to their components for translation. It is the job of a good dictionary to give one the semantic components of the meaning of a word.

Back in 1963, Katz and Fodor proposed a semantic theory based on such semantic components. The theory floundered because the components that had to be posited seemed to be very large—almost as large as the language itself. But they had an interesting discussion of 'the colorful ball'. Consider the sentence: <u>Barbara threw a colorful ball</u>; and its two meanings: 'She gave a party', and 'She caused a round object to move through the air'. In such a sentence, the components of meaning of 'throw', 'colorful', and 'ball' must all be compatible. 'Throw' can mean 'to sponsor with a flourish' or 'to cause something to move through the air'. 'Colorful' can mean 'abounding in contrast or variety of colors' as applied to a social event or to a physical object. 'Ball' can mean 'an occasion for social dancing' or 'a small spherical object'.

The two combinations of meaning in the one clause above are meaningful only if the semantic components of the words fit together properly. When we translate or speak a foreign language, we make wrong or funny sentences when we choose words whose semantic components are not compatible and do not fit together properly. The problem is especialy severe in translation, where one is introducing new ideas and new collocations.

B. Scope and structure

Another phase of semantic study is the study of the 'scope' of certain items. For example, Gene Loos (in Landerman and Frantz) gives the following Capanahua sentences:

1. <u>cochi</u>   <u>ta</u>   <u>ca -ha -x -qui</u>
   pig   decl   go -past -3 -decl

   'The pig went.'

2. <u>cochi</u>   <u>ta</u>   <u>ca -yama -ha -x -qui</u>
   pig   decl   go -neg -past -3 -decl

   'The pig did not go.'

3. <u>hochitinin</u> <u>ta</u>   <u>cochi</u> <u>ca -ma -yama -ha -x -quin</u>
   dog   decl   pig   go -cause -not -past -3 -decl

   'The dog didn't cause the pig to go.'

4. <u>hochitinin</u> <u>ta</u>   <u>cochi</u>   <u>ca -yama -ma -ha -x -quin</u>
   dog   decl   pig   go -not -cause -past -3 -decl

   'The dog caused the pig not to go.' or
   'The dog prevented the pig from going.'

<u>5.</u> <u>hochitinin</u> <u>ta</u>   <u>cochi ca -yama -ma -yama -ha -x -quin</u>
    dog   decl   pig   go -not -cause -not -past -3 -decl

   'The dog didn't cause the pig not to go.' or
   'The dog allowed the pig to go.'

157

Notice how each suffix in the verb modifies what precedes it. We could diagram the semantics of the verb in #5 as follows:

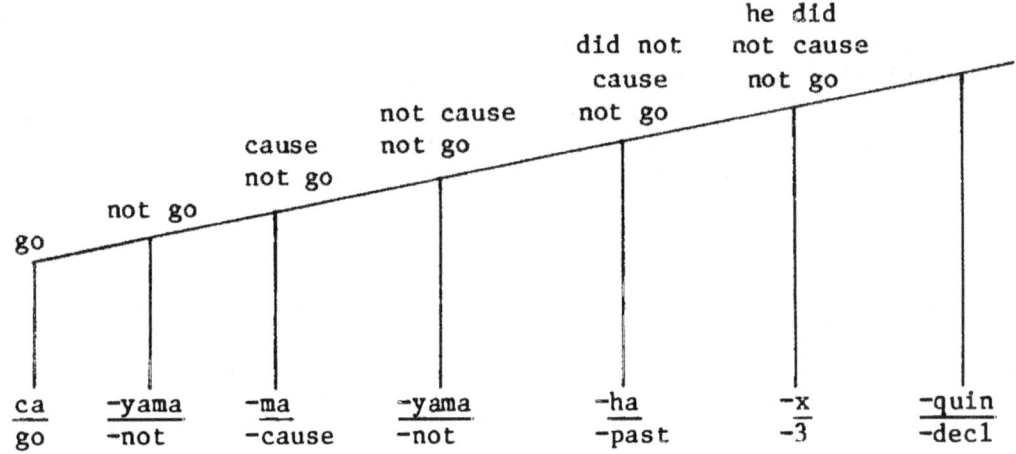

David Weber found a similar semantic structure in Quechua.

Zeno Vendler (1968. <u>Adjectives and Nominalizations</u>) found a similar phenomenon governing the order of adjectives in the English noun phrase. The most adjectivelike adjectives come first and the most nonadjectivelike modifiers come last. He was able to distinguish more than a dozen different classes of adjectives by using paraphrases and transformations.

A noun phrase such as 'big rectangular green Chinese carpet' would be diagrammed semantically as follows:

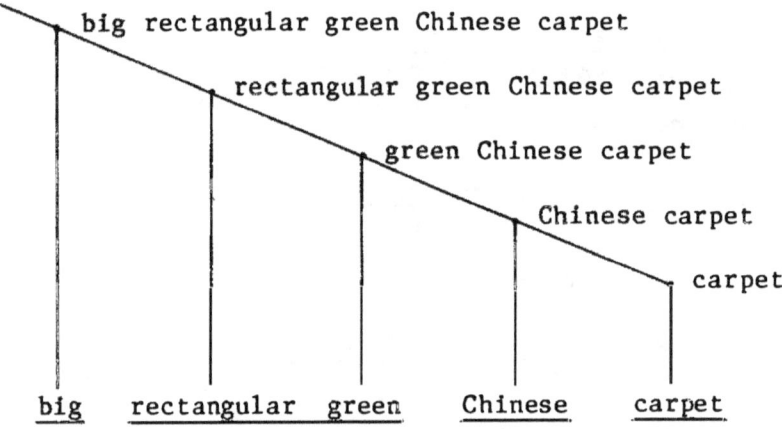

However a phrase such as 'big rectangular red and green Chinese carpet' would have the following diagram:

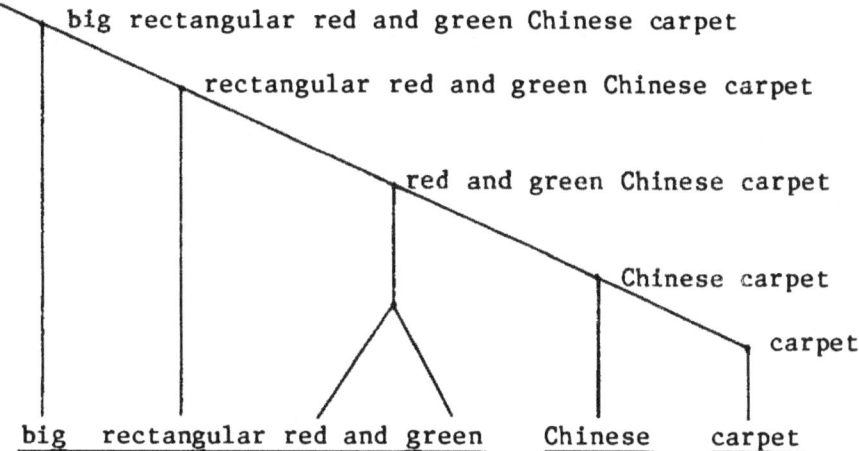

Notice how adjectives of different ranks cannot be coordinated, such as *'big rectangular red green and Chinese carpet'. For a more complete discussion, see Vendler, 1968.

A comparison of the Capanahua diagram with the English diagrams shows how in Capanahua modifiers follow the main item and in English they precede the main item.

C. Lexical properties of nouns

When one studies which nouns can go with which verbs, certain semantic properties of nouns are relevant. Wallace Chafe (1970, <u>Meaning and the Structure of Language</u>) brought many of these ideas together, and what follows is taken largely from his book. First, nouns in English are either count nouns or mass nouns. Count nouns can take a numerical quantifier; mass nouns cannot.

<u>some</u> <u>air</u>	<u>some</u> <u>apples</u>
*<u>six</u> <u>airs</u>	<u>six</u> <u>apples</u>
*<u>a</u> <u>dozen</u> <u>airs</u>	<u>a</u> <u>dozen</u> <u>apples</u>
*<u>dozens</u> <u>of</u> <u>airs</u>	<u>dozens</u> <u>of</u> <u>apples</u>

In other languages, nouns may be divided into obligatorily possessed and optionally possessed (and sometimes obligatorily unpossessed) classes, which affects the kinds of noun phrases they can occur in.

Secondly, many verbs require an animate or a human subject, as the following two impossible sentences demonstrate:

*<u>The</u> <u>rock</u> <u>saw</u> <u>the</u> <u>fish</u>.

*The fern studied the worm.

So one component of noun meaning is whether it is animate or human or not.

Chafe points out that there are verbs that require a 'potent' noun as subject, such as cut, hit,

The river cut through the dike.

The hail hit our roof.

The wind eroded the sand dunes.

Most of these verbs can also take animate subjects. Hence the broadest class of noun is 'potent'. A subset of 'potent' nouns are 'animate', and a subset of 'animate' nouns is 'human'. A verb like erode takes a 'potent' but 'non-animate' subject. A verb like study takes a 'human' subject.

Some verbs require certain kinds of objects. Erode takes a 'concrete' object that has certain characteristics. Annoy takes an animate object; amaze takes a human object.

Other characteristics of nouns that might be relevant in other languages are generic versus specific versus random (any one). Some may make a difference between concrete and abstract.

In some languages, whether the object is inhabited by a spirit, or not, will be relevant to some part of the grammar. For example, in Cheyenne, rocks are animate, as far as grammar is concerned.

D. Semantic derivations

A consideration of verbs uncovered three basic components of verb meaning: state, process, and action.
Some verbs describe a 'state' that is unchanging, such as:

The clothing is dry.   The water is hot.

The glass is broken.   The animal is dead.

The road is narrow.

In general, these are descriptive clauses and cannot be made imperative.

The next class of verbs describes a change of state, or a 'process,' such as:

The clothing is drying.   The animal is dying.

The water is warming up / getting hot.

These clauses all have a component of 'beginning' or 'becoming'. Chafe called this component 'inchoative'.

There is a class of related transitive verbs, called 'action-process' verbs, such as:

She is drying the clothing.   I am heating the water.

He is breaking the glass.   He is killing the animal.

In these clauses, another participant is added who causes the change of state.

There is also a fourth class of active intransitive verbs, called 'action' verbs, such as in:

They are dancing.   Harry sneezes a lot in the summer.

He is singing in the shower.

These verbs involve an activity but not a change of the state of something.

Walter A. Cook (1972. 'A Case Grammar Matrix') took these four classes of verbs and put them into a derivation chart.

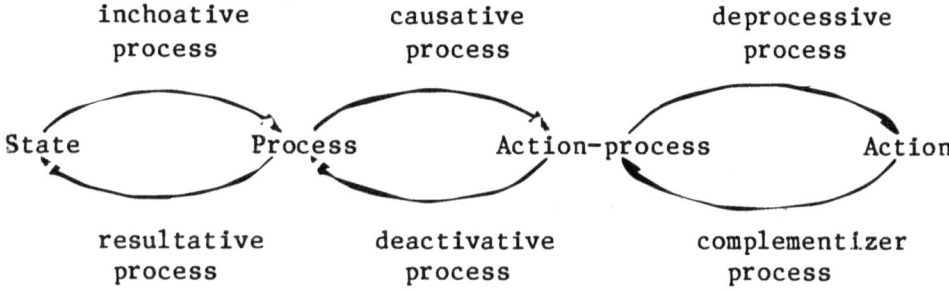

These derivation processes are illustrated further in the clauses below:

Inchoative process:
    dry (state) -> dry out (process)
    hot (state) -> heat up (process)

Resultative process:
    widen (process) -> wide (state)
    die (process) -> dead (state)

Causative process:
    die (process) -> kill (action-process)
    break (process) -> break (action-process)

Deactivative process:
    kill (action-process) -> die (process)
    widen (action-process) -> widen (process)

Deprocessive process:
    cut (action-process) (transitive) -> cut (action)
        (intransitive: This knife cuts well.)

Complementizer process:
    dance (action) -> dance (action-process)
        (Maria dances the tango.)

    sing (action) __> sing (action-process)
        (Maria is singing vs. Maria is singing a ballad.)

In the array above, action-process verbs derived from action verbs cannot take 'deactivative process', and action-process verbs derived from process verbs cannot take 'deprocessive process'.

Cook integrated these verb classes with Fillmore's case grammar, as we shall see later.

E. Case grammar

Case grammar dates from Charles Fillmore's germinal paper 'The Case for Case', which was published in 1968 in <u>Universals in Linguistic Theory</u> (ed. by Bach and Harms). It circulated in mimeographed form for a year before it was published and excited much interest.

Fillmore began with sentences such as the following:

    <u>John broke the window.</u>
    <u>A hammer broke the window.</u>
    <u>John broke the window with a hammer.</u>
    <u>The window broke.</u>

    <u>John opened the door.</u>
    <u>This key opened the door.</u>
    <u>John opened the door with this key.</u>
    <u>The door opened.</u>

and impossible sentences such as:

    *<u>John and a hammer broke the window.</u>
    *<u>John and this key opened the door.</u>

Obviously something is going on in addition to the surface structure. So he set up some case notions, namely:

    Agentive (A) (sometimes called 'agent' or 'actor')

    Instrumental (I)

Dative (D) (others call it 'patient' or 'undergoer')

Factive (F) (others call it 'objective')

Locative (L) (others have split this into 'source' and 'goal')

Objective (O)

By 1970, he had revised his case notions (as reported by Walter Cook (1971: 'Improvements in Case Grammar' 1970)):

A	Agentive	instigator of the action, animate
E	Experiencer	affected by the action, animate
I	Instrumental	force or object causing action or state
O	Objective	semantically most neutral case
S	Source	the origin or starting point
G	Goal	the object or end point
L	Locative	spatial orientation of the action
T	Time	temporal orientation of the action
C	Comitative	accompaniment role, animate
B	Benefactive	benefactive role, animate

Before going further, we should note that a clause is divided into two parts: its verb and its case-related nominals on the one hand and the tense, aspects, mood, negative, and other marginal items (all grouped together under the term 'modality') on the other hand. Case grammar deals with the first part and ignores the modality part. So case grammar cannot capture all there is in language.

Locative and time margins are always included in the modality except when they are vitally related to the verb. Sentence-level benefactive also is left in the modality (Platt's outer benefactive).

To account for the clauses earlier in this chapter, Fillmore set up a selection hierarchy for the subject. The hierarchy is A-E-I-O-S-G. If A is present, it is subject. If A is absent and E is present, E is subject. If A and E are both absent and I is present, then I becomes the subject. If A, E and I are absent and O is present, then O becomes subject.

For the object, there is a different selection hierarchy, namely, E-O-G for most verbs. Some verbs have an O-E-G object hierarchy.

Different verbs take different selections of cases; each verb has its own case frame or case frames. For example, 'break' and 'open' have A-I-O, where A and I are optional and O is obligatory. Fillmore symbolized these case frames as [_____(A)(I)O]. L, T, and B are also possible but are nondiagnostic and are left in the modality, because they go with most verbs. The parentheses around A and I shows that they are optional.

Case frames for other verbs are:

    kill   [_____ E (I)(A)] where either I or A or both must occur, thus the linked parentheses.

    murder   [_____ E (I) A]

    be true [_____ O]

    want   [_____ E O]

    say   [_____ A O (E)]

    persuade [_____ A E O_s] where O_s is a proposition.

    withdraw [_____ A O S] but A and O may be coreferential.

    hear   [_____ E O]

    listen to [_____ A O]

Fillmore stresses that the case system has to be determined anew for each language. We tend to treat cases as universals, so Fillmore's point is well taken. In your language, you can begin with the system presented here (for English), and adapt it to fit your language.

If you adopt a fine enough grid, you can come up with many cases and case frames. The problem then is to group the cases into 'emic' cases with etic variants. By so doing, we hope you will arrive at some kind of emic case system for your language.

F. Case matrices

Walter Cook (1972. 'A Case Grammar Matrix') combined Chafe's derivation ideas and Fillmore's case grammar and made a 4x4 matrix.

	(A) Basic verb	(B) + Experiencer	(C) + Benefactive	(D) + Locative
S t a t e	1. Os verb broken, adj dry, adj dead, adj tight, adj	1. Es O verb know like want doubt	1. Bs O verb have have got own	1. Os L verb (be) in (be) on (be) under
P r o c e s s	2. O verb break, iv die, iv dry, iv tighten, iv	2. E O verb feel hear see	2. B O verb find lose win	2. O L verb come go move
A c t i o n	3. A verb dance laugh play sing	3. A E verb frighten please answer question	3. A B verb arm bribe help supply	3. A L verb come go run walk
A c t i o n P r o c e s s	4. A O verb break, tv dry, tv kill, tv tighten, tv	4. A E O verb ask speak say teach tell remind show	4. A B O verb buy give sell accept	4. A O L verb bring place put take

Here are some example clauses using the verbs in Cook's matrix:

A.1. Os verb: The dish is broken. The wood is dry.
A.2. O verb: The ice is breaking. The wood is drying.
A.3. A verb: The kids are playing in the backyard. Ethel sings in the shower.
A.4. A O verb: William is breaking dishes. He is tightening the rope.

B.1. Es O verb: We know the national anthem. We like it.
B.2. E O verb: I felt an earth tremor. Can you see me?
B.3. A E verb: He is deliberately frightening the baby. I'll answer your question, if I can.
B.4. A E O verb: Sally said 'hello' to Mary. She told her the good news.

C.1. Bs O verb: I have a car now. He owns two dogs.
C.2. B O verb: I've found my maps. Seymore won the booby prize.

C.3. A B verb: The U.S. is arming Egypt. You have to bribe him to get anything done.
C.4. A B O verb: Henry buys the groceries for the family. I accepted the cheque on behalf of the church.

D.1. Os L verb: Your book is on your desk. The paper I want is under that stack of papers.
D.2. O L verb: July is coming soon. The desert in North Africa is moving south.
D.3. A L verb: I'm coming to your room to see you. Helen is walking to the store.
D.4. A O L verb: Stanley took his car to the garage. Marty brings her knitting to lectures. I put my important papers in a special drawer.

Whenever there is an agentive in a case frame, the verb can be made imperative because an agentive generally exerts some decision of the will to do the action. An experiencer, on the other hand, is a passive participant who cannot be commanded to participate. Thus see takes an experiencer, look at takes an agentive. You can't command anyone to experience some action, but you can command him to try to experience it.

The benefactive of column C and the locative of column D are inner benefactive and inner locative in Platt's terms. They are required by the verb and its case frame. Outer locative (on sentence level) can go with almost any clause, and outer benefactive can go with any clause that contains an agentive. An example with an outer locative is:

'In small communities, children walk to school.'

An example with an outer benefactive is:

'For you, I'll sell your car to the highest bidder.'

(For you is an outer benefactive, and the highest bidder is an inner benefactive, encoded as an indirect object.)

G. Longacre's case system

Robert Longacre (1976) set up some new cases, namely 'patient', 'range', 'measure', and 'path'. 'Patient' is an inanimate entity of which state or location is predicated or which undergoes a change of state or location. It was included in Fillmore's 'objective' case. It involves such verbs as throw, slide, fall, and other motion or causative motion verbs.

'Range' is the nominal that completes or further specifies a verb, in such combinations as sing a song; fight a battle; study a lesson; play a game; eat food, and so on. It was a part of the 'Objective' case in Fillmore's system.

'Measure' is the nominal that completes a predication by quantifying it, for example: weigh a kilogram; cost ten dollars; gain ten yards; buy something for ten dollars; and so on.

'Path' is added to 'locative', 'source', and 'goal'. 'Path' is the course of movement attached to a verb.

Longacre's total case system may be summarized as follows:

A agent
   a. the animate entity that exercises some volition in performing the action of the verb
     'Tom (A) opened the door.'

  *b. some inanimate forces of nature and some abstract entities that cause or perform the action of the verb
     'The wind (A) blew the tree down.'

  * There are differences of opinion concerning nonanimate agents. If they are not counted as agents, then they must be patients or sources, which creates other problems (see below).

E experiencer
   a. the animate entity whose registering nervous system is relevant to the action of the verb
     'He frightened me (E).'
     'Mary (E) likes sour apples.'

G goal
   a. the end location of a motion
     'Hank threw the ball to Joe (G).'

   b. the owner in a possession clause
     'That coat is Joan's (G).'

   c. the final owner in a transfer
     'Hank sold his car to Joe (G).'

   d. the entity at which the activity of a verb is aimed and which is not affected by the activity of the verb
     'Mary accused Joe (G).'
     'Jerry loves Helen (G).'

I instrument
   a. the entity that an agent uses to accomplish the activity of the verb
     'John hit Bill with a club (I).'

   b. the entity that triggers (a change in) an emotional state
     'Sally is afraid of snakes (I).'

   c. the price in a transfer using with
     'John bought a shirt with his gift certificate (I).'

L locative
   a. the locale of an activity

'We keep our car in our garage (L).'
'My parents live in California (L).'

M measure
    a. the nominal that quantifies the activity of a predicate
       'I've gained five pounds (M).'

    b. the price in a transfer with no preposition or with for
       'It costs ten dollars (M).'
       'They bought their house for fifty thousand dollars (M).'

P patient
    a. the entity that undergoes a change in state or location
       'The rope (P) broke.'
       'He broke the axe handle (P).'
       'John threw his clothes (P) into the closet.'

    b. the entity of which a state or change of state is predicated
       'That tree (P) is very old now.'
       'Measles (P) is contagious.'
       'Anthony (P) was a saint.'

Path path
    a. the locale transversed in a motion
       'We returned from Australia by way of Europe (Path).'

    b. the transitory owner or bearer in a transaction
       'Sally gave Wilson (Path) a recipe for his wife.'

R range
    a. the product of the activity of a verb
       'Beethoven composed several symphonies (R).'
       'Mary sang a song (R).'

    b. the entity involved in the activity of the verb but not affected by that activity
       'Bart is learning to speak Chinese (R).'

    c. the entity that completes or further specifies the verb
       'Our team played a good game (R).'

    d. the entity or quotation that is spoken, written, thought, known, guessed, dreamed, surmised, and so on
       'Josh knows a lot of jokes (R).'
       'I said, "Come here" (R).'

S source
    a. the beginning place from which an entity moves
       'The boat drifted from its moorings (S).'

    b. the source of physical sensations
       'The chief heard an owl (S).'
       ['The chief (E) heard the sound (R) of an owl (S).']

c. the original owner in a transfer
   'Sam bought a motorcycle from Roscoe (S).'

In general, there can be only one of each case in a predication (simple clause), which means that there can be only one agent, one patient, one experiencer, one locative, and so forth. If there is more than one constituent in the surface structure of a clause requiring the same case assignment, then those constituents are conjoined as a coordinate encoding of a single case.

Consider the following:

'Julius(A) wrote the paper with his associate, John Weston (A).'

Julius, and his associate, John Weston are all a complex but singular AGENT in the clause.

We allow nominals to fill more than one role. For example, in the following clauses, the subjects are, respectively, AGENT / SOURCE, AGENT / GOAL, AGENT / EXPERIENCER:

'I (A/S) gave my notes (P) to Harry (G).'

'Harry (A/G) grabbed his coat (P) and ran.'

'We (A/E) listened to the ball game (R) on the radio (Path) last night.'

'We (A/E) listened to some records (S) last night (T).'

And in the following clause, the object is both a PATIENT and an EXPERIENCER:

'John (A) hurt his younger brother (P/E) in the scuffle.'

In the next clause, the object may be both PATIENT and MEASURE:

'They (A/S) gave Nancy (G) five hundred dollars (P/M) for her car.'

Saksena, 1980, points out that there is a difference, syntactically, in Hindi, between affected AGENTs and unaffected AGENTs. For example, the AGENTs in the two clauses below are affected AGENTs:

'Ross (afA or A/E) ate dinner early last night.'

'Ross (afA or A/E) showered before dinner last night.'

We might capture the affectedness by assigning both AGENT and EXPERIENCER to the affected subjects, but this solution may not be acceptable for some languages.

Unaffected AGENTs are AGENTs who do something to something else but are not affected themselves:

'Harry (unafA) burned his old papers in the incinerator.'

'Harry (unafA) wrote a nice term paper last semester.'

In Hindi, affected AGENTs are demoted to dative in causative clauses, but unaffected AGENTs are demoted to intrumental (see Saksena's article).

Saksena also mentions the INSTRUMENT may have to be divided between passive INSTRUMENT and active (volitional) INSTRUMENT. Consider the following clauses:

'Ben painted his room with a paint applicator (passive I).'

'Ben sent some of his luggage home by the Johnsons (active I).'

'Ben got his new job on Harry's recommendation (active I).'

In the first clause, the INSTRUMENT is an inanimate object. But in the second and third clauses, the INSTRUMENT involves people who exercise some volition in the action. In English, we have so few instances of active INSTRUMENT that the distinction does not seem useful to us. You will have to decide how useful the distinction between active and passive INSTRUMENTs is in your language.

One other problem is the assignment of nonanimate causers to something besides the agent case. If we assign it to 'patient', then there may be two patients in a single clause, for example:

'The hail (P) damaged our roof (P),'

in which 'hail' and 'roof' are hardly a coordinate patient entity. If we assign inanimate causers to 'source', we may have another conflict, for example:

'The wind (S) blew the boats out of the harbor (S),'

where 'wind' and 'harbor' are not coordinate sources. So for the lack of a suitable case to which to assign inanimate causers, we either posit a new case for them or assign them to 'agent', as we have done above.

As another suggestion, we might take the discourse genre into account in defining the cases. For narrative discourse, we might have one definition of 'agent', and in an expository discourse, we could allow a different definition of 'agent' to include logical nonanimate 'agents.' For example, consider the following example:

'Various scientific findings (A) have changed

ourideas (P) about some diseases.'

Perhaps another way to view the problem is increase the depth of our analysis. The previous example at a deeper semantic level might be:

'Because of various scientific findings (I), we (E) have changed our minds (P) about some diseases.'

Consider another sentence:

'Bill paid the taxi fare (P/M) for me.'

At the highest level taxi fare is a patient, but at some deeper level, it is a measure. These are some of the problems with case grammar.

Robert Longacre also elaborated on Cook's 4x4 matrix. Longacre's matrix has an overall 2x2 plan, - Agent vs. + Agent and + Experiencer vs. - Experiencer. Each quadrant is subdivided by occurrence and nonoccurrence of instrumental, measure, range, path, and patient. His matrix is a 4 x 12 matrix. (See pages 42 to 49 of his An Anatomy of Speech Notions. See also Echerd, 1979.)

H. Conclusion

We accept case grammar as the deep structure of clause level. For the analysis of some languages, you may find that case grammar is not particularly useful. For others it is very useful. In the Philippines, case grammar has helped explain articles on noun phrases and d inflections on verbs. See Teresita V. Ramos: The case system of Tagalog verbs; and Edward Ruch: Role combinations and verb stem classes in Kalamian Tagbanwa.

Bibliography

Chafe, Wallace L. 1970. Meaning and the structure of language. Chicago: The University of Chicago Press.

Cook, Walter A. 1971. Improvements in case grammar 1970. Georgetown University working papers in languages and linguistics, number 2. Washington, D.C.: Georgetown University Press.

_____. 1972. A case grammar matrix. Georgetown University working papers in languages and linguistics, number 6. Washington, D.C.: Georgetown University Press.

Echerd, Stephen M. 1979. Of men, machines and planets. Papers on case grammar, Research papers of the Texas S.I.L. at Dallas no. 6. Dallas: S.I.L.

Fillmore, Charles J. 1968. The case for case. Universals in linguistic theory, ed. by Emmon Bach and Robert T. Harms. New York: Holt, Rinehart and Winston, Inc.

Katz, Jerrold J. and Jerry A. Fodor. 1963. The structure of a semantic theory. Language, vol 39, part 2.

Landerman, Peter L. and Donald Frantz. 1972. Notes on grammatical theory. Lima, Peru: S.I.L.

Longacre, Robert E. 1976. An anatomy of speech notions. Lisse: The Peter de Ridder Press.

Platt, John T. 1971. Grammatical form and grammatical meaning, a tagmemic view of Fillmore's deep structure case concepts. Amsterdam: North Holland Publishing Company.

Ramos, Teresita V. 1974. The case system of Tagalog verbs. Pacific Linguistics, Series B. Number 27. Canberra: The Australian National University.

Ruch, Edward. 1974. Role combinations and verb classes in Kalamian Tagbanwa. Pacific Linguistics, Series A, Number 41. Canberra: The Australian National University.

Saksena, Anuradha. 1980. The affected agent. Language 56:4.812-26.

Vendler, Zeno. 1968. Adjectives and nominalizations. Papers in formal linguistics, Number 5. The Hague: Mouton.

Weber, David. 1976. Suffix as operator analysis and the grammar of successive encoding in Llacón (Huánuco) Quechua. Documento de trabajo No. 13. Yarinacocha, Perú: Instituto Lingüístico de Verano.

Chapter 11

Sentence-level structures

A sentence is a cluster of clauses and other constructions that communicates some logical relationship between the events represented by the clauses. As such, it is the threshold of real communication. A phrase refers to some entity, a clause describes some event or state, but a sentence puts events and states together into some statement about the world.

In general, we can divide sentence structures into a nuclear part, an inner peripheral part, and an outer peripheral part. See Longacre, 1970, from which most of this chapter is taken.

A. Outer-peripheral tagmemes

The outer-peripheral tagmemes include sentence introducers, sentence modifiers, exclamations, vocatives, responses, disclaimers, and some others. Typically, they are expounded by single words and short phrases, and they are elided when a sentence is embedded.

1. Sentence introducer

Sentence introducers are expounded by conjunctions such as: <u>then, and then, so, later, next, and,</u> and <u>however.</u>

2. Sentence modifier

Sentence modifiers are expounded by expressions of the speaker's concern, such as: <u>for sure, certainly, hopefully, really, regretfully,</u> and other such adverbs. Such sentence modifiers have been the subject of studies about 'sentence performatives' among transformational grammarians.

3. Exclamation

Exclamation is expounded by particles such as <u>oh</u> or <u>well</u>.

4. Vocative

Vocative tagmeme is expounded by a name, a kinship term <u>(brother)</u>, or an honorific term <u>(sir)</u>.

5. Response margin

The response margin is expounded by <u>yes, no,</u> or <u>maybe,</u> indicating the speaker's agreement or disagreement with the preceding sentence.

6. Disclaimer margin

The disclaimer margin tagmeme is expounded by a particle or a verb: <u>they say / said,</u> or a phrase: <u>according to our ancestors</u> or <u>according to the experts.</u> The disclaimer usually occurs at the end of the sentence, but in some languages, can be placed anywhere in the sentence. The <u>you know</u> of current American English usage is probably some kind of disclaimer.

7. Summary of outer-peripheral tagmemes

All the outer-peripheral tagmemes are more or less permutable to other places in the sentence. Sometimes the permutation is obligatory, as, for example, in Greek, certain outer-periphery particles must occur after the first word of the sentence. It is often preferable, in English, to move the however back into the sentence somewhere. In some languages, the disclaimer can occur almost anywhere in the sentence.

Usually, when a sentence is embedded in another sentence (except in quotations), the outer-periphery tagmemes are elided. Rarely, a disclaimer or a conjunction may remain, such as however or they say. Here is a sample array of the outer-peripheral part of a sentence:

Outer-peripheral tagmemes

± Sentence introducer	± Sentence modifier	± Exclamation margin
and and then then so so later next however immediately but	for sure surely hopefully regretfully certainly surprisingly verily	oh

± Vocative margin	± Response margin	± Disclaimer margin
name or name phrase kinship word or phrase honorific word or phrase	yes no maybe	you know they say supposedly so I've heard so I gathered

Note: These tagmemes are usually permutable among themselves and in among the other sentence tagmemes.

B. Inner-peripheral tagmemes

The inner-periphery tagmemes are tagmemes expounded by phrases, dependent (relator-axis) clauses, or clauses with special inflections on their verbs. Inner periphery-tagmeme exponents generally convey background or fill-in information. They are usually somewhat permutable to fore and aft positions in a sentence, and they can occur on almost all kinds of sentences. In English, they are marked by subordinating conjunctions, by conjunctions, by participial inflection, and/or by their movability. In other languages, they may be so slightly marked that it is hard to know whether they are peripheral or not. But in some languages, they are clearly marked.

1. Time margins

Perhaps the most common inner-periphery tagmemes are sentence-level time tagmemes. We generally divide these into prior time, simultaneous time, and subsequent time. It is important to distinguish sentence-level time tagmemes from clause-level tagmemes. Consider the following.

'Next week, we plan to work late on Monday and Tuesday and take off some time on Friday.'

The next week is sentence level; it modifies all the sentence. The various day-name phrases are clause level.

a. Prior-time margin

The prior-time is the most common time margin:

'When school is over, we plan to stay home and rest a while.'

'We plan to stay home and rest a while when school is over.'

'After school is over, we will have a short vacation.'

'When the heat persisted, water supplies ran low in many communities.'

'Once the study is completed, the commission will have to decide how much stress is too much to justify restarting the reactor.'

Note that When school is over, 'After school is over, and When the heat persisted, are dependent (relator-axis) clauses, each with a relator expounded by a subordinating conjunction. Prior time can also be expounded by a phrase, such as after summer school, or after Monday.

In many languages, in narrative and procedural discourses, the prior-time margin is used to summarize the preceding sentence, which is called recapitulation. A typical sequence might be:

> 'They crossed the river.
>
> Having crossed the river, they proceeded up the trail.
>
> When they arrived, they found the village deserted.
>
> When they found the village deserted, they talked about why the people had left.'

Note how some of the recapitulating margins repeat the preceding verb or clause, and other margins mark the completion of the preceding sentence. The recapitulation may be fairly exact, or may be more generic. See Longacre's _Philippine Languages_ and his _Anatomy of Speech Notions_ for more discussion of recapitulation.

Recapitulations may occur on every sentence, or only at the beginning or at some point in a paragraph. Their appearance may, or may not, be significant at higher levels.

b. Simultaneous time margin

Simultaneous time margin tagmeme exponents are marked by the subordinating conjunctions _while, meanwhile, at the same time,_ and _as._ For example:

> 'At the same time that I was approaching the intersection, that other car was coming, too!'
>
> 'That other car was coming at the same time that I was approaching the intersection.'
>
> 'As they rounded the bend in the river, they saw the village.'
>
> 'They saw the village as they rounded the bend in the river.'
>
> 'While you were sleeping, I baked some bread.'
>
> 'Besides having some extra money, he also had some extra time to spend.'
>
> 'In addition to liking modern music, she really likes modern art, too.'

The simultaneous-time margin may also be expounded by a participial clause in English:

> 'Rounding the bend in the river, they saw the village.'

'Glancing at his watch, Sam saw that he had to go.'

In English, there is sort of a negative simultaneous-time margin that uses a participial clause introduced by without.

'Without looking at the clock, Sam ran as never before and won the race.'

c. Subsequent-time margin

Subsequent, or future, time margin tagmeme exponents are marked by before, as in:

'Before you leave, be sure to empty the garbage and lock the back door.'

d. Indefinite-time margin

There is another time margin that is called 'indefinite time margin', which borders on the conditional margin. The indefinite time exponent is marked by when or whenever and conditional tagmeme is marked by if. In some languages they are merged, and the subordinating conjunction means both 'when' and 'if'. In English there is a slight difference:

'When you buy your next car, go to your discount car dealer and buy a Hwizit.'

vs. 'If you buy another car, go to your discount car dealer and buy a Hwizit.'

'Whenever you are in town, look me up.'

'If you are ever in town, look me up.'

2. Condition margins

a. Condition margin

The conditional margin is marked by the subordinating conjunctions if and in case in English. Often the clause following the if is subjunctive or marked in some other way. Some examples are:

'If the weather is good and my car is working, we'll go to the rodeo.'

'We can finish the work by five o'clock and go home, if we all work a little harder.'

'In case Prof. Smith is able to come to class today, we will have him speak in the phonetics class.'

'In case interest rates come down, try to make some
    provision for reducing the monthly payments.'

The conditional margin may also be expounded by a contrary-to-fact type of clause:

'If I were you, I would try to get a personal interview
    with the manager.'

'If I cast out demons by the power of Beelzebub,
    by whose power do your people cast them out?'

Unless is a negative condition marker.

'Unless the summer rains start soon,
    the country will be in trouble.'

b. Circumstance margin

The circumstance margin tagmeme exponents are introduced by since, in that, or seeing that, or are floating participial (or gerundial) clauses, in English; for example:

'Since the stock market is bound to rise, the investors
    are buying into it.'

'In that the stock market is bound to rise, the
    investors are buying into it.'

'Seeing that the stock market is bound to rise, the
    investors are buying into it.'

'The stock market showing signs of rising, the
    investors are buying into it.'

(The seeing that... might also be interpreted as a clause modifying the subject of the first clause.)

c. Concessive margin

The concessive margin tagmeme is expounded by a dependent clause or a phrase introduced with although, in spite of, regardless of, despite, or even if.

'Although he studies hard, he still fails his
    examinations.'

'In spite of his studying hard, he still fails
    his examinations.'

'Regardless of how hard he studies, he still fails
    his examinations.'

'Despite his studying hard, he still fails his
   examinations.'

'Even if she does get that job, she won't be satisfied.'

The 'even if' margin is perhaps the weakest concessive margin. It borders on being a conditional margin.

Notice that these margins often set up an expectation which is frustrated in the nuclear clauses.

3. Logical margins

The following tagmemes may be nuclear in some languages and peripheral in other languages. They involve 'logical' relationships such as cause, result, purpose, contrast, added afterthought, and echo question. (The following examples may not be good English; they are given to illustrate other languages.)

a. Reason or cause margin

The reason or cause tagmeme is inner peripheral in English. Its exponent is introduced with 'because' or 'since.'

'Because it is hot outside, we stay inside
   our air-conditioned houses.'

'We stay inside our air-conditioned houses because
   it is hot outside.'

'Soren works hard because he wants to get ahead.'

'I want to buy some paint and paint the garage, because
   I want to get it ready for winter.'

'Susan dosen't drive to work any more since her new job
   is within walking distance.'

b. Purpose margin

The purpose tagmeme is peripheral in English, its exponents are introduced with in order to, or so that.

Examples are:

'In order to get ahead, Walter worked hard,'

'Carl worked hard in order to get ahead,'

'Lonnie studies hard so that he can get good grades.'

c. Result margin

The result tagmeme is nuclear in English because it is not permutable. Its exponents are introduced with so.

'He worked hard, so he got ahead.'

'We had only a little work to do, so we took the
    weekend off.'

d. Contrast margin

The contrast margin tagmeme is permutable and thus an inner-periphery tagmeme in English. Its exponents are introduced with rather than, instead of, or regardless of.

'Rather than submit, he fled.'

'Instead of telling us, he left without a word.'

'Regardless of what he should have done, he left
    without a word.'

Note that all these are permutable in English.

e. Similarity margin

The similarity margin is expounded by dependent clauses with the subordinating conjunctions like, as if, as though.

'They don't build houses as you might expect them to.'

'As you might imagine, I was very tired by the time
    the day was over.

'We continued to work on the project as though
    our very lives depended on it.'

'He throws a baseball like a woman throws one.'

'Unlike the survivors of the atomic bombs in Japan,
    the residents of Three Mile Island do not appear
    to be numbed by their experience.'

'As the newspaper account suggests, the usual
    human reaction to seeing blood is not so much
    compassion or anger as it is physical revulsion,
    disgust or squeamishness.'

> 'But, unlike the 'railbirds' who leaned on the fence and at least acknowledged the horses when they dashed past, the gambler was bored by the animals and was entertained only by the scoreboards that announced the odds for the coming race.'

4. Other margins

a. Sentence topic margin

The sentence topic is an inner-periphery tagmeme that occurs early in the sentence. It is expounded by a noun phrase or by a nominalized clause or sentence that is not a part of any of the nuclear clauses, but is coreferential with some noun or pronoun somewhere in the nuclear clauses. It announces beforehand the semantic topic of the following clauses.

Some languages forefront a clause constituent to give it some emphasis. The sentence topic is similar to a fronted clause constituent, except that it is in addition to the clause constituent, which itself may not be forefronted at all. Consider the following examples and note how the sentence topic exponent is coreferential with something in the following clause:

> 'My grandfather, he moved to this river and made his house here.'

> 'My grandfather, I remember his working hard in his garden.'

> 'That garden, my grandfather used to work there a lot.'

> 'The man who is hospitable, he gets ahead and people admire him.'

> 'Whoever is hospitable, he gets ahead, and people admire him.'

> 'That medicine you gave us, it really made us well.'

> 'Whichever model you choose, I am sure you will like it and find it a great labor saver.'

> 'That all living things are derived from a common ancestor and are thus related, almost all evolutionists hold this statement to be a fact.'

Sentence topics are not considered to be good form in written English except is certain contexts. One such context is in a listing of options or projects, such as:

> 'Now the old science hall, we need to refinish the floors in the hallways.'

> The library, its floors need some attention, too,
> especially in the reading rooms.

b. Location margin

The sentence-level location margin tagmeme must be distinguished from a clause-level location tagmeme:

> 'In the tropics, people build their houses on river
> banks and make their fields around the village.'

In the tropics is a sentence level margin; and the on river banks and around the village are clause-level margins. Some more examples of the sentence-level location margin tagmeme are:

> 'In both University laboratories and in commercial
> laboratories, scientists are working on
> recombinant chromosomes in bacteria in an
> effort to make insulin plentifully and cheaply.'

> 'In the developed countries the birth rate
> is declining and the population is expected to
> stabilize by the year 2000.'

> 'In Chicago, we were able to find a place to live
> and after only a short time I found a
> good-paying job.'

> 'Anywhere you find people, you will also find refuse
> heaps that will tell you a lot about their material
> culture.'

> 'Wherever you finally find a job and settle down,
> please write to me and I'll send you your books.'

c. Benefactive margin

Like sentence-level location, sentence-level benefactive is usually expounded by a prepositional phrase:

> 'For the sake of peace, I'll give in and I'll make
> it right.'

> 'For you, I'll bake a cake and write 'happy birthday'
> on it.'

d. Afterthought margin

The added afterthought tagmeme occurs in conversational English. In some Papua New Guinea languages, it occurs frequently on almost any kind of a sentence. Typically a clause with a final verb terminates a sentence, and then another nonfinal clause or noun phrase is added.

An example from Abulas (data from Patricia Wilson):

de	wunat	kera -e	/	kut -de -ka /
he	me	get -same.subj		hold -he -simult.diff.subj

naané	giyaa -k	/ (sentence terminated)
we	come.down -past	

anat	Kudama	wale // (afterthought)
us.two	Kundama	with

'He drove me and we all came down, me and Kundama.'

e. Tag question

The echo or tag question is nuclear in English, but is peripheral in some languages. In English, it is optionally attached to a yes-no positive question:

'Are you going, or not?'

(In English, the tag question may be expounded by other reduced clauses such as 'are you', 'isn't he'.) In some languages, the equivalent of 'or not' can be attached to any kind of a sentence. It can mean 'maybe', or it may be a device to elicit hearer response.

'You are going to study tonight, aren't you?'

'We surprised the Russians, didn't we?'

'We will go to market next Saturday, or not.'

'They had a singsing last month, or not.'
   (Maybe they did, I don't know.)

5. Summary

To summarize this discussion of possible sentence margins, we will use a partial bidimensional array:

Inner-periphery tagmemes

Other sentence tagmemes	± Prior time margin	± Simultaneous time margin	± Subsequent time margin
	prior time phrase or clause or sentence	simultaneous time phrase or clause or sentence	indefinite time phrase or clause or sentence
	'after' 'when'	'while' 'at the same time' 'as'	'before'

	± Indefinite time margin	± Condition margin	± Circumstance margin	± Concession margin
	indefinite time clause or sentence or phrase	condition clause or sentence or phrase	circumstance clause or sentence or phrase	concession clause or sentence or phrase
	'whenever' 'when' 'if ever'	'if' 'unless'	'since' 'in that'	'although' 'in spite of' 'regardless'

± Reason margin	+ Purpose margin	± Result margin	± Contrast margin
reason clause or sentence or phrase	purpose clause or sentence or phrase	result clause or sentence or phrase	contrast clause or sentence or phrase
'because'	'in order to' 'so that'	'so'	'rather than' 'instead of'

± Similarity margin	+ Sentence topic	± Location margin	± Benefactive margin
similarity clause or sentence or phrase	noun phrase nominalized clause or sentence	location clause or sentence or phrase	benefactive clause or sentence or phrase
'like' 'as though' 'as' 'as if'		'in' 'at' 'where'	'for' 'for the sake of'

Nuclear sentence tagmemes	± After-thought margin	± Tag question margin
	noun phrase clause	formulaic clause or phrase

In all the arrays that follow in this chapter, the above arrays will be abbreviated as ± Margins. There are probably some coocurrence restrictions on the margin tagmemes, but we will not work them out here.

C. Nuclear tagmemes

The nuclear tagmemes are somewhat different for each different sentence type. There are many different sentence types possible, and languages differ in the richness of their sentence level. What is presented here is taken from only a few different languages.

To all the sentence arrays below, almost any peripheral tagmemes can be added. The peripheral tagmemes are not included in the arrays in the interest of economy. If all the possible peripheral tagmemes were added to each array, each array would be very long.

1. Simple sentences

a. Simple sentence

The simple sentence consists of a single sentence base expounded by a single clause plus some sentence peripheral tagmemes. The marginal tagmeme exponents may be very complex, but if the nuclear part is a single clause, the construction is a simple sentence:

> <u>When a cold front blows in, the temperature goes down, because the wind is cold</u>.

> <u>If the inflation continues and prices keep going up, people's buying power will go down</u>.

Simple sentence

± Margins	+ Simple base	± Margins
Dependent clause or sentence	any single clause	Dependent clause or sentence

Rule: At least one margin must be present.

b. Juxtaposed sentence

The juxtaposed sentence is common in some languages. A juxtaposed sentence is a sequence of clauses without any intervening conjunctions or links. The implied relationship between the clauses can be almost any of the sentence types described below. We can simulate it a bit in English as follows:

<u>I'm going home, I'm dog tired.</u>

<u>Cecil may come this afternoon, keep watching for him.</u>

<u>Anita may ask for your book, Loren may ask for it, too.</u>

<u>She isn't sick, she is quite well.</u>

Juxtaposed sentence

± Sentence margins	+ Juxtaposed base-1	+ Juxtaposed^n base-2	± Sentence margins
	any clause any sentence	any clause any sentence	

2. Time-oriented sentences

a. Narrative sentence

Perhaps the most common sentence type is the narrative sentence or the sequential sentence. In some languages, there is a conjunction meaning 'then' or 'and then' which serves to link the clauses in a sequence, for example:

<u>I graduated from college in 1975, and then I went to work for an advertising firm in Chicago for two years and then I moved to New York.</u>

Other languages may simply juxtapose the clauses.

Narrative sequence sentence

+ Sentence margins	+ Sequence base-1	+(+ Seq link link	+ Sequence base-2)^n	+ Sentence margins
	any declarative verbal clause	and then	any declarative verbal clause	

or:

Narrative sequence sentence

+ Sentence margins	+(+Sequence base-1	+ Sequence)^n link	+ Sequence base-2	+ Sentence margins
	any declarative medial verbal clause	and then	any declarative final verbal clause	

The difference between the two arrays above is in how the links are treated.

For the language without the conjunction, simply omit the Seq-link tagmeme.

Note that all the clauses expounding the sequential bases are arranged in a time-sequence order.

Here is an example without links, from the Asaro language of P.N.G. (data by David Strange).

<u>eze</u> <u>ningo</u> <u>vo</u> <u>halekavo,</u> <u>aza</u> <u>nene</u>
him having.seen having.gone having.hidden he this

<u>mine</u> <u>lamine'</u> <u>ogo</u> <u>ningine'</u>
remain good being he.looked

'Having seen and having gone and hidden, he stayed there very still and watched.'

(The first three clauses are a recapitulation of the previous sentence.)

Here is an example with links, from Kiowa of North America:

'hao'tekhi	'a'tho:ya	/	gɔ	'habe:
several.days	they.traveled		and.then	one

te:'gi:gyæ	'a'tsan	/	'sangyæ'	gɔ	'ɔ:pehɔ
evening	they.came		plain.at	and.then	right.there

gyæ'kʰɔ:yi	gɔ	'emde:mɔ	/
it.got.dark	and.then	they.lay.down	

'They traveled several days and then one evening they came
to a plain and there it got dark and they lay down.
for the night.'

b. Simultaneous sentence

The simultaneous sentence says that two activities occur at the same time. It is closely related to a simple sentence with a simultaneous time margin. In English, we use meanwhile and simultaneously. Here are two examples:

The Russians have been developing more nuclear weapons,
    meanwhile, the Americans have not been idle either.

We have been working on splicing new genetic material
    into bacteria; simultaneously, the other laboratory
    has done the same with mice.

Simultaneous sentence

+ Sentence margins	+(+Simultaneous base-1	+ Simultaneous link)^n	+ Simultaneous base-2	+ Sentence margins
	any activity clause or sentence	meanwhile simultaneously	any activity clause (often somewhat parallel to the preceding clause)	

3. Quotation-oriented sentences

The direct quotation, indirect quotation, sensation, and indirect question sentences are a group of similar sentences, because their last constituents are like direct objects to the initial clauses.

a. Direct quotation sentence

The direct quotation sentence consists of a repetition of what someone said with preceding, following, or bracketing formulas involving such verbs as say, reply, shout, whisper, and cry.

Direct quotation sentence

± Sentence margins	+ Direct quotation$_n$ formula	+ Direct quotation^n	± Sentence margins
	any clause or sentence whose last verb is a a verb of 'saying', with no object	any word, phrase, clause, sentence, paragraph, or discourse	

The exponent of the direct quotation tagmeme is an exact repetition of what someone said or is reputed to have said, as in:

    Jeanne said to her father, "When you get home tonight, would you let us have the car to go to the swimming pool?"

In other languages, the direct quotation formula, or some variation of it, may follow the quotation, or may interrupt it.

    "No, honestly, I won't hurt you," said the tiger to the monkey.

    "You go to your uncle's place," said the father to his two sons, "and ask him for work," he said.

b. Indirect quotation

The indirect quotation sentence resembles the direct quotation sentence in that it may have the same formula, and it may encode the same speech, but with a difference. In indirect quotations, the person pronouns and tenses in the quotation are changed to be appropriate to the time of the quotation.

Indirect quotation sentence

+ Sentence margins	+ Indirect quotation formula	+ Indirect quotation marker	+ Indirect quotation	+ Sentence margins
	any clause or sentence whose last verb is a verb of saying	that	indirect quototion of any utterance	
	no object		Tenses and person pronouns are altered	

Some examples are:

Rita said that she would help me.

(Note, in direct quotation, she said, "I will help you". The indirect quotation changed the 'I' to 'she', the 'will' to 'would', and the 'you' to 'me'.)

Mike said that he is surprised at you.

c. Sensation sentence

The sensation sentence is much like the indirect quotation sentence. Its formula has a verb of sensation rather than of saying. In English, the sensation is only a variant of the indirect quotation sentence, but in other languages, they may contrast and be separate.

Sensation sentence

+ Sentence margins	+ Sensation formula	+ Sensation marker	+ Sensation quote	+ Sentence margins
	any clause or sentence whose final verb is a verb of sensation	that	any clause, sentence or paragraph	
	lacks an object			

Rule: Some sensation formulas can be permuted to later in the sentence, in which case, the sensation marker is deleted and the sensation sentence becomes a disclaimer margin.

Examples are:

Alice felt that all was well between Clara and herself.

I think that it is time to water the lawn.

It is time to water the lawn, I think.

We saw that they had left already.

I heard that you are engaged.

You are engaged, I heard.

With verbs such as seem, appear, strike, occur, and look, the quotation formula exponent has a different, more passivelike structure.

It seems to me that the weather is about to change.

It appears to me that we are heading for trouble.

It strikes me that your idea may be the best one yet.

It occurred to me that I had forgotten your birthday.

It looks to me like this lot is not really level.

d. Perceived description sentence

If we take the last group of examples above and permute the topic to the initial subject position, we come up with a somewhat different sentence type. Here are some examples:

The weather seems to me to be about to change.

These scissors appear to be new.

These scissors seem new.

These scissors look brand new to me.

The exam appeared to some students to be too long for them.

The exam appeared to be too long to some students.

The weather seems to change quite frequently here in the spring.

Walter seems to earn a good salary at his new job.

Perceived description sentence

+ Subject	+ Perception predicate	± Perceiver	+ Description	+Margin
noun noun phrase	perception verb such as seem	to prep phrase	infinitival clause or sentence	

Rule: The perceiver is permutable to a position following the description.

The to and the copula of an infinitival description clause expounding the description may be omitted.

e. Indirect question sentence

For English, Longacre found a related sentence, the indirect question sentence.

Indirect question sentence

+ Sentence margins	+ Indirect question formula	+ Indirect question marker	+ Indirect question	+ Sentence margins
	any clause or sentence whose final verb is ask, wonder and others	if whether interrogative pronoun	any clause sentence	
	exponent lacks an object		exponent lacks the tagmeme that is questioned	

Examples are:

They asked me if I knew anything about the case.

We wondered whether you would like to come along with us or come later with the others.

He asked why you aren't going.

She tried to figure out what he wanted for his birthday.

I wonder whose shoes these are.

If reflects a yes-no question, whether reflects an alternative interrogative, while the interrogative pronouns reflect information questions.

Some languages may use quotationlike sentences for other purposes. For example, Guerrero Amuzgo (data by Marjorie Buck, personal communication) uses a quotationlike sentence to encode aspectual meanings.

ma'ndii	tyochjoo	na	makaan	skwela
leaves	boy	that	goes.he	school

'The boy stops attending school.'

seiyu' katsian na nleinoom

| | agreed | tiger | that | will.run.he |

'The tiger agreed to run.'

nnanndyo	na	nnsts'aaya	ts'iaan'ñeen
will.ability.I	that	will.do.I	work.that

'I'll be able to do that work.'

lkwiya	na	ñetso
woke.up.I	that	was.sleeping.I

'I woke up from sleeping.'

siekjeeñe	na	tyoch'een	ts'iaan
hurried.he	that	was.doing.he	work

'He worked quickly.'

maju'naanñena'	na	nlanaanya	ñ'oom'ñeen
permits.it	that	will.talk.we	message.that

'We have opportunity to talk about that matter.'

Aspectual sentence in Guerrero Amuzgo

+ Aspect	+ Link	+ Activity
clause with verb of aspect (personal or impersonal)	na 'that'	clause

4. Logical structure sentences

Another group of similar sentences is the coordinate, antithetical, alternative, conditional, contrafactual, concessive, reason, result, and causation sentences. They all have some logical relationship between their tagmemes.

a. Coordinate sentence

The coordinate sentence is similar to the narrative sequence sentence. In the coordinate sentences, the link is expounded by a bound or free conjunction meaning 'and', which links two or more clauses into a coherent whole. The coordinate sentence may encode sequential time or simultaneous time, or it may encode some logically coordinated statements. It may have the same subject throughout or have different subjects. Examples from English are:

Wally bet on the horses and won some money.

<u>Nestor</u> <u>bet</u> <u>on</u> <u>the</u> <u>horses,</u> and <u>Wally</u> <u>bet</u> <u>on</u> <u>his favorite</u> <u>football team.</u>

<u>Theresa stayed home,</u> and <u>Betty</u> went to a movie.

<u>Holly went</u> <u>to</u> <u>a</u> movie and came home late.

Coordinate sentence

+ Sentence margins	+ Coordinate base-1	+ Coordinate link	+ Coordinate base-2	+ Sentence margins
	any clause	and	any clause	
	any sentence		any sentence	

The repetition may be indicated by one of the following, depending upon links and inflections:

$$+ \text{Coord base-1} + (+ \text{Coord link} + \text{Coord base-2})^n$$

or $\quad + (\text{Coord base-1})^n + \text{Coord link} + \text{Coord base-2}$

The difference between the two formulas is in the distribution of the link.

b. Antithetical sentence

The antithetical sentence's link is expounded by <u>but</u>. The sentence has only two bases, and usually there must be two or more significant contrasts between the clauses expounding the bases.

Antithetical sentence

+ Sentence margins	+ Thesis	+ Adversative link	+ Antithesis	+ Sentence margins
	clause	but	clause	
	sentence	<u>only</u>	sentence	

The antithetical sentence encodes frustrating outcome, unexpected outcome, contrasting parallelism, counterbalancing consideration, and contrasting exception.

Frustrating outcome:
> Jerry worked hard, but he wasn't able to finish painting his house.

Unexpected outcome:
> We went to the show not expecting much, but it turned out to be good.

> Al worked hard for the party, only to be passed over by the election committee.

Contrasting parallelism:
> Jerry is a carpenter, but William is an auto mechanic.

Counterbalancing consideration:
> He has a good job now, but if there is a recession, he may lose it.

Contrasting exception:
> Everyone was there, but Anna could not come.

c. Alternative sentence

The alternative sentence is marked by having its link expounded by or.

> We will see you next week, or we'll telephone you later.

> Jimmy has to sell his car, or he won't have money for school.

> Sally will help you, or Janice will come to help later.

Alternative sentence

± Margin	+ Alternative intro	+ Alternative base-1	+ Alternative link	+ Alternative base-2	± Margin
	either	any clause	or	any clause	
	neither	any sentence	nor	any sentence	

Note that there is always some contrast between the exponents of the alternative bases. Contrasts involve actors, actions, times, locations; any clause-level constituents.

If the alternative intro is omitted then alternative base-1 can be repeated any number of times.

197

There is a variant of the alternative sentence that involves undesirable alternative:

You had better help him, or he won't finish on time.

We asked her to let us know when she was coming, otherwise we wouldn't know when to meet her.

In some languages, the undesirable alternative sentence is called a warning sentence:

You had better go home now, or it will get dark on you.

Eat your breakfast, or you'll get hungry before lunch.

The alternative link exponent may be a clitic and may occur on both parts of the alternation:

You can work this weekend-or you can work next weekend-or.

In most languages there is no grammatical difference between inclusive (A or B or both) and exclusive (A or B but not both) 'or' constructions. However, Todd S. Ireland (private communication) has informed me that Latin made such a distinction, as shown in the following examples:

(Aut) puer aut puella viam transiet.

'Either the boy or the girl (but not both) will cross the street.'

(Vel) puer vel puella viam transiet.

'Either the boy or the girl (or both) will cross the street.'

Mortuus est aut vivit.

'He is either dead or living.'

Mortuus est vel vivit.

'He is dead, living, or somewhere between.'

d. Conditional sentence

The conditional sentence is the result of bringing a conditional margin into the nucleus, which is done by changing the apodosis clause in such a way that it cannot stand alone, and/or the two tagmemes are not permutable. In English, we do this by adding a 'then' to the second clause.

Conditional sentence

+ Sentence margins	+ Conditional protasis	+ Conditional apodosis	± Sentence margins
	conditional clause or sentence	any clause or sentence	
	Usually marked by a protasis marker	Usually marked by an apodosis marker	

Examples in English are:

    If you eat your vegetables, then you can have dessert.

    If the price of oil keeps increasing, then the prices of
        manufactured items are sure to rise.

In other languages, the if and then may be bound morphemes, affixes or clitics, appearing inside the clauses.

e. Contrafactual sentence

The contrafactual (counter-to-fact) sentence is like the conditional sentence but its exponents are both false. It states the opposite of the truth to emphasize the truth.

    If it had not rained, we wouldn't have got stuck.

    If there had been animals, we would have killed them and
        brought them home.

    Had there been animals, we might have found them.

    Had you taken better care of your cornfield,
        you would have more corn.

Contrafactual sentence

± Sentence margins	+ Contrafactual protasis	+ Contrafactual apodosis	± Sentence margins
	concessive clause or sentence	any clause or sentence	
	Both exponents have contrafactural marking.		

Note that usually both clauses involve subjunctivelike clauses or sentences. A past perfect clause expounds the protasis, and a future-plus-past 'would' auxiliary marks the exponent of the apodosis.

In another language, the order of the tagmemes may be different.

f. Concessive sentence

The concessive sentence is similar to a sentence with a concessive margin. The difference is that the exponent of the apodosis is different in such a way that it cannot stand alone and/or the two tagmemes are not permutable. In English, we cannot bring the concessive margin into the nucleus, so the examples below can only represent what may occur in another language.

Concessive sentence

± Sentence margins	+ Concessive protasis	+ Concessive apodosis	± Sentence margins
	concessive clause or sentence	any clause or sentence (marked for concession)	
	Usually marked by a clitic or a particle	Usually marked by a clitic or a particle	

(Or the order might be different in another language.)

> Even though the carrots aren't ready, the children are pulling them up.

> In spite of mechanical difficulties, the plane took off.

g. Reason sentence

The reason sentence consists of a statement and a reason for it. The tagmemes may come in either order, depending upon the language. It is similar to a sentence with a reason margin, but here the reason is not marginal. The reason sentence in English has a <u>for</u> link.

> We gave up the attempt, for we could not see any way to finish it.

> The president is concerned about inflation, for that seems to be what voters are concerned about.

Reason sentence

± Sentence margins	+ Statement	+ Reason link	+ Reason	± Sentence margins
	any clause or sentence	for	any clause or sentence	

Some languages approximate the reason sentence by merely juxtaposing two clauses and letting the meanings of the clauses signal the functional relationship.

> The president is concerned about inflation; that's what the voters are concerned about.

h. Result sentence

The result sentence consists of a statement and a result.

> Rori married a woman of the Toucan clan, so he gets a share of their land.

> We don't have much money, therefore we have to work all the time.

> His behavior so alarmed and disgusted his father that he was disinherited, cut off from any access to his father's modest fortune.

> The downturn in business has resulted in reduced business taxes and the drought has reduced the income of many people, forcing them to ask for governmental aid, which has all worked together to strain the government's financial resources.

Result sentence

+ Sentence margins	+ Statement	+ Result link	+ Result	+ Sentence margins
	any clause or sentence	<u>so</u> <u>therefore</u> <u>which</u>	any clause or sentence that is the result of the statement	

i. Caution sentence

The caution sentence comprises a reason plus a command, or a foreseen undesirable result plus a command. Examples of the first type are:

<u>It's raining, come inside!</u>

<u>You're late, so hurry!</u>

Examples of the second type are:

<u>You might get there late, so hurry.</u>

<u>Lest you fall off, walk carefully!</u>

The two formulas are:

+ Reason   + Command

or,   + Foreseen result   + Command

The tagmemes may come in either order, or may be permutable in a language.

5. Parallel-structure sentences

The next group of sentences involves some repetition. They are the parallel sentence, the paraphrase sentence, the recapitulation sentence, the amplification sentence, the covariant sentence, the comparative sentence, and the evaluation or summary sentence. It is doubtful that these would all be emically different in any one language.

a. Parallel sentence

The parallel sentence involves identical or similar clauses in which the exponent of one tagmeme is varied systematically.

> I hate war, Eleanor hates war, we all hate war.
>
> I bought some tomatoes, I bought some onions, I bought some milk.
>
> We will work Monday, we will work Tuesday, we will work Wednesday.

Often parallel sentences are used to reduce the semantic load in any one clause. For example, the last example above is taken from a Papua New Guinea language that does not allow coordinate time phrases in a clause. Another example might be:

> He worked as hard as two men, he made a house for his family, he made it on their farm.

Here, the language would not allow a long manner phrase, a long benefactive phrase, and a location phrase all in one clause.

Parallel sentence

± Sentence margins	+ Parallel base-1	+ Parallel base-2^n	± Sentence margins
	any clause	any clause nearly identical to preceding clause(s)	
	All the exponents should have a parallel structure.		

The clauses are all nearly identical, contrasting in only one constituent.

b. Paraphrase sentence

The paraphrase sentence consists of a statement and then a paraphrase of that statement in different words. For example:

> I flunked that phonetics test; I couldn't answer half the questions.
>
> He bought some worthless bonds; he really wasted his money.

Paraphrase sentence

± Sentence margins	+ Statement	+ Paraphrase	± Sentence margins
	any clause or sentence	any clause or sentence that paraphrases the statement	

c. Recapitulation sentence

The recapitulation sentence consists of a statement tagmeme and a recapitulation tagmeme whose exponent uses many of the same words as the exponent of the statement. The recapitulation may be longer or briefer than the statement.

Examples (from Longacre, 1970):

I went home; I went home to see what was really going on.

We suspected something; we suspected that something was wrong.

Recapitulation sentence

± Margin	+ Statement	+ Recapitulation	± Margin
	any clause or sentence	a clause or sentence recapitulating the preceding one	

d. Amplification sentence

The amplification sentence is similar to the preceding two sentence types. It consists of a statement and an amplification of that statement:

We cook rice, we boil it with onions and herbs.

They are studying now, they are memorizing their Latin sentences.

They make brooms, all the people in that village make brooms in their homes.

Amplification sentence

± Sentence margins	+ Statement	+ Amplification	± Sentence margins
	any clause or sentence	a clause or sentence amplifying the statement	

In English, I find it difficult to distinguish the above sentence types, but the terms are there if you ever need them.

e. Covariant sentence

The covariant sentence says that two processes or actions increase or decrease with each other. Exodus 1:12 says 'But the more the Egyptians oppressed the Israelites, the more they increased in number and the farther they spread through the land.' (TEV)

Other examples are:

The more you spend, the less you have left.

The harder you work on your garden, the better it will grow.

Covariant sentence in English

± Sentence margins	+ Covariant statement	+ Covariant statement	± Sentence margins
	clause sentence	clause sentence	
	Exponents must have a fronted comparative adjective or adverb phrase preceded by the definite article the	Exponents must have a fronted comparative adjective or adverb phrase preceded by the definite article the	

The covariant statements are much reduced in certain English idioms:

The more, the merrier.

The bigger, the better.

Pacoh has a similar array except for an added link before the second correlative quantity. (Data by Dick Watson, personal communication):

li -mm	pit	na:y	pad m	kŏh	li -mm
equal -however	big	they	oppress	thus	equal -however

klin	va:ih	ape	Ihra'en
plentiful	became	they	Israel

'However much they oppressed them, that many the Israelites became.'

Vietnamese (data from Dick Watson) would have a reversed array:

tr :y	mi	chin	na:w	thi k	mok	len	čin	áy
sky	rain	however	much	so	grass	grows	up	so much

'The more it rains, the more the grass grows.'

Covariant sentence in Vietnamese

+ Covariant statement-1	+ Covariant quantity-1	+ Covariant link	+ Covariant statement-2	+ Covariant quantity-2
clause	quantity phrase-1	thí 'thus/so'	clause	quantity phrase-2

f. Comparative sentence

The comparative sentence can come out in various ways. In some languages without comparative adjectives and adverbs, two clauses with contrasting subjects and contrasting attributes are juxtaposed, as in:

This stick is long, that one is short.

(= 'This stick is longer than that one.' In relation to the rest of the world, both may be short or long.)

Another example is:

My dog is a good hunter, yours isn't a good hunter.
(= 'My dog is a better hunter than yours.')

Comparative sentence

+ Sentence margins	+ Comparative Statement	+ Comparison	± Sentence margins
	any clause	any clause	
	The exponents must show two pairs of semantic contrasts.		

English has comparative adjectives and adverbs. Our comparative sentences are as follows:

This rice is nicer than that sugar.

Johnson's eyes are darker than his father's (eyes are).

We spend more on arms than the Russians spend on agriculture.

So in English, the array for the comparative sentence is:

Comparative sentence in English

± Margin	+ Comparative Statement	+ Comparative Link	+ Comparison	+Margin
	any clause with a comparative adjective or adverb	than	any clause parallel to the first clause	

In Pacoh (data from Dick Watson) the comparative sentences are:

pe:ŋ nnɛh dyeam   tilət   pe:ŋ   nkoh
bread this delicious more.than   bread that

'This bread tastes better than that bread.'

akay kī: ta'   bẹñ   tilət   akay nay
son   my   works strong   more.than   son   your

'My son works harder than your son.'

Comparative sentence in Pacoh

+ Comparative Statement	+ Comparative link	+ Comparison
any clause	tilət 'more.than'	noun phrase

The noun phrase expounding the comparison tagmeme contrasts with the subject of the first clause.

g. Evaluation and summary sentences

There are some other sentence types similar to the above sentences. Barai (Olson) has an evaluation sentence with from one to three statements and then an evaluation.

ro	na	kuar -ia,	kuar -ia,	kuar -ia,	ije	fu	ise
but	I	talk -you	talk -you	talk -you	this	it	bad

'But I talk to you and talk and talk, and this is bad.'

ire	maje	no	ke	vaj -uo	no	i -dufuo -je	/
food	good	we	take	give -we	we	eat -purpose -topic	

no	dabe	ije	abere -eva -je	/
we	take	this	lose -past.dep -topic	

fu -ka	be
it -really	different

'Concerning the food that is for exchanging with one another and eating; concerning this (food) that we took and lost; it is certainly different.'

Evaluation sentence in Barai

+ Statement$^{n=1-3}$	+ Evaluation
any clause or sentence	equational clause

Barai also has a summary sentence:

uru -ko -ko	/	bu	ve	kuke	suke
dance -simult -diff.subj		they	then		drinks

m -ia -kinu	/	miane ifa -j -ia -kinu

```
    give -they -same.time   fire    fix -benef -they -simult
```

<u>ijegere</u>
do.like.this

'While they were dancing, the others gave them refreshments again and fixed the fires for them; they did like this.'

Summary sentence in Barai

+ Action$^{n=1-7}$	+ Summary
any clause or sentence (medial inflection)	clause based on verb 'do (like) this' (final inflection)

Barai (data from Olson) has another summary sentence that is similar to the paraphrase sentence. The Barai summary tagmeme exponent is a short emphatic formulaic paraphrase of the first statement and the effect of the sentence is to emphasize its statement.

<u>o</u>	<u>na-</u>	<u>a-</u>	<u>mad</u>	<u>-a</u>	<u>-vo</u>	<u>baki</u>
no	I-	you-	angry.at	-you	-pres	no

'No, I'm not angry with you, certainly not.'

<u>fu</u>	<u>gare</u>	<u>mitini</u>	<u>gare</u>	<u>fu</u>	<u>ma</u>	<u>ije</u>
it	that	meeting	that	it	good	this

'The meeting is a good one, it certainly is.'

The summary is also an evaluation of the preceding statement.

Summary sentence in Barai

+ Statement	+ Summary / Evaluation
any sentence	descriptive clause with an evaluative adjective

Here are two examples of summary sentences in Pokomchí (data by Ted Engel, personal communication):

ma'atob	ni-	puhbal	pa	ri-	puhnox	kar
not.good	my-	rifle	for/to	its-	shoot	fish

reh	banox	kar	
for	doing	fish	(summary)

'My rifle isn't any good for shooting fish.'

išpon	ri-	raq	taqe	winaq
he.arrived	he-	found	plural	men

kamanik	inka'n	/	banox	abiš
work	they.do		doing	cornfield

banox	kinaq'
doing	beans

inka'n	
they.did	(summary)

'When he encountered the men, they were planting corn and beans.'

Summary sentence in Pokomchí

+ Statement^n	+ Summary
any series of clauses, usually parallel in structure	clause with 'do' as verb

6. Equation-structure sentences

The equational sentence that Longacre posits for English is broken into two sentence types by others: pseudocleft and cleft sentences.

a. Pseudocleft sentence

The two parts of the pseudocleft sentence are paraphrases of a question and its answer (see Jones, p. 185).

What the president wants is to balance the budget.

What we are having for dinner today is macaroni and cheese.

What we all want is that something be done about inflation.

The president's wish is to balance the budget.

<u>To decrease taxes now would be to increase the
magnitude of the budget deficit next year.</u>

Pseudocleft sentence

± Margin	+ Pseudocleft question	+ Copula	+ Pseudocleft answer	± Margin
	any phrase 'what' nominalized clause	'be' (inflected)	any phrase infinitival clause 'that' nominalized clause	

The main restriction is that both tagmemes cannot be expounded by phrases. If both are expounded by simple phrases, the construction is probably an equational clause. The order of the two tagmemes can be reversed.

<u>Macaroni and cheese is what we had for dinner.</u>

b. Cleft sentence

The cleft sentence is like the pseudocleft except that the question is transposed to the end and a dummy pronoun <u>it</u> is put in its place.

Cleft sentence

± Margin	+ Dummy subject	+ Copula	+ Cleft answer	+ Cleft question	± Margin
	<u>it</u>	be (inflected)	any phrase nominalized clause or sentence	<u>that</u> / <u>who</u> nominalized clause or sentence	

Examples are:

<u>It was in the dining room that I saw your book last.</u>

<u>It was with a flourish that the senator ended his speech.</u>

<u>It is the economy that is occupying Congress's time these days.</u>

<u>It is reducing taxes that people see as the main issue in</u>

the next election.

c. Evaluation cleft sentence

The evaluation cleft sentence is similar in structure to the cleft sentence but it does not reflect a question and answer structure. It consists of an evaluation and a proposition. The evaluation is expounded by an adjective or an adjective phrase. The proposition is expounded by dependent or nominalized clause or sentence. Here are some examples:

It would be good if you could get there before noon.

It was kind of you to remember to lock my door for me.

It will be disastrous if they decide to build the new road through our property.

It's a shame that we didn't buy our house earlier.

Is it O.K. with you if I borrow your laundry soap?

Is it worthwhile to phone Sam yet about that job for tomorrow?

It might be interesting to trace the historical rise of capitalism.

Wouldn't it be interesting to attend a Rock Concert just once?

To try to repair that vase now would be useless.

Evaluation cleft sentence

+Margin	+ Dummy	+ Copula	+ Evaluation	+ Proposition	+Margin
	it	inflected form of be	adjective adjective phrase	dependent conditional clause or sentence that nominal clause or sentence infinitival clause or sentence	

Omit the dummy subject and/or the copula if either or both are not used in your language.

212

The proposition may be permuted to the subject position,
replacing the _it_.

In other languages, the text may be expounded by other types of clauses, for example:

<u>Maybe</u> <u>good</u> <u>that</u> <u>you</u> <u>sell</u> <u>your</u> <u>rice</u> <u>now</u>.

<u>Surely bad that we planted our rice too early.</u>

7. Merged sentences

When two clauses in a sentence share a clause constituent and one or both of the clauses probably cannot stand alone, we call the construction a merged sentence.

English has a large system of merged sentences, most of them encoding aspectual meanings. In all of them, the second clause lacks a subject. The understood subject is the object of the first clause, if there is one, or otherwise is the subject of the first clause. Longacre (1970) organized them into a 2x5 system, making ten kinds of merged sentences in English. The first five consist of two clauses which have the same subject, which means that the first clause never has an object. The second five consist of two clauses which may have the same or may have different subjects. If the subjects are different, the subject of the second clause is the object of the first clause. That is, there is a nominal with dual function between the two clauses.

Within each group of five, the merged sentences are ranked according to how restricted the form of the second clause is. The first merged sentence of each group may have a full infinitive clause as the second part. The second, third, and fourth types may have only a minimal infinitival clause as the second part. The fifth type may have only a single verb word or a participial clause as the second part.

a. Manner merged sentence

The manner merged sentence must have the same subject in both clauses, and the second clause may be a full infinitive clause or a participial clause. The verb of the first clause modifies the second clause; it is often paraphrasable with a cognate manner adverb. The verb in the first clause is <u>come</u>, <u>hasten</u>, <u>seem</u>, <u>happen</u>, <u>chance</u>, <u>risk</u>, or <u>try</u>.

Some examples are:

<u>He</u> <u>chanced to make some money.</u> (by chance)

<u>He</u> <u>appeared to succeed.</u> (apparently)

<u>He</u> <u>won't</u> <u>fail</u> <u>to</u> <u>do</u> <u>it.</u> (without fail)

<u>He proceeded to wrap it up.</u>

He happened to have been seen there two days before.
(full infinitive)

He risked doing it again. (He took a risk and did it again.)

He tried rigging up a connection. (He rigged up a
connection as an experiment.)

Manner merged sentence in English

± Margin	+ Manner formula	+ Manner statement	± Margin
	manner formulaic clause	full active or passive infinitival clause participial clause	
	Lacks an object	Lacks a subject	

b. Conative merged sentence

The conative merged sentence may have only a minimal infinitive clause or a participial clause in its second part, and the two clauses must have the same subject.

Conative merged sentence:

± Margin	+ Conative formula	+ Conative statement	± Margin
	conative formulaic clause	minimal active or passive infinitive clause participial clause	
	Lacks an object	Lacks a subject	

Here are some examples:

She is attempting to outperform her brother.

214

> She is trying to accomplish something.
>
> He tried to help.   He tried helping them.
>
> Strive to be regarded well. Try noticing how they do it.

Notice how the first clause is formed around a verb whose action is an effort directed toward the second clause.

c. Predispositional merged sentence

The predispositional merged sentence consists of a first clause built around the verbs remember and forget, and the second clause must be a minimal active infinitival clause.

Predispositional merged sentence

± Margins	+ Predispositional formula	+ Predispositional statement	± Margins
	predisposition formulaic clause	minimal active infinitival clause	
	Lacks an object.	Lacks a subject.	

Examples:

> I remembered to go.   I forgot to tell you.

215

d. Obligation merged sentence

The obligation merged sentence has a formulaic clause built around need and want, and the second clause is a minimal active or passive infinitive clause or is a participial clause. The first verb is sort of a modal to the second verb.

Obligation merged sentence in English

± Margin	+ Obligation formula	+ Obligation statement	± Margin
	obligation formulaic clause	minimal active or passive infinitive clause participial clause	
	Lacks an object	Lacks a subject	

Examples:

He needs to clean the car.   The car needs cleaning.

The car needs to be cleaned.

He wants watching. (= He needs to be watched.)

e. Passive merged sentence

The passive merged sentence has the verb get in its formulaic clause and a participial verb or a gerundial verb in the second clause.

Passive merged sentence in English

± Margin	+ Passive formula	+ Passive statement	± Margin
	passive formulaic clause	gerundial clause (-en) verb	
	Lacks an object	Lacks a subject	

Examples:

> They got married.   He gets punished all the time.
>
> He hasn't been getting punished quite so regularly as before.

We now begin the second group of five merged sentences. In all of the following merged sentences, there may be a shared nominal between the two clauses, which serves as the object of the first clause and the subject of the second clause. If the nominal is a pronoun, it must be the objective form of the pronoun, so we will include it as the object of the first clause in the surface structure.

f. Telic merged sentence

The telic merged sentence consists of a formulaic clause involving some mental or vocal activity that points to the second clause. The second clause is a full active or passive infinitive clause or is a participial clause. The verbs that may occur in the formulaic clause are: agree, ask, expect, intend, advise, warn and want.

Telic merged sentence in English

± Margin	+ Telic formula	+ Telic statement	± Margin
	telic formulaic clause	full active or passive infinitive clause participial clause	
	Optional object	Lacks a subject	

Examples:

> I expect to tell about it.
>
> I expect to be telling about it soon.
>
> I want to know the reasons.
>
> They advised me to go.
>
> I expect him to be defeated.
>
> I intend to have finished by then.

217

I intend finishing by then.

I propose ignoring that proposal.

g. Aspectual merged sentence

The aspectual merged sentence has a verb in its formulaic clause that functions as an aspect for the second clause. The second clause is a minimal active or passive infinitival clause or a minimal active or passive participial clause. This sentence is divided into three subtypes. The verbs for subtype (a) are: begin, start, continue, and cease. Subtype (a) permits both infinitival and participial clauses in the second tagmeme.

Examples are:

He began to talk.   He began talking.

He continued to be talked about.

He continued to be considered undesirable.

He ceased talking about his past achievements.

Subtype (b) permits only a participial clause in the second tagmeme and prohibits the occurrence of the shared nominal. Verbs for this subtype are: keep (on), finish, stop, and get.

Examples are:

He keeps (on) talking.   She stopped doing it.

When the factory finishes being retooled, it will be able to resume production.

Subtype (c) has different actors, hence it must have the shared nominal. The verbs for this subtype are: start, set, keep, and stop.

Examples are:

He started them talking about the upcoming football game.

He kept them going.   He stopped them stealing.

Aspectual merged sentence

+ Margin	+ Aspectual formula	+ Aspectual statement	+ Margin
	aspectual formulaic clause	minimal active or passive infinitival clause	
		minimal active or passive participial clause	
	Object is optional	Lacks a subject	

h. Reciprocal merged sentence

The reciprocal merged sentence has a formulaic clause with a verb of help, or let. with or without an object for a shared nominal. If the object is absent, it is implied. The second clause is a minimal active infinitival clause or is a clause with an uninflected verb. The examples are:

'Help' may occur with either type of second clause:

I helped (to) paint the house.

I helped them (to) paint the house.

Please help (to) put the books away.

Please help me (to) put the books away.

'Let' requires the uninflected verb type of clause:

They let him go.

They let him hurt her badly.

He was let stay there too long.

He let fall that he would be coming. (idiomatic)

He let go the rope.

Reciprocal merged sentence in English

+ Margin	+ Reciprocal formula	+ Reciprocal statement	+ Margin
	reciprocal formulaic clause	minimal active participial clause clause with uninflected verb	
	Object is optional	Lacks a subject	

i. Causative merged sentence

The causative merged sentence consists of a formulaic clause expressing causation of the second clause. The verbs that occur in the formulaic clause are: have, get, make, and cause. The second clause may be a minimal active or passive infinitival clause, a clause with an uninflected verb, or a participial clause. There are restrictions on the statement clause depending on the formulaic verb, as may be seen in the following examples:

<u>I</u> had <u>him</u> tell <u>me</u> all about <u>it</u>.

I've had him writing another essay.

<u>I</u> got <u>him</u> to go.   <u>I</u> got <u>him</u> going.

He was got to go.   He made me do it.

I caused him to pay attention.

I caused him to get elected.

I'll cause you to feel differently about it.

Causative merged sentence

+ Margin	+ Causative formula	+ Causative statement	+ Margin
	causative formulaic clause	minimal active or passive infinitival clause	
		clause with uninflected verb	
		participial clause	
	Object is optional	Lacks a subject	

j. Sensation merged sentence

The sensation merged sentence resembles the indirect quotation sentence. Its formula is expounded by a clause with a verb of speech, perception, or cognition, with an object that is shared with the second clause. The statement tagmeme is expounded by a clause with an uninflected verb, by a participial clause, and by a clause with the -en inflection (the passive form). There are three subtypes of this sentence.

Subtype (a) has one of the following verbs in the formulaic clause: hear, feel, smell, see, watch, and notice. The second clause may be any one of the three mentioned above.

> I saw them cross the river.
>
> I saw them crossing the river.
>
> I saw our team beaten badly.
>
> I heard it played by a symphony orchestra.
>
> I noticed him mowing (not mow) the front lawn.
>
> They were last seen crossing the river.

(Passive see and hear require the participial form.)

> They were last heard radioing for help.

Subtype (b) has one of the following verbs in its formula: catch, find, and observe, and the statement clause must be participial.

221

<u>They were caught stealing cookies.</u>

<u>Grandma caught them stealing cookies.</u>

<u>They were found sleeping.</u>

Subtype (c) has <u>remember, forget, regret, recollect,</u> and <u>recall,</u> and the second clause must be participial. The formulaic clause must be active.

<u>He</u> <u>remembers</u> <u>me</u> <u>saying something like that.</u>

<u>I'd</u> <u>forgotten him doing that.</u>

<u>I'd</u> <u>forgotten his saying that.</u>

<u>I'd</u> <u>forgotten his having said that.</u>

Sensation merged sentence in English

± Margin	+ Sensation formula	+ Sensation statement	± Margin
	sensation formulaic transitive clause	clause with uninflected verb participial clause clause with past participial (passive) verb	
	Must have an object if clause is active	Lacks a subject	

Longacre found merged sentence in the Trique language in Mexico. At first he called them 'colons' and he set up a colon level between clause level and sentence level. Later, however, from a study of hierarchy, he concluded that the colon level was a 'mezzanine' level in the hierarchy and did not fit in well. So he moved the colon level up to the sentence level and called the constructions 'merged sentences.'

Merged sentences in other languages may not be just like the ones in English. Many of the merged sentences in English make up for the lack of aspectual inflections on verbs. In other languages, certain serialized verb constructions may be analyzed as merged sentences. In still other languages close-knit clause clusters should be analyzed as merged sentences.

8. Dependent sentences

a. Relator-axis dependent sentences

A relator-axis sentence is formed when a sentence receives a preposed subordinating conjunction, in English. Such sentences are called dependent sentences, and they function in the margins of other sentences. For example, the conditional margin of the following sentence is expounded by a relator-axis sentence:

'If Warren will only telephone us or get word to us somehow, we will know when to meet him.'

The if Warren...has a relator-axis structure and is called a dependent condition sentence.

Dependent condition sentence

+ Condition relator	+ Condition axis
if	any clause or sentence

Other dependent sentences are possible. Here is a dependent time sentence expounding the prior time margin of another sentence:

'When classes are over and we've had time to leave our books in our rooms, let's go shopping and try to get back in time for supper.'

Dependent prior-time sentence

+ Prior-time relator	+ Prior-time axis
when after	any clause or sentence

b. Embedded sentences

Sentences can be embedded as exponents of nuclear tagmemes of other sentences, for example:

'<u>Mary</u> attends all the <u>P.T.A. meetings, takes the children to scout meetings, and tries to be a good suburban mother</u>, but <u>when she thinks about it</u>, <u>she dreams of the day when she can have some free afternoons</u>.'

In the example above, a coordinate sentence expounds the thesis of an antithetical sentence. It isn't hard to find other examples.

Bibliography

Ballard, D. Lee, Robert J. Conrad and Robert E. Longacre. 1971. The deep and surface grammar of interclausal relations. Foundations of language 7.70-118.

———. 1971. More on the deep and surface grammar of interclausal relations. Language data, Asia-Pacific series, no. 1. Santa Ana, California: S.I.L.

Foreman, Velma M. 1974. Grammar of Yessan-Mayo. Language Data, Asia-Pacific series, no. 4. Santa Ana, California: S.I.L.

Jones, Linda Kay. 1977. Theme in English expository discourse. Lake Bluff, Illinois: Jupiter Press.

Longacre, Robert E. 1968. Philippine languages: discourse, paragraph, and sentence structure. Santa Ana: S.I.L.

———. 1970. Sentence structure as a statement calculus. Language, 46.783-815.

———. 1976. An anatomy of speech notions. Lisse: The Peter de Ridder Press.

Murane, Elizabeth. 1974. Daga grammar from morpheme to discourse. S.I.L. publications in linguistics and related fields, no. 43. Norman: S.I.L. and the University of Oklahoma.

Olson, Michael L. 1973. Barai sentence structure and embedding. Language Data, Asia-Pacific series, no. 1. Santa Ana: S.I.L.

Wilson, Patricia R. 1973. Abulas sentences. Workpapers in Papua New Guinea languages, vol. 1. Ukarumpa, E.H.D., Papua New Guinea: S.I.L.

Chapter 12

Propositional Calculus

Propositional calculus as a deep structure for sentences was first worked out by Robert Longacre and Robert Conrad in the Ballard, Conrad, and Longacre papers (1971). Others have worked on it, including Bob Conrad, Steve Echerd, Bud Frank, Tom Godfrey and Bill Leal. Stephen Echerd's revision was published as part of the Introduction in volume 1 of Discourse Grammar (Longacre and Woods, 1976). The version presented here was suggested by Bill Leal in 1978. It is similar to previous versions but treats the arguments of the predicates a bit differently. The new symbolization permits better accounting of participants and their case roles. In general, P is a predicate, and P123 is a predicate with three arguments. Arguments are all optional and occur in ordered positions: subject, object, and other. $P1^a 6^e$ means that participant number one is an argument of predicate P and is in an agent role, and participant number six is in an experiencer role to the predicate.

The case system we will use here is taken from a previous chapter and is as follows:

a   agent   -- the typically animate entity which acts, or the entity which instigates a process

c   course   -- (or Path) -- the locales transversed in a motion, or, the bearer in a transaction

e   experiencer   -- the animate entity whose registering nervous system is relevant to the predication

g   goal   -- the ending location of a motion, or
the final owner in a transfer, or
the entity at which the activity of the predicate is aimed but which is not affected or changed by the activity of the predicate

i   instrument   -- the entity that an agent uses to accomplish the activity of the predicate, or
the entity that triggers (a change in) an emotional state, or
the price in a transfer (with <u>with</u>)

ℓ locative   -- the locale of a predication

m   measure   -- the nominal that quantifies the activity of the predicate, or
the price in a transfer, or
any manner modifiers of the predicate (for our purposes here)

p   patient   — the entity of which a state is predicated, or
              the entity which undergoes a change of state
                  or location

r   range   — the product of the activity of the predicate, or
              the entity involved in the activity of the
                  predicate, but which is not affected by the
                  activity, or
              the entity that completes or further specifies
                  the predicate, or
              the quoted proposition that complements such verbs
                  as speak, say, write, think, dream, guess,
                  and ask

s   source   — the beginning place from which something moves
                  or emanates, or
              the source of physical sensations, or
              the original owner in a transfer

Note that the modality (tense, mood, aspects, outer location, and benefactives) is not accounted for in either case grammar or in propositional calculus. Some aspects will be included as prefixes on the predicate symbols. (See section D.1.)

We will present basic structures in section A, rhetorical elaborated structures in section B, frustrative structures in section C, and a full definition of symbols in section D, following Longacre's presentation.

A. Basic deep structures include nonsequential conjoining and sequential conjoining. The first is nonsequential; that is, there is no sequential relationship between the clauses in a sentence.

A.1. Conjoining without temporal or logical sequence

A.1.a. Conjoining with 'and', no contrast emphasized.

A.1.a.1. Coupling with same first term

'She's blonde and (she's) beautiful.'

$P1^P \land Q1^P$

(Here predicate P is 'be blonde' and predicate Q is 'be beautiful.' Participant 1 'she' is patient in each predicate.)

A.1.a.2. Coupling with different first terms (without reciprocity)

'He paints and his wife collects postage stamps.'

$P1^a \wedge Q2^a3^p$

(Here P is 'paints' and Q is 'collects'; 1 is 'he', 2 is 'his wife' and 3 is 'postage stamps'.)

This could also be written as:

$P1^a \wedge Q2^a$

where Q is now 'collects postage stamps'.

(The above is an example of how a predicate can be defined to include more than just the verb. This is a convenient convention we will use frequently. Languages differ in how much is included in a verb, anyway. For English, we might coin a derived verb stem 'philatelize' for 'to collect postage stamps'; now it is all one verb!)

A.1.a.3. Coupling with different first terms (with reciprocity)

'She nags him, and he pays scant attention to her.'

$P1^{as}2^{eg} \wedge Q2^a1^s$

(where participant 1 'she' is the source of the sound waves and the goal of his attention.)

A.1.a.4. Parallel coupling

'I'll pay for your clothing, I'll pay for your books, and I'll pay for your tuition, but you'll have to earn your own spending money.'

$P1^a2^p \wedge P1^a3^p \wedge P1^a4^p \wedge oQ5^a6^p$

(where P is 'pay for', 2 is 'your clothing', 3 is 'your books', 4 is 'your tuition', and 6 is 'your own spending money', and oQ 'will have to earn'.)

'The men, women, and children speak the trade language.'

$P1^a \wedge P2^a \wedge P3^a$

(where P is 'speak the trade language'),

or $P1^{a_4{}^r} \wedge P2^{a_4{}^r} \wedge P3^{a_4{}^r}$

(where P is 'speak' and 4 is 'the trade language', which has a 'range' role in the predicate.)

A.1.b. Conjoining with 'but', emphasizing contrast.

A.1.b.1. Contrast by negation

'I got a raise, but he didn't.'

$P1^e \wedge \bar{P}2^e$

(where P is 'got a raise' and $\bar{P}$ is 'did not get a raise'.)

A.1.b.2. Contrast by antonyms

'She works as a business executive during the day, but she has to revert to being a mother and housewife in the evening.'

$P1^{a}{}_2{}^r t^1_2 \wedge P1^{ae}{}_2{}''{}^r t^2_3 \wedge (t^1_3 = Ut)$

(Ut = universe of time, 2 is 'a business executive', 2" is 'mother and housewife'.
A more rigorous symbolization might be:

$P1^{a}{}_2{}^r t^1_2 \wedge P1^{a}{}_3{}^r t^2_3 \wedge (t^1_2 = \bar{t}^2_3) \wedge (2 = \bar{3})$

which says that t^1_2 and t^2_3 make up the universe of time, and 2 and 3 make up the universe of culture.)

A.1.b.3. Contrast by exception

'Everyone went to church except grandfather.'

$P(U-1)^{ap}3^g \wedge \bar{P}1^{ap}3^g \wedge (1 \varepsilon U)$

(where P is 'went', $\bar{P}$ 'did not go', 3 is 'church', U is 'everyone', and 1 is 'grandfather', and 'grandfather' is a member of the 'everyone' group.)

'Nobody went to church except grandfather.'

$\bar{P}(U-1)^{ap}3^g \wedge P1^{ap}3^g \wedge (1 \varepsilon U)$

A.1.c. Conjoining for comparison

    'Bill is bigger than John.'

    $P1^e x^m \land P2^e y^m \land (x^m > y^m)$

    (where P is 'have size', x and y are degrees of size, so the formula says 'Bill has size x and John has size y, and x is greater than y.')

    'John loves Mary as much as he loves Sue.'

    $P1^e 2^g x^m \land P1^e 3^g y^m \land (x^m = y^m)$

    (where > means 'is greater than', = means 'is equal to', and < means 'is less than', and x and y are unspecified measure role fillers.)

A.1.d. Conjoining for alternation with 'or'.

A.1.d.1. Two alternatives

A.1.d.1.a. Alternation by negation, two alternatives

    'Either he did it, or he didn't.'

    $P1^a \veebar \overline{P}1^a$

    'Do you want to buy it, or not?'

    $dP1^a 2^g \veebar d\overline{P}1^a 2^g$

A.1.d.1.b. Alternation by antonyms, two alternatives

    'Is he dead or alive?'

    $P1^e \veebar Q1^e \land ((P \cup Q) = U)$

    (where P is 'be dead' and Q is 'be alive', and P and Q together make up the universe of possibilities. $\veebar$ means that one or the other is true but not both.)

    'Either the man is working or his wife is working.'

    $P1^a \lor P2^a$

    Here v stands for 'inclusive or' where one or the other or both must be true.)

    'Are you going to your village by canoe or by plane?'

    $P1^a P2^g 3^i \lor P1^a P2^g 4^i$

A.1.d.2. Alternation of more than two alternatives

'Either John will come, or Mary will come, or Sue will come.'

$P1^a \lor P2^a \lor P3^a$

'Let's beg, borrow, or buy a stopwatch.'

$P1^a{}_2{}^p \lor Q1^a{}_2{}^p \lor R1^a{}_2{}^p$

'He'll come today, tomorrow, or sometime next week.'

$P1^a t_1 \lor P1^a t_2 \lor P1^a t_3$

or $Pt_1 \lor Pt_2 \lor Pt_3$

(where P now means 'he will come'.)

A.2. Sequential conjoining

A.2.a. Temporal sequence

A.2.a.1 Overlapping

A.2.a.1.a. Coterminous continuous events

'He whistled as he worked.'

$P1^a t_2^1 \land Q1^a t_2^1$

(where t_2^1 is the same for both predicates.)

A.2.a.1.b. Punctiliar with a continuous event

'He glanced back as he walked on.'

$P1^a t_2 \land Q1^a t_3^1$

(where t_2 lies within the span of t_3^1.)

'While he was walking, he stumbled.'

$P1^a t_3^1 \land Q1^e t_2$

A.2.a.1.c. Two overlapping punctiliar events

'As he turned the corner, another car hit him.'

$P1^a{}_3{}^\ell t_1 \land Q2^a{}_1{}^p t_1$

A.2.a.2 Succession in time, 'and then'

A.2.a.2.a. Continuous plus continuous events

'They played tennis for an hour, then swam for another hour.'

$P1^a2^rt_2^1 \land Q1^at_4^3$

A.2.a.2.b. Punctiliar plus continuous events

'He put the wood on the stove, then sat there for an hour.'

$P1^a2^P3^gt_1 \land Q1^a4^\ell t_3^2$

'It rained all morning but cleared up about noon.'

$Pt_2^1 \land Qt_3$

A.2.a.2.c. Punctiliar plus punctiliar events

'He sat down, took the book and opened it.'

$P1^at_1 \land Q1^{ag}2^Pt_2 \land R1^a2^Pt_3$

'He gave her some water, and she drank it.'

$P1^{as}2^P3^g \land Q3^a2^P$

(lit: He gave some water to her, and she drank it.)

A.2.b. Logical succussion - implication, 'if...then'

A.2.b.1. Conditionality

A.2.b.1.a. Hypotheticality

'If he comes, I'll go.'

$P1^a ==> Q2^a$

'If she doesn't go, I won't go either.'

$\bar{P}1^a ==> \bar{P}2^a$

A.2.b.1.b. With universal quantifier

'Wherever you go, I'll be thinking of you.'

$\forall x, P1^{aP}x^g ==> Q2^{ae}1^g$

(for all x's, if you go to x, I will think of you.)

'Whomever we sent got lost.'

$\forall x, \; Pl^a x^e ==> Qx^{pe}$

'Everyone who goes to Alaska gets rich.'

$\forall x, \; Px^{ap}l^g ==> Qx^{pe}$

A.2.b.1.c. Contingency - temporal condition

'If you pay a deposit, you can have a key.'

$Pl^a 2^r t_1 ==> uQl^{eg} 3^p t_3^2$

A.2.b.1.d. Proportional covariance - correlative

'The bigger they are, the harder they fall.'

$\forall x \; \& \; y, \; (Px^P a^m \land Py^P b^m \land (a^m > b^m)) ==>$
$(Qx^P c^m \land Qy^P d^m \land (c^m > d^m))$

'The harder I work, the less I seem to earn.'

$\forall x^m \; \& \; y^m, \; ((Pl^a x^m \land Pl^a y^m) \land (x^m > y^m)) ==>$
$((Ql^e c^m \land Ql^e d^m) \land (c^m < d^m))$

A.2.b.2. Causation

A.2.b.2.a. Efficient cause (preceding cause)

'You came because your wife made you come.'

$Pl^a t_2 \land oQ3^a l^e t_1 \land (oQ3^a l^e t_1 ==> Pl^a t_2)$

(Here oQ indicates obligation; oQ = 'make to come'.)

A.2.b.2.b. Final cause (future cause)

'They went to the stadium early in order to get good seats.'

$Pl^{ap} 2^g t_1 \land A(Pl^{ap} 2^g t_1 ==> Ql^a 3^P t_2)$

('They went to the stadium early (t_1, earlier than the game at time t_2) and arriving early implies the expectation of good seats at time t_2.')

A.2.b.2.c. Circumstantial cause

'Since he's doing his best, let's leave him alone.'

$P1^a{}_2{}^m \land (P1^a{}_2{}^m ==> wQ3^e(oP4^a{}_1{}^e)^r) \land oP4^a{}_1{}^e$

Literally: He is doing his best and (if he is doing his best, then I think we should leave him alone) so we should leave him alone.

'Since it was raining outside, we stayed in the shopping center a while longer.'

$P1^\ell \land (P1^\ell ==> wQ2^e(oR2^a{}_3{}^\ell t_2^1)^r) \land R2^a{}_3{}^\ell t_2^1$

Literally: It was raining outside and (if it was raining outside, then we thought that we should stay in the shopping center a while longer) we did stay in shopping center a while longer.

A.2.b.3. Contrafactuality

'Had he come, I would have come too.'

$(P1^a t_1 ==> P2^a t_1) \land \bar{P}1^a t_1 \land \bar{P}2^a t_1$

'If it had not rained last week, the ground would be too hard to dig now.'

$(\bar{P}t_2^1 ==> Q2^p t_3) \land Pt_2^1 \land \bar{Q}2^p t_3$

A.2.b.4. Warning - with undesirable foreseen result

'We shouldn't let our torches go out because if we do let our torches go out we won't find our way home.'

$((pP1^a{}_2{}^p ==> \bar{Q}1^a 3^g) \land dQ1^a 3^g) ==> p\bar{P}1^a{}_2{}^p$

(Here, P = 'go out', pP = 'permit to go out', Q = 'find way'; dQ = 'desire to find way'. This is read, 'If we let our torches go out, then we won't find our way home and we want to find our way home so we should not permit the torches to go out.')

'We shouldn't let our torches go out, or we won't find our way home.'

(Same deep structure as above. Note that this example lacks the conditional portion in the surface structure, but implies it.)

'We should warn them, or they may not do the assignment right.'

$$(\bar{P}1^a2^e \implies m\bar{Q}2^a3^p) \wedge (dR1^e(Q2^a3^p)^r \implies oP1^a2^e)$$

(Here, Q = 'do', mQ = 'might do'.)

B. Rhetorical elaboration structures include nonreportive and reportive elaboration structures.

B.1. The nonreportive rhetorical elaboration structures include paraphrase and illustration.

B.1.a. Paraphrastic structures

B.1.a.1. Equivalent paraphrase

'He drives a small car, he drives a Mini Minor.'

$$P1^a \wedge Q1^a \wedge G(PQ)$$

(where G(PQ) means P is more generic than Q, G is a two place 'generic' predicate.)

'We purchased a big new refrigerator, we bought a big avocado-colored, double-door model.

$$P1^a2^g \wedge Q1^a3^g \wedge H(PQ) \wedge H(2^g3^g)$$

(here, H(PQ) means that P and Q are synonymous.)

B.1.a.2. Paraphrase with a negated antonym

'He gave her a big diamond, not just a little one.'

$$P1^{as}2^{eg}3^p4^m \wedge \bar{P}1^{as}2^{eg}3^p5^m \wedge (4^m > 5^m)$$

'He didn't give her a small diamond, but he gave her a big one.'

(Same structure as above, but the surface structure manifests a reversal of terms.)

B.1.a.3. Paraphrase with negated higher degree

'It's not hot, but it is warm.'

$$\bar{P}1^m \wedge P2^m \wedge (1^m > 2^m)$$

'They are a good ball team but they are not unbeatable.'

$$P1^p2^m \wedge \bar{P}1^p3^m \wedge (2^m < 3^m)$$

B.1.a.4. Paraphrase with negated extremes

> 'It's neither hot nor cold; it's just lukewarm.'

$$\bar{P}1^m \wedge \bar{P}3^m \wedge P2^m \wedge (1^m > 2^m > 3^m)$$

B.1.a.5 Paraphrase with generic and specific

> 'They cook lots of potatoes in a day, they french fry them.'

$$P1^a 2^p \wedge Q1^a 2^p \wedge G(PQ)$$

(where P is more generic and Q is more specific.)

B.1.a.6. Paraphrase with amplification

> 'They sang only a little bit; they sang only two songs.'

$$P1^a 2^m \wedge P1^a 3^m \wedge G(23)$$

> 'He was unconscious; Debony, a woman, had knocked him unconscious.' (Inibaoi, Philippines)

$$P1^p \wedge cP2^a{}_1{}^p$$

(P = 'be unconscious' and cP = 'cause to be uncounscious'.)

> 'The store is closed; it closed at noon today.'

$$P1^p t_2 \wedge P1^p t_1$$

B.1.a.7. Paraphrase with specific and generic

> 'They dug up some Assyrian ruins; they did a lot of excavation.'

$$P1^a \wedge Q1^a \wedge G(QP)$$

B.1.a.8. Paraphrase with contraction in the second part

> 'I won't go to see him; I just won't go.'

$$\bar{P}1^a 2^g \wedge \bar{Q}1^a \wedge H(PQ)$$

> 'She knocked him unconscious; he's out cold.'

$$P1^a 2^p \wedge Q2^p \wedge H(PQ)$$

> 'We'll bury the fish in the ashes; we'll hide it.' (Wik-Munkan, Australia)

$$P1^a 2^p 3^\ell \wedge Q1^a 2^p \wedge G(QP)$$

B.1.a.9. Paraphrase with a summary

>'John works at the sawmill; Jim works at the repair shop; and Al works at the print shop--that's what they're all doing these days.'
>
>$P1^a{}_2{}^\ell \land P3^a{}_4{}^\ell \land P5^a{}_6{}^\ell \land QUt_1 \land (1 \cup 3 \cup 5 = U) \land G(QP)$

B.1.b. Illustration

B.1.b.1. Simile

>'My love is like a red, red rose.'
>
>$\ell P1^P{}_2{}^r \land Q2^P$
>
>(read: 'My love is like a rose and red the rose.')
>
>'You're acting like a child.'
>
>$Px^a{}_y{}^m \land P1^a{}_y{}^m$
>
>('A child acts a certain way, and you act that same certain way.')

B.1.b.2. Exemplification

>'Take any green vegetable, for example, spinach.'
>
>$P1^a{}_U{}^P \land P1^a{}_2{}^P \land (2 \; \varepsilon \; U)$
>
>'Any color will do: either red, white, green, or blue.'
>
>$PU^P \land P1^P \land P2^P \land P3^P \land P4^P \land (\{1, 2, 3, 4\} = U)$

B.2. The reportive rhetorical elaboration includes deictic structures and speech or sensation attribution structures.

B.2.a. Deixis

B.2.a.1. Introduction

>'There was an old cow that died from the cold; we boiled boiled and ate it.' (Inibaloi)
>
>$\exists 1^P \land P1^P t_1 \land Q2^a{}_1{}^P t_2 \land R2^a{}_1{}^P t_3$

B.2.a.2. Identification

'The Spanish picked him up on their way, and he was the one who showed the way up here.' (Inibaloi)

$P1^a{}_2e{}_3{}^\ell \quad \wedge \quad E2(Q2^a1^e{}_4{}^g)$

'Kimboy got a hammer, and that was what they used.'

$P1^a{}_2{}^p \quad \wedge \quad E2(Q3^a{}_2{}^i)$

B.2.a.3. Other identification and introduction

'There was a man called Al; he was an electrician.'

$\exists 1^p \quad \wedge \quad PU^a1^e{}_3{}^r \quad \wedge \quad Q1^p$

(read: 'There was a man and people called him Al and he was an electrician.')

'Al was and electrician; he worked for Thomas Smothers.'

$P1^p \quad \wedge \quad Q1^a{}_2{}^g$

B.2.b. Speech and awareness attribution – quotations

B.2.b.1. Speech attribution

'"Yesterday," he said, "I saw her at the fair."'

$wP1^a(Q1^e{}_2{}^r{}_3{}^\ell{}_{t_1})^r{}_{t_2}$

(here, wP is a words predicate, an internal or external speech predication.)

'He thought to himself, "I've seen her somewhere before."'

$wP1^{ae}(Q1^e{}_2{}^r{}_3{}^\ell{}_{t_1})^r{}_{t_2}$

B.2.b.2. Awareness attribution, knowledge, and sensation

'I knew that something was wrong.'

$aP1^e(Q2^p)^r$

'I saw that he was in a bad mood.'

$aP1^e(Q2^p)^r$

C. The third and last major type of deep structures comprises the frustration structures. They are different because the structure must include both the expected and the unexpected results. The full general formula is:

$$A(P \Longrightarrow Q) \land P \land R \land Q_\beta \land S$$

where $P \Longrightarrow Q$ is the basic expected cause and effect, P is the cause or circumstance, R is the intervening, blocking circumstance, Q_β is the opposite of Q, the expected outcome, and S is the substitute action taken as a result of Q_β. Not all structures have all these terms, because not all are relevant to all situations.

C.1. Basic frustration structures

C.1.a. Frustrated, nonsequential coupling

'We have some medicine but it doesn't do anything.'

$$A(P1^P \Longrightarrow Q1^P) \land P1^P \land \bar{Q}1^P$$

(where 'medicine' implies 'being effective' is the background supposition (in parentheses), and $P1^P$ and $Q1^P$ are the actual states. The frustration is that $Q1^P$ would be expected but $\bar{Q}1^P$ (not $Q1^P$ is what actually exists.)

C.1.b. Frustrated sequence

C.1.b.1. Temporal sequence

C.1.b.1.a. Overlapping frustration

'He drives down crowded streets, but doesn't look out for pedestrians.'

$$A(P1^a{}_2{}^\ell t^1_2 \Longrightarrow oQ1^a{}_3{}^g t^1_2) \land P1^a{}_2{}^\ell t^1_2 \land \bar{Q}1^a{}_3{}^g t^1_2$$

'He drives down crowded streets but doesn't look out for pedestrians, so he struck a child the other day.'

$$A(P1^a{}_2{}^\ell t^1_3 \Longrightarrow oQ1^a{}_3{}^g t^1_3) \land P1^a{}_2{}^\ell t^1_3 \land \bar{Q}1^a{}_3{}^g t^1_3 \land S1^a{}_4{}^P t_2$$

C.1.b.1.b. Succession frustration

'I studied the material, but my mind went blank and I couldn't answer the questions.'

$$A(P1^a{}_2{}^r t^1_2 \Longrightarrow Q1^e{}_3{}^r t_2) \land P1^a{}_2{}^r t^1_2 \land R4^P{}_5{}^m t_2 \land \bar{Q}1^e{}_2{}^r t_2 \land$$

$$H\ (23) \land G\ (14)$$

C.1.b.2. Frustrated implications

C.1.b.2.a. Frustrated conitionality

C.1.b.2.a.1. Frustrated hypotheticality

'Even if I could loan you some money, I'm not going to, I want to invest it in some real estate.'

$$A(mP1^a2^P3^g ==> P1^a2^P3^g) \land mP1^a2^P3^g \land \bar{P}1^a2^P3^g \land dQ1^a2^P4^g$$

C.1.b.2.a.2. Frustrated contingency

'Even if I get a scholarship, I'll still have to work part time.'

$$A(P1^g2^Pt_1 ==> o\bar{Q}1^at_2) \land P1^g2^Pt_1 \land oQ1^at_2$$

C.1.b.2.b. Frustrated causation

C.1.b.2.b.1. Frustrated preceding cause

'He was poisoned, but he did not die.'

$$P1^e \land A(P1^e ==> Q1^e) \land \bar{Q}1^e$$

C.1.b.2.b.2. Frustrated foreseen cause

'He seemed to have all the qualifications, but he didn't get the job.'

$$sP1^P \land A(sP1^P ==> Q1^e2^P) \land \bar{Q}1^e2^P$$

C.2. Rhetorically elaborated frustration structures

C.2.a. Frustrated attribution

'He <u>says</u> that she is intelligent.'

'He says that she is intelligent, but, really, she isn't.'

$$wP1^a(Q2^P)^r \land A(wP1^a(Q2^P)^r ==> Q2^P) \land \bar{Q}2^P$$

C.2.b. Mistaken idea

'I thought you were wrong, but you weren't.'

$$wP1^a(Q2^P)^r \land A(wP1^a(Q2^P)^r ==> Q2^P) \land \bar{Q}2^P$$

C.3. Frustrated modality

C.3.a. Frustrated intent

'I intended to go, but some friends dropped in, so I didn't.'

$$iP1^a \land A(iP1^a \Longrightarrow P1^a) \land R2^a \land \bar{P}1^a$$

C.3.b. Frustrated obligation

'I should have gone, but I didn't.'

$$oP1^a \land A(oP1^a \Longrightarrow P1^a) \land \bar{P}1^a$$

C.3.c. Frustrated facility or ability

'I could have promoted him, but I didn't.'

$$uP1^a2^e \land A(uP1^a2^e \Longrightarrow P1^a2^e) \land \bar{P}1^a2^e$$

D. Definition of terms

D.1. Predicates whose arguments are terms

P, Q, R, S are general purpose predicate symbols that stand for whole clauses minus the arguments that are specified following the predicate symbols.

$\bar{P}, \bar{Q}, \bar{R}, \bar{S}$ are the negations of P, Q, R, and S.

Q_β is the opposite of Q.

Q" is the antonym of Q.

∃ is 'there is, or was'.

E = 'someone was the one who'.
    E often has two arguments, the second being an expression.

∀ is 'all' or 'for all' or 'every' or 'for every'.

A(... ==> ...) stipulates if the condition is true then it is expected that the result will also be true, where the ...'s are replaced with predicates or propositions.

aP means that the first argument is aware of the second argument, which is usually an expression.

cP means that first argument is the agent or causer of the predicate P.

dP means that the first argument desires the action or state of predicate P.

eP means that the first argument expects the action or state of predicate P.

iP means that the first argument intends the action or state of predicate P.

ℓP means that the predicate P predicates some likeness to its arguments.

mP means that the predicate P has a 'may or might' aspect.

oP means that the predicate P has an 'obligation' aspect, 'must', 'have to'.

pP means that the predicate P has a 'permission' aspect, 'permit'.

sP means that the predicate P has a 'seem to' aspect.

uP means that the predicate P has a 'possibility or ability' aspect, 'may' or 'might'.

wP means that the first argument speaks the second argument, which is usually an expression.

D.2. Predicates whose arguments are predicates

G means that its first argument is more generic than its second argument.

H means that its arguments are equivalent paraphrases.

D.3. Terms that serve as arguments of predicates.

a, b, c, d, ... are nonspecific terms.

x, y are nonspecific terms, usually time or location.

1, 2, 3, 4, ... are specific terms, usually participants.

t_1, t_2 are point in time.

t_2^1, t_3^2, ... are spans of time from $time_1$ to $time_2$ and from $time_2$ to $time_3$.

$\bar{t}$ is the negation of t

1", 2", ... are antonymous terms to 1, 2, i.e., 1 and 1" are antonyms within the universe of the sentence.

U   is the whole set, the whole universe of that set of items or possibilities

Ut is the whole set of items

D.4. Role symbols (superscripts)

a   agent role

c   course role (= path)

e   experiencer role

g   goal role

i   instrument role

ℓ location role

m   measure role, manner role

p   patient role

r   range role

s   source role

D.5. Apparatus, and conjunctions

ε 'is a member of'

$\wedge$ 'and', 'but'

$\vee$ 'or'

$\underline{\vee}$ 'exclusive or', 'but not both'

$\overline{P}, \overline{2}$ 'not' (written over terms or predicates)

$>$ 'is greater/more than'

$<$ 'is less than'

$=$ 'equals'

$\Longrightarrow$ 'implies', 'should result in'

&   'and all', used between subterms of $\forall$ 'all'

$\cup$ 'and', conjoins subsets into a set

( ) used to group expressions and terms

... 'and other similar elements' (in D.3. above)

Propositional calculus, as a deep structure for sentence level, symbolizes the relationships between clauses in a sentence, and ignores most of the semantic content. Usually, there are several ways to say something, so one formula will symbolize several surface structures. If the propositional calculus formulas were in a one-to-one correspondence with the surface structures, they would be of little interest. But just because they are not one-to-one but many-to-one and one-to-many, they are useful.

In Inibaloi, Ballard, Conrad and Longacre found that most surface structures could encode more than one calculus relationship, and most calculus relationships could be encoded by more than one surface structure. So they drew up a long (vertically) diagram with the calculus relationships listed down the left side and surface structures listed down the right side. Then they drew criss-crossing lines connecting each calculus formula with all its appropriate right-hand surface structures.

A translator needs to have such a chart internalized; he needs to know intuitively all the possible alternative ways to express each idea. More importantly, he or she needs to know when to use each different alternative.

Bibliography

Ballard, D. Lee, Robert J. Conrad and Robert E. Longacre. 1971. The deep and surface grammar of interclausal relations. Foundations of Language 7.70-118.

_____. 1971. More on the deep and surface grammar of interclausal relations. Language Data, Asian-Pacific Series No. 1. Santa Ana: S.I.L.

Longacre, Robert E. 1976. An anatomy of speech notions. Lisse: The Peter de Ridder Press.

_____ and Stephen Echerd. 1976. Appendix to introduction to volume 1. Discourse grammar, studies in indigenous languages of Colombia, Panama, and Ecuador, ed. by Robert E. Longacre and Frances Woods. Dallas: S.I.L. and the University of Texas at Arlington.

Chapter 13

Paragraph-level structures

A paragraph is a cluster of sentences held together by a single theme or setting and organized according to some pattern. Or, looking at a paragraph from the larger perspective of discourse level, it is a small chunk of discourse that functions as a single constituent. (If you make detailed span charts of discourse, you will find seams where several semantic vectors end and others begin. These are paragraph breaks.)

(Paragraphs in written English are usually set up on orthographic-appearance criteria as much as on structure. In fact, some writers can write without forming structurally well-formed paragraphs, and have their text broken into paragraphs two or three inches long, rather arbitrarily.)

(The material in this chapter is taken almost entirely from the works of R. E. Longacre; see the bibliography.)

Some paragraphs are peculiar to certain discourses and play a large part in forming such discourses. These include the narrative, explanatory, and procedural paragraphs. Other paragraphs tend to be smaller and to occur embedded in other paragraphs. These include the sentencelike paragraphs treated last in this chapter.

Paragraphs derive much of their flavor from the discourse in which they occur. A contrast paragraph in a narrative discourse will differ from a contrast paragraph in a hortatory discourse. We will allow such variation in order to avoid having to set up a much larger inventory of paragraphs.

A. Paragraph boundaries

1. Paragraph boundaries in chronological discourses

Paragraph boundaries in narrative discourse are marked by a change of time, place, and cast of participants. They may be marked also by special sentence constituents such as sentence introducers, recapitulation, sentence time margins, location margins, and sentence topics. In a Pocomam narrative text in Guatemala (data by Sonya Eidsvoog and Susan Baird), paragraph boundaries are signaled by a generic type of clause at the end of one paragraph and a more specific, more active clause in the beginning of the next paragraph.

Sometimes, in the absence of clear grammatical signals, paragraph boundaries have to be determined by the patterns of intersentence relationships, the scripts or frames of paragraph structure. (See: Papers in Discourse Grammar, ed. by Longacre and Woods, 1977.)

Paragraph boundaries in procedural paragraphs are marked by changes in time, location, or activity. Very often there will be a paragraph break after some subpart of the product is finished, or when one stage in the procedure is finished and another is begun.

2. Paragraph boundaries in logical discourses

Paragraph boundaries in expository and behavioral discourses are signaled by a change in theme or topic and by seams between paragraph structures. A new topic sentence signals a new paragraph, along with any sentences that are closely related lead-ups to that topic sentence. Often, a series of sentences fit a paragraph structure, and a following series fits another; we then posit a paragraph break between the two paragraph structures without further overt signals.

Paragraph breaks in epistolary discourse are signaled by changes in topic and mode. There is a paragraph break between a narrative passage and an exhortation passage, between a petition section and a narrative section, and so on.

B. Discourselike paragraphs

Paragraphs form a grammatical level between discourse level and sentence level, so they share some of the properties of discourses, and some of sentences. We will discuss the discourse-related paragraphs first, paragraphs unique to paragraph level second, then the sentencelike paragraphs last.

1. Narrative paragraph

Narrative paragraphs are similar to narrative discourse and to the narrative sequence sentence. They encode sequences of events in a narrative time ordering.

Narrative paragraph

$\pm$ Setting	+ Buildup-1^n	+ Buildup-p	$\pm$ Terminus
sentence	sentence	sentence	sentence
paragraph	paragraph	paragraph	paragraph

The exponent of the setting is usually a clause or sentence or paragraph containing descriptive clauses, motion clauses, existence clauses, and the like. The exponent of the setting is not a part of the story line and does not encode any action of the narrative. Instead, it encodes background and setting information.

The exponents of the buildups are narrative paragraphs or sentences or compound, alternative, or parallel sentences or paragraphs. They encode events in the story line. If the exponents are paragraphs, very often the paragraphs will include some background and setting information.

Buildup-p is the climactic, peak buildup. Since it is on paragraph level, it is not as high a climax as is the climax of a narrative discourse. Sometimes it is difficult to see any climax in Buildup-p.

The terminus is a conclusion to the paragraph and is usually brief or absent. It encodes evaluative material, subsequent secondary events, and transitional material.

Often, the initial peripheral tagmemes of the first sentence will act as the setting, and final peripheral tagmemes of the last sentence will act as terminus. Sometimes only one part of a sentence will expound BU-p. Such mismatching of sentences and paragraph slots is common in some languages. One way to handle such mismatch is to say a sentence or part of a sentence simultaneously expounds two tagmemes, one on sentence level and one on paragraph level.

Quotation sentences may expound narrative buildups. Such quotation sentences may be quite important in narrative structure, or important to narrative style (for example, see Mildred Larson, 1978, The functions of reported speech in discourse).

In contrast to other paragraph types, the principal participants are first and third person (rarely second person), and the time is set at a point in history and events are related in a chronological sequence.

Narrative paragraph=

BU-1   Having stood up, they jumped down together (from the house), since the invaders had already fired their guns.

BU-2   Then Boro jumped out.

BU-3   When he jumped out, he got caught on the fence at the side of the house.

BU-4   Then the invaders surrounded him.

BU-5   Then the strong men, Adon, Magadan, Komanyan also jumped out, because their father was already surrounded.

BU-6   At the time when the invaders arrived near their father, they pushed the old man, Boro, up off the fence, freed him, then distracted the invaders from him.

BU-p	They were fighting the invaders, while others carried the old man away because he was weak already.
TERM	The old man didn't want to go because he wanted to fight, he was already emboldened. (from Phil. Lang., p. 63)

Narrative paragraph=

SETTING	And then it was afternoon now.
BU-1	And we were playing volleyball.
BU-2	And I wasn't (playing) very long and I saw Nini come up to me.
BU-3	(And when she had come) she said, "Father, they said for you to come home."
BU-4	And when I heard that, I went home.
BU-5	And arriving at the house, Uyen said to me, "They said for you to go upstairs."
BU-6	And when I heard that, then I went upstairs.
BU-7	And when I arrived upstairs, then Barb said to me, "Have Uyen come up also."
BU-8	And when I heard that, then I said to Uyen, "She said for you to come up."
BU-9	(When she heard this) then Uyen came up also.
BU-10	And when Uyen arrived beside us, Barb said to us, "Sit down."
BU-11	And when we were sitting, Barb said to me, she said, "A letter has just arrived...big mother is very sick, you are to go home, it says."
BU-12	And when I heard that, first I was just silent, for a long time I didn't speak.
BU-13	And when I was able to talk, then I said, "They wouldn't send that letter here quickly if mother hadn't died, but she is already dead."

BU-14   And when we had finished talking about the letter,
        then we cried.

BU-p   And I said, "Oh, it is really so that mother has already
        died." (Phil. Lang., p. 68)

2. Explanatory paragraph

Explanatory, expository, or attestation paragraphs are related to expository discourse and to logically structured sentences. An explanatory paragraph is organized around a single text which is expounded by a single sentence or paragraph. The other constituents reinforce, explain, or elaborate on that text.

Explanatory paragraph

± Preliminary	+ Text	+ Exposition^n	± Terminal
sentence	sentence	sentence	sentence
paragraph	paragraph	paragraph	paragraph

The text is the peak tagmeme, and the expositions reinforce it by giving reasons, evidence, and logical entailments to support it.

Some of the paragraphs described later in this chapter, such as the warning paragraph, the comment paragraph, the exemplification paragraph, are very similar to the explanatory paragraph. Generally, if the text is accompanied by a single exposition or by more than one similar exposition, the paragraph can be assigned to one of the latter types. But if a text is accompanied by two or more different kinds of expositions, then this explanatory paragraph structure is useful.

In an expository discourse or behavioral discourse, the explanatory paragraph expounds one of the point tagmemes. In narrative or procedural discourses or paragraphs, the explanatory paragraph gives background and explanatory material to the events or procedural steps.

In contrast to other paragraph types, the person in an explanatory paragraph is usually inanimate third person, but can be any person. The sentences tend to be static (nonactive), often equational or habitual in structure or have stative aspects. Temporal sequence is absent, usually.

Comment paragraph=

    TEXT   She stopped off at an all-night cafe for a quick
            coffee and joked a bit with the waiter to
            amuse herself.

COMMENT: Explanatory paragraph=

  TEXT She always felt comfortable in an all-night cafe when she was lonely.

  EXPO Some of the excitement of her first job as a counter girl rubbed off on her, back from the days when her life was less complicated.

  EXPO She had a wry nostalgia for her younger days when people were friendlier to each other.

- -

Explanatory paragraph=

  TEXT Another reason some managers fail to go up the ladder is their failure to learn to delegate authority.
  EXPO As effective young managers, they learned to get things done by their own efforts.

  EXPO They had their fingers on all departments under them and were personally responsible for any success or failure.

  EXPO But as a manager gets promoted, he reaches a level where he must change and learn to delegate the responsibility.

  EXPO He must promote a team effort among the managers under him.

  EXPO And if he meddles at some lower level, he is not just meddling in a department, he is meddling in another manager's work, and it causes real problems.

  EXPO If a manager is to continue to go up the ladder of promotion, he has to make a radical shift, and some fail to make the change.

3. Procedural paragraph

Procedural paragraphs are generally constituents of procedural discourse, although they can also expound tagmemes in other kinds of discourses and paragraphs.

Procedural paragraph

± Setting	+ Step^n	± Target Step	± Terminus
sentence	sentence	sentence	sentence
paragraph	paragraph	paragraph	paragraph

A procedural paragraph's sentences often have prior time tagmemes and condition tagmemes which help link the steps together and give proper timing to the procedure.

The steps in a procedural paragraph do not have to be all sequential. There may be simultaneous steps that are to happen at the same time. And there may be alternative steps, where there are two ways to continue the procedure. So in the array above, one could add 'simultaneous steps' and 'alternative steps' or posit a simultaneous or an alternative paragraph expounding one step of the procedural paragraph.

In contrast to other paragraph types, procedural paragraphs usually have imperative verbs. They may also be couched in first person plural habitual mood, 'We always do it this way'. Occasionally, a procedural paragraph may have third person indefinite, 'the one who wants to do this should do...'.

Some languages have an impersonal, timeless verb that they can use for procedural discourse. (Be careful of procedural discourses elicited out of context, that is, when you are not actually ready to do the procedure. You may get an activity discourse (see the next chapter of this book) that is a blend of procedural and expository, which may account for the use of different verb types.)

The procedural paragraph has sequential time but it is not time pinned down to a point in history. The time frame is a sequence of time starting whenever the person doing the procedure begins.

Procedural paragraph=

STEP-1   Put the thermometer into the water bath, stir, and measure the bath temperature.

STEP-2   If the solution temperature hasn't reached $38^{o}C$, but the water bath has, add hot water to the water bath until it is about $38^{o}C$, then rinse the thermometer and return it to the solution.

STEP-3   Continue to monitor the solution temperature and raise water bath temperature as necessary until the solution comes to $38^{o}C$.

STEP-4   Once the solution is at the right temperature, the water bath must also be brought to 38°C.

STEP-5   Alternative P =

    ALTERNATIVE-1: Proc P =

        STEP-1   If the water bath temperature is too high, add ice cubes to bring it down.

        STEP-2   Measure the water temperature carefully while stirring it with the thermometer.

        STEP-3   As soon as it reaches the proper temperature, remove the ice immediately.

        TERM   Try to avoid overshooting the mark.

    ALTERNATIVE-2: Procedural P =

        STEP-1   If, however, the water bath is below 38°C, add hot water to it slowly, stirring constantly with the thermometer.

        TERM   Try to avoid overshooting the mark.

TARGET STEP   Once you manage to get both the solution and the water bath at 38°C, you can begin the experiment.

(Note the alternate procedures at step 5.)

The last example showed one way to handle alternative steps in the procedure. The following example shows some simultaneous steps:

Procedual paragraph=

SETTING It takes cooperation between the pilot and the photographer to get good aerial pictures of a big fire.

STEP-1   First, you should have arranged with the pilot ahead of time, so that you can contact him and get into the air in a minimum of time.

STEP-2   Be sure your equipment is in good shape and is tied down, so that it won't fall out or move about in the plane.

STEP-3: Simult P =

    SIM-EVENT-1 When you approach the scene, the pilot must keep a safe altitude and a safe distance as he makes passes near the fire.

    SIM-EVENT-2 While the pilot makes his passes, shoot as many pictures as you can, beginning early and shooting as long as you can, in order to get as many angles as possible.

STEP-4   As soon as you have landed and can get to your laboratory, have the films developed and printed.

TARGET STEP If you are successful, you can sell your pictures for enough to pay your expenses and have some left over.

4. Hortatory paragraph

The hortatory paragraph is similar to the explanatory paragraph but has an exhortation instead of a text. Like hortatory or behavioral discourse, the hortatory paragraph is concerned with changing someone's behavior.

Hortatory paragraph

$\pm$ Prelim	+ Exhortation	+ Reinforcement^n	$\pm$ Terminal
sentence	sentence	sentence	sentence
paragraph	paragraph	paragraph	paragraph

The exhortation is the peak of this paragraph and it usually occurs near the beginning of the paragraph. But in some langauages, the peak exhortation may occur near the end of the paragraph.

The reinforcements may be evidential reasons, logical reasons, foreseen results, warnings, motivations, and so on. Sometimes a 'closure' tagmeme is inserted before the terminal tagmeme.

The hortatory paragraph is not at all time oriented; it is logical in structure. The person in focus is usually second person plural or singular. Imperative and hortatory moods are most common.

Hortatory discourse occurs most often at weddings and initiations when older members of the community instruct young people in proper behavior. Sometimes a hortatory paragraph occurs in a sermon. Political orations may also contain hortatory paragraphs.

A hortatory paragraph is preachy, often uncomfortable, so it is not common in daily social intercourse.

The exhortations may be mitigated exhortations if the social situation calls for deference. We can rank exhortations on a scale of direct versus mitigated and increasingly mitigated exhortations. Here are some examples:

'Go out and get a job!'

'You had better go out and get a job.'

'A young fellow like you should go out and get a job.'

'It would be good if you could get a job.'

'If you expect to get ahead, you should go out and get a job.'

'If you would go out and get a job,
    you could be more independent.'

'Please go out and look for a job.'

'Why don't you go out and look for a job?'

'You must go out and look for a job.'

'You should go out and look for a job.'

'After all, you could begin earning your own money.'

'Young fellows like you always go out and look for a job.'

'Any young fellow worth his salt goes out and looks for a job.'

The social situation and custom determine the kind of exhortation that is appropriate. Parents can use very direct commands with their children. Only people with obvious authority can use strong commands, as well as hints and very mitigated commands and expect them to be obeyed. People of lower status must use somewhat mitigated commands such as requests and suggestions, if he or she is to avoid offending a person of higher status. A preacher may use mitigated exhortations to keep his audience with him. (One interesting question is why the first epistle of John contains such mitigated exhortations.)

Hortatory paragraph=

PRELIM   Now, son, you are going off to school today.

EXHORTATION I want you to behave yourself.

REINF-1	I don't want the teacher to say you are disobedient in school.
REINF-2	I don't want to have to mend torn clothes, so don't get into fights.
REINF-3	If I find out that you haven't behaved, I will punish you here at home.
TERMINAL	So be a good boy.

- - - - - - - - - - - - -

Hortatory paragraph=

EXHORTATION	Today you are getting married, and now you must forget your childish ways and be a good woman and wife.
REINF-1	Prepare your husband's food as a good wife should.
REINF-2	Take good care of your possessions, and your husband's possessions, your clothing, your house, your garden.
REINF-3	If you don't do these things, you will bring shame on your family.
REINF-4	The spirits of our ancestors expect you to continue in the good way.

- -

Exhortation paragraph=

PRELIM	You know that we have the festival of Saint James next month.
EXHORTATION	And you, brother, Luis, should sponsor the fiesta this year.
REINF-1	We know it will cost you much money, but it is your turn to sponsor it, and you must do it.
REINF-2	All the other men in your generation have sponsored a fiesta, except you and Nestor, and Nestor is too stupid and poor to sponsor a fiesta.

    REINF-3   Your father sponsored this fiesta when he
                was alive, and his spirit is telling you
                now that you should do it, too.

    REINF-4   Your grandfather's spirit says you are too lazy
                and selfish to make a good fiesta, but your
                father's spirit says you are a good son who
                respects his ancestors and sponsors a fiesta
                for them.

    TERMINAL   So, what do you say?

5. Embedding of paragraphs

   Nonnarrative paragraphs are quite frequently embedded in other paragraphs, especially in some discourse styles. Embedded explanatory paragraphs, for example, may expound a narrative buildup. In this case, the text of the explanatory paragraph would expound the buildup by itself, but it has some explanatory sentences following it, so the would-be exponent of the buildup plus the explanatory sentences constitute an explanatory paragraph that expounds the buildup. For example, if we are in a narrative sequence encoding a series of events and we encounter the following sequence:

    Sentence 1   encodes an event
    Sentence 2   encodes an event
    Sentence 3   encodes an explanation of the event in S.2
    Sentence 4   encodes a further explanation of the event in S.2
    Sentence 5   encodes another event following the event in S.2

we would posit sentences 2, 3, and 4 as an explanatory paragraph, and our analysis of the narrative paragraph would be:

    BU-1   S.1
    BU-2   Explanatory paragraph
    BU-3   S.5

and the structure of the Explanatory paragraph would be:

    TEXT   S.2
    EXPO   S.3
    EXPO   S.4

For example: Narrative paragraph=

    BU-1   And after having fallen asleep, I woke up,
            and I got up.

    BU-2   And I peered out of the doorway and I heard
            a sound like a man moaning.

BU-3: Comment Paragraph=

    TEXT   As I listened carefully, "Oh," I said, "that is the carabao."

    COMMENT   Cyclical contrast Paragraph=

        TEXT   The thought in my mind was that he was really tired from plowing and that was why he was gasping.

        CONTRAST   I never thought that he might be sick and I never thought that he might be bitten by a snake.

        TEXT'   What I thought was that he was tired from pulling the plow because the plow went so deep that the overturned soil was as wide as a mat in the wake of the plow along the edge of my farm where I was plowing.

    BU-p   So I went back to bed and wrapped up in my blanket and got under the mosquito net. (Phil. Lang. p. 82)

C. Repartee paragraphs

Repartee paragraphs encode conversations. The dialogue paragraphs use quotation sentences and the dramatic paragraphs use any kind of sentences--sentences just as the participants spoke them.

1. Dialogue paragraph

Dialogue paragraphs encode chunks of conversational exchange. Longacre devotes a whole chapter to repartee in his <u>An Anatomy of Speech Notions,</u> and Larson discussed the importance of reported speech in her book.

Dialogue paragraph

± Setting	+ Initiating utterance	+ Continuing utterance^n	+ Resolving utterance	+ Terminating utterance
sentence	quotation sentence	quotation sentence	quotation sentence ------ sentence	quotation sentence ------ sentence
preliminary narration	question ------ proposal ------ remark	counter question ------ counter proposal ------ counter remark	answer ------ response ------ evaluation	aquiescence rejection

The initiating utterance is expounded by a quotation sentence that encodes a question, a proposal, or a remark spoken by the (leading) first participant. The second participant responds in a resolving utterance that is an answer to the question, a response to the proposal, or an evaluation or response to the remark. This is the minimal dialogue paragraph, called the 'simple dialogue paragraph'.

The response may be nonverbal, an action, or a gesture that serves the same purpose as a resolving utterance.

Simple dialogue paragraph=

INIT-UTT   "So you're buying me," retorted Nayal.

RESOL-UTT "We're offering a contract and making it worth your while," replied Silver quietly.

- -

Simple dialogue paragraph=

INIT-UTT   "My, what large ears you have, grandmother," said Red Riding Hood.

RESOL-UTT "The better to hear you, dear," said the wolf.

Simple dialogue paragraph=

INIT-UTT   Starkley noted the stranger's appearance inquisitively, and after a moment suggested, "Let's step into a joint where we can have some coffee and talk some more."

RESOL-UTT   The stranger agreed, "I know a good place nearby."

The second participant may, however, decide not to respond in the expected manner. He may produce a counterquestion, a counterproposal, or a counterremark. Now the first speaker must produce a resolving utterance, or he may produce another continuing utterance, causing the second participant to respond, and so on. A dialogue paragraph containing continuing utterances is called a 'complex dialogue' paragraph.

Complex dialogue paragraph=

SETTING: Description paragraph=

         And just ahead, he could see the black outline of an island.

         On either side, he could see the bright reflections on the river.

INIT-UTT   "Get ready!" he yelled, "We're going to swim for the island when we're a little closer."

CONT-UTT   "Swim nothing," growled Greg, "let's go back home. Why not?"

CONT-UTT   "Don't argue, do as I tell you!" commanded Bart.

RESOL-UTT   Greg was surprised at Bart's insistence but managed to say "O.K., you're boss."

TERM-UTT   "That's better," Bart replied.

2. Compound dialogue paragraph

A dialogue paragraph may occur alone, embedded in a narrative paragraph or discourse, or it may be a part of a larger reported conversation. We describe the longer conversation as a compound dialogue paragraph.

Compound dialogue paragraph

± Setting	+ Exchange-1	+ Exchange-2^n	± Terminus
sentence paragraph	dialogue paragraph	dialogue paragraph	sentence

Each exchange is expounded by a dialogue paragraph, and all the exchanges cohere as a single conversation which is a single constituent of some larger construction.

Compound dialogue paragraph=

SETTING I could see antiaircraft shells exploding under us.

EXCH-1 Control asked the pilot, "Can you see the searchlight beams at the front line?"

The pilot replied, "I can see them and we're not more than three minutes away."

EXCH-2 Control ordered, "Head right between them."

"I'm getting nearer, but my engine isn't running so well. I'm losing altitude," called the pilot.

EXCH-3 After a couple of minutes, control said, "You should be crossing the river soon."

My pilot replied, "I just crossed it, and I'm still losing altitude. Do you think we can make it home?"

Control said, "I don't know. Maybe..."

TERM Control had to turn his attention to other planes while we limped back to base.

3. Dramatic paragraph

A dramatic paragraph is similar to a dialogue paragraph in that it has the same tagmemes and deep structures. But it differs in the exponents of the utterances. The exponents are sentences and paragraphs as actually spoken, without quotation formulas and quotation sentences.

Dramatic paragraph

± Setting	+ Initiating utterance	+ Continuing^n utterance	+ Resolving utterance	± Terminus
sentence paragaph	sentence paragraph	sentence paragraph	sentence paragraph	sentence
preliminary narrative	question	counter question	answer	acquiescence
	proposal	counter proposal	response	rejection
	remark	counter remark	evaluation	

The exponents of the utterance tagmemes are directly quoted sentences and paragraphs:

Simple dramatic paragraph=

    INIT-UTT   "Is that you, Higgins?"

    RESOL-UTT   "Yeah, it's me."

- - - - - - - - - - - - - - -

Simple dramatic paragraph=

    INIT-UTT   "Let's step outdoors for some fresh air."

    RESOL-UTT   "Good idea."

- - - - - - - - - - - - - - -

Complex dramatic paragraph=

    INIT-UTT   "Helen, where is that book I've been reading?"

    CONT-UTT   "Where did you leave it last?"

    CONT-UTT   "I was reading here in my easy chair, and I left it on this table."

    RESOL-UTT   "Well, I haven't seen it."

- - - - - - - - - - - - - - -

Complex dramatic paragraph=

INIT-UTT	"He couldn't have given you a higher compliment."
CONT-UTT	"I know, but I didn't do anything so wonderful."
CONT-UTT	"You didn't make a mistake under all that pressure and everyone knows it."
CONT-UTT	"I only did what came as a reflex."
CONT-UTT	"That was more than most of us could do."
RESOL-UTT	"Well, thank you for the compliment."

4. Compound dramatic paragraph

The compound dramatic paragraph is similar to the compound dialogue paragraph.

Compound dramatic paragraph

± Setting	+ Exchange-1	+ Exchange-2^n	± Terminus
sentence paragraph	dramatic paragraph	dramatic paragraph	sentence paragraph

Compound dramatic paragraph=

SETTING	After breakfast, the young one got ready to go outside.
EXCH-1	"Mother, I'm going outdoors." "O.K., son."
EXCH-2	"Teep teep teep." "Who is that saying, 'teep teep teep'?" "It's me."
EXCH-3	"Where are you?" "I'm up here in the tree."
EXCH-4	"Who are you?" "I'm the spirit of your father's arrows."
EXCH-5	"What do you want?" "I've come to help you hunt."
TERMINUS	And so it was that the boy gained the power of his father's arrows.

D. Other paragraph structures more or less unique to paragraph level

The following paragraphs have interconstituent functions that usually occur on paragraph level.

1. Simple paragraph

A simple paragraph comprises a single text with a preliminary statement, or a single buildup with a setting. It is the minimal form of all the other paragraphs. It consists of one nuclear tagmeme and one or more peripheral tagmemes.

Simple paragraph

± Margins	+ Simple base	± Margins
	sentence	

Rule:
One or more marginal tagmemes must be present.

Simple paragraph=

SETTING   Samson's hair had grown back and he had regained his strength.

BUILDUP   When the Philistines held a banquet and were making sport of him, he pulled the supports of the banquet hall down causing the building to collapse on the guests.

TERMINAL   Were they ever surprised!

- - - - - - - - - -

Simple paragraph=

PRELIM   Let us go back in history a little.

TEXT   The need for adequate energy supplies was obvious to some people as early as 1960.

2. Comment paragraph

The comment paragraph consists of a text and one or more comments. This paragaph may occur in almost all kinds of discourse. The text is a regular constituent of another paragraph or discourse. The comments are almost parenthetical additions to the discourse or paragraph, and are often equational clauses or sentences.

    BU-i   The game continued for several more minutes with no one making any goals.

    BU-i+1: Comment paragraph=

        TEXT   In the final moments of the third period, Reeves made a goal that tied the score.

        COMMENT   Reeves, you may remember, was on the injured list much of last season.

    BU-i+2   After Reeves, Callum had a turn but failed to complete a goal.

Comment paragraph=

TEXT: COMMENT P=

    TEXT   The next day, the men perform the yam ceremony in the village and in the fields.

    COMMENT   This is the ceremony that was described earlier by J. C. Swatt.

    EXPOSITION The yam ceremony requires the participation of the whole extended family and takes a whole day to complete.

Comment paragraph

+ Text	+ Comment
sentence	sentence
	paragraph

Sometimes, an Addition paragraph is posited. Such a paragraph is very similar to the comment paragraph. It has a Text and an Addition. The Addition is somewhat parenthetical, just as the Comment is. The Addition, however, would add more relevant information to the Text than a Comment does.

3. Description paragraph

The description paragraph consists of a text and reinforcing descriptions. It occurs frequently in the introductory stage tagmemes of narrative discourses and in some scientific writings. This paragraph also handles descriptions interposed in a narrative paragraph, where the text is one of the buildups of the paragraph, but with one or more descriptive sentence added. The text and its desctiptive followers are combined into a descriptive paragraph, which expounds the buildup tagmeme that the text itself would otherwise expound. At other times this paragraph consists of a series of descriptions with or without a conclusion or summary.

Description paragraph

± Setting	± Text	+ Description^n	± Summary	± Conclusion
sentence	sentence	sentence	sentence	sentence
paragraph	paragraph	paragraph	paragraph	paragraph

Description paragraph=

SETTING   There were many animals in the bush, resting in the heat of the day.

DESCR-1   There was a tiger resting under the tree, but he was uncomfortable, he had fleas.

DESCR-2   There were many fleas on him.

DESCR-3   There was a monkey who was in the tree above the tiger.

CONCLUSION   The tiger thought maybe the monkey could help him get rid of his fleas.

In the paragraph above, the conclusion sets the theme for the following story about what the monkey did to the tiger.

The following example is a description paragraph that occurs in an explanatory discourse. It is describing some language learning lessons:

Description paragraph=

DESCR-1   Each lesson begins with a small dialogue or text that forms the core of that lesson.

DESCR-2   All the drills and exercises in the lesson will be based upon the dialogue or text.

DESCR-3   The approximate English translation of the dialogue or text will be provided in a right-hand margin near the dialogue or text.

DESCR-4   Ideally, these lessons would be accompanied by a tape recording of the dialogue or text with pauses between the utterances for repetition and eventual memorization.

DESCR-5   The language data in the lessons will be written phonetically unless otherwise noted.

One characteristic of the description paragraph is the lack of cohesion among the descriptions. Each description seems to be about something else. In such cases, the cohesion lies in the outside world being described. In the example above, the cohesion is fairly well maintained by the repeated references to lessons.

4. Induction paragraph

The induction paragraph is a reversal of the explanatory paragraph. In the induction paragraph, several evidences are lined up to support the conclusion.

Induction paragraph

± Prelim	+ Evidence^n	+ Conclusion
sentence	sentence	sentence
	paragraph	paragraph

Induction paragraph=

- PRELIM   Over a year ago, the Iranians took the United States embassy staff as hostages.

- EVID-1   Now, over a year later, many of the hostages have not been heard from for several months.

- EVID-2   Some have written complaining of boredom and lack of medical attention.

- EVID-3   And no Westerner has been allowed to see them for several months.

- CONCL   So the United States has charged Iran with cruel and inhuman treatment of the prisoners.

The induction paragraph is a kind of a reversed explanatory paragraph. It leads up to its conclusion or text, while the explanatory paragraph begins with a text and then adds reinforcements. In some types of discourse, the induction paragraph may be the paragraph of choice.

When the explanatory paragraph and the induction paragraph are combined and the text is placed both at the beginning and at the end, then we have a cyclical explanatory paragraph, which will be treated later in this chapter.

5. Warning paragraph

The warning paragraph consists of a text and a warning. This paragraph occurs in procedural paragraphs where a warning is appended to a step of the procedure. It can occur in other paragraphs also, such as explanatory and hortatory wherever a warning is used as part of the development of a discourse. The warning paragraph is often a subtype of the larger explanatory paragraph.

Warning paragraph

+ Text	+ Warning	± Conclusion / Summary
sentence	sentence	sentence
paragraph	paragraph	paragraph

Warning paragraph=

    TEXT   The price of gasoline keeps going higher and higher.

    WARNING We must drive our cars less or budget more money for gasoline.

Warning paragraph=

    TEXT   There is an epidemic of rabies among the wild animals in this area.

    WARNING Stay away from any animal that is acting strangely or is sick.

6. Exemplification paragraph

The exemplification paragraph consists of a text and examples of the text. Since the examples tend to reinforce the text, this paragraph is quite similar to the explanatory paragraph. The exemplification paragraph occurs whenever examples are introduced in the development of a discourse.

Exemplification paragraph

± Prelim	+ Text	+ Example^n	± Conclusion
sentence	sentence	sentence	sentence
paragraph	paragraph	paragraph	paragraph

Exemplification paragraph=

    TEXT   The burden of paper work generated by the requirements of governmental bureaucracies costs the average consumer no small sum every year.

EXAMPLE-1   Businesses, large and small, have to hire extra people just to prepare all the reports that have to be submitted to various agencies.

EXAMPLE-2   Hospitals have to spend large amounts on keeping records and submitting reports.

EXAMPLE-3   The auto industry is saddled with a whole bagful of expensive regulations and restrictions that add to the costs of cars.

CONCLUSION No business or service activity is immune to the requirements for added paperwork.

7. Execution paragraph

The execution paragraph is similar to the narrative paragraph in that it describes events in a narrative sequence. The first event is a plan suggested by someone, and the second event is the following out of that plan by the same person alone or with some of his companions.

Execution paragraph

± Setting	+ Plan	+ Execution	± Terminus
sentence paragraph	sentence paragraph	sentence paragraph	sentence
	Includes some quoted material.	Fulfills the plans made earler.	

The execution is often expounded by a narrative paragraph.

Execution paragraph=

    PLAN: Narr P

        The men were sitting around late in the afternoon.
        They were talking about making a long hunting trip.
        "Let's go tomorrow and plan to be back in three days.
        Let's go up river to the next tributary and hunt
        there," said one of the older men, and everyone agreed.

    EXECUTION: Narr P

        So they all set to making preparations.
        The men checked their arrows and their bows, and
        made minor repairs as needed.
        The women began to prepare food for the trip.
        And the next morning, they set off, happy and
        excited at the prospect of a good hunt.

8. Stimulus-response paragraph

The stimulus-response paragraph is similar to the execution paragraph and to the dialogue paragraph. It comprises a stimulus and a response to that stimulus by someone else. This paragraph is a bit like the quotation paragraph.

    Stimulus-response paragraph=

    STIMULUS   His mother warned him not to let his little
                          brother play in the street.

    RESPONSE   So he did his best to keep his brother
                          inside the house all afternoon.

- -

Reason paragraph=

REASON: Stimulus-response paragraph=

    STIMULUS   His friends told him to quit rocking
                          the boat.

    RESPONSE   But he just kept on playing and
                          rocking the boat.

TEXT   Finally, without warning, the boat
                      tipped over and spilled everyone
                      into the water.

- -

Stimulus-response paragraph=

STIMULUS   Silver approached the stranger and asked him for help in finding the address that was on the slip of paper in his hand.

RESPONSE   The stranger appeared to be friendly and tried to help, but he was not familiar with that part of the city, either.

Notice how this paragraph involves two participants, as the dialogue paragraph does, while the execution paragraph has only one participant.

Stimulus-response paragraph

± Setting	+ Stimulus	+ Response	± Terminus
	sentence paragraph	sentence paragraph	

9. Rhetorical question-answer paragraph

The rhetorical question-answer (R-QA) paragraph consists, as its name implies, of a rhetorical question and its answer. This paragraph occurs in expository and behavioral discourses where it emphasizes a point or introduces a new section, as, for example, in Paul's epistle to the Romans.

Rhetorical question-answer paragraph

± Prelim	+ Rhetorical question	+ Answer
sentence paragraph	sentence (interrogative) paragraph	sentence paragraph

Rhetorical question-answer paragraph=

RHET-QUESTION   What were the local ball players like last weekend?

ANSWER   They were a bunch of novices who could not handle the ball, could not throw, could not catch, and could not block their opponents' plays.

Rhetorical question-answer paragraph=

    RHET-QUESTION   Why do we need a tax cut every two or three years?

    ANSWER   Inflation is the culprit. As our incomes rise, they fall into higher tax brackets and we become subject to higher percentage taxes. So we need tax cuts just to keep the old percentages.

10. Hypothetical paragraph

The hypothetical paragraph consists of a supposition of a hypothetical situation and the consequence of that hypothetical setup. The paragraph can occur in narrative, expository, and behavioral discourses.

Hypothetical paragraph

± Setting	± Topic	± Supposition	± Result
	sentence	paragraph	sentence
	paragraph	sentence	paragraph

Hypothetical paragraph=

    TOPIC   I read that scientists think they will be able to unlock the secrets of the aging of cells and organisms within a decade, and they will learn how to prevent aging.

    SUPPOS   It set me to thinking what life would be like if scientists could keep us from growing old.

    RESULT   There are two possibilities. One is that only a few people could afford the treatment. They would continue to live while the rest of the people would die. After a hundred years of being twenty five, what sort of characters would they be? The other possibility is that everyone could obtain the treatment. Then the population boom would have to stop at once. We would have to have only enough children to replace the people we would kill. But what kind of people would we be after a century of being the same age?

E. Sentencelike paragraphs

There are a number of possible paragraphs that resemble sentence structures. They are not single sentences because they comprise two or more separate sentences by the general criteria for sentencehood. Such sentencelike paragraphs include the alternative paragraph, the contrast (antithetical) paragraph, the parallel paragraph, the simultaneous paragraph, the result paragraph, the reason paragraph, the quotation paragraph, and possibly some others.

1. Alternative paragraph

The alternative paragraph presents two or more alternatives, each encoded in a sentence or a paragraph.

Alternative paragraph

± Intro	+ Alternative-1	+ Alternative-2^n	± Conclusion
sentence paragraph	sentence paragraph	sentence paragraph	sentence paragraph

Alternative procedural paragraph=

    INTRO   When it comes to painting your house, there are two ways to do it.

    ALTERN-1   You can do it yourself, but it will take a lot of your time and work to scrape off the old paint and to apply the new.

    ALTERN-2   Or you can hire a painting contractor who will have the ladders and tools and can do the job quicker and better.

2. Contrast paragraph

The contrast paragraph, or antithetical paragraph, has a text and a contrast; two contrasting statements.

Contrast paragraph

± Prelim	+ Text	+ Contrast	± Conclusion
sentence paragraph	sentence paragraph	sentence paragraph	sentence paragraph

Contrast paragraph=

TEXT   When a Democratic president takes office, he tends to choose academic people for his cabinet officers.

CONTRAST   But when a Republican president takes office, he tends to choose business executives for his cabinet.

CONCLUSION   Perhaps this represents the chief difference between the two parties.

3. Parallel paragraph

The parallel paragraph comprises two or more parallel sentences or paragraphs.

Parallel paragraph

$\pm$ Prelim	+ Parallel-1	+ Parallel-2^n	$\pm$ Summary
sentence	sentence	sentence	sentence
paragraph	paragraph	paragraph	paragraph

The exponents of the parallel tagmemes must all be alike; in other words, all narrative sentences, narrative paragraphs, explanatory paragraphs, and so on.
The parallel paragraph may be a parallel narrative paragraph, a parallel procedural paragraph, or a parallel explanatory paragraph.

Parallel paragraph=

PARALLEL-1   The men worked on baling the hay.

PARALLEL-2   The women were busy preparing meals.

PARALLEL-3   As for the children, they did the regular chores.

SUMMARY   In short, everyone had something to do.

- -

Parallel expository paragraph=

PARALLEL-1   In a surprise move, J. L. Tupping tendered his resignation at last night's board meeting, citing personal reasons.

PARALLEL-2   It was only a month ago that H. F. Culle
              submitted his resignation at the monthly
              board meeting, saying that he needed a
              change.

PARALLEL-3   And at their meeting only two months ago, M. P.
              Sales had submitted his resignation,
              explaining that he wanted to retire and
              move to another state.

SUMMARY   Thus, over half of the board members have
              resigned in the last two months.

4. Simultaneous paragraph

The simultaneous paragraph describes simultaneous activities, either narrative or procedural.

Simultaneous paragraph

± Setting	+ Simultaneous event-1	+ Simultaneous event-2^n	± Terminal
sentence paragraph	sentence narrative paragraph procedural paragraph	sentence narrative paragraph procedural paragraph	sentence paragraph

Simultaneous narrative paragraph=

SIMUL-EVENT-1   Some people were trying to take care of the
                 victims.

SIMUL-EVENT-2   Meanwhile, other people had gone to get help.

Note that the exponent of Simultaneous event-2 and following simultaneous events must commence with a conjunction or sentence margin that indicates simultaneous time.

Simultaneous procedural paragraph=

SIMUL-STEP-1   Bring the mixture to a boil and let it boil
                ten minutes.

SIMUL-STEP-2   While it is boiling, place the remaining ingredients in a small pan with two tablespoons of oil and fry them just until their color brightens.

TERMINUS   The two mixtures should be ready to be combined at about the same time.

5. Reason paragraph

The reason paragraph comprises a statement and a reason for that statement. It is also closely related to the explanatory paragraph.

Reason paragraph

$\pm$ Prelim	+ Text	+ Reason^n	$\pm$ Conclusion
sentence	sentence	sentence	sentence
paragraph	paragraph	paragraph	paragraph

Reason paragraph=

TEXT   Roberta Smithson, who lives in the western part of the city, isn't happy with the zoning in her part of the city.

REASON-1 A concrete company lies to the south of her home.

REASON-2 To the north is a trucking company and an oil distribution yard.

REASON-3 And now, a steel construction company wants to locate across the street from her.

6. Result paragraph

The result paragraph comprises a statement and a result of that statement.

Result paragraph

± Prelim	+ Text	+ Result	± Conclusion
sentence	sentence	sentence	sentence
paragraph	paragraph	paragraph	paragraph

Result paragraph=

TEXT   The company delivered five hundred thousand dollars to the consortium of banks, but that was far short of the three million dollars that was due.

RESULT   The banks reacted quickly by declaring the company to be in default on its bonds and by instituting legal procedures against the company.

CONCL   The financial world is keeping its collective fingers crossed as it studies the situation.

Result paragraph=

TEXT   The book's designers wanted to include all the photographs, charts and long captions, and they did this by reducing the size of the printing and illustrations.

RESULT   The result is that the book is cluttered, frequently illegible and frustrating to use.

Parallel paragraph=

PARALLEL-1: Result paragraph=

    TEXT   Like computer word processors that allow an author to alter his paragraphs, we now have computer picture processors that can clear up fuzzy pictures, accentuate colors, and delete or add details to a picture.

    RESULT   The result is that what passes as a photograph in a magazine or newspaper may be a seriously doctored derivative of a colored photograph.

PARALLEL-2:   Result paragraph=

TEXT   Darkroom operators have always been able to cut and paste together parts of different black and white photographs, and some publications have been famous for such tactics.

RESULT Now with color photography and computer color processors, the reader is again thrown back upon the integrity of those in the media business.

7. Quotation paragraph

The quotation paragraph is like a quotation sentence except that the quote formula is a separate sentence that sets the stage for the quotation. This paragraph is very useful when the quotation formulas are separate sentences by all the criteria of sentencehood.

Quotation paragraph

± Setting	+ Quote formula^n	+ Quotation	± Terminus
sentence paragraph	sentence paragraph	sentence paragraph	sentence paragraph

The quote formula may follow the quotation, and may interrupt the quotation, as well as precede the quotation. There may be more than one quote formula, distributed before, during, and after the quotation.

Quotation paragraph=

QUOTE FORMULA   The reporter began with a stock question.

QUOTATION   "How do you feel now, Mr. Burney?"

— —

Quotation paragraph=

QUOTE FORMULA   Miguel spoke to his companions.

QUOTATION   "Let's go to the city and get jobs and make some extra money, and then maybe we can buy some land."

QUOTE FORMULA   He did say.

277

F. Cyclical paragraphs

Nathan Waltz (Longacre and Woods, 1976, vol. 1) found cyclical paragraphs in Guanano. A cyclical paragraph has a repetition of the first part placed at the end, to give an ABA pattern. By recognizing embedding, the ABA sequence results in ABA, ABCA, ABCBA, ABCCBA, ABBA, and ABAB. Almost any type of paragraph may have the cyclical modification.

Here are some of Waltz's examples:

Cyclical reason paragraph

TEXT		He arrived at another place again.
REASON:	Reason P =	
	TEXT	He, the turtle, was beginning to question the tapir's droppings.
	REASON	He was following him to kill him.
TEXT'		He arrived another year again.

- - - - - - - - - - - - - - -

Cyclical contrast paragraph

TEXT	The food in this village is good.
CONTRAST	It isn't like the food in my land.
TEXT'	Now I eat good food here.

- - - - - - - - - - - - - - -

Cyclical circumstance paragraph

TEXT		Wow! He (the deer) ran past two hills he had cleared and fell down.
CIRCUM:	Circum P =	
	TEXT	He ran too much.
	RESULT	Thus being, his heart quit.
TEXT'		The poor old deer died.

Waltz says the cyclic paragraph is used to resume a narrative after an interruption, to signal the climax of a narrative, and to be an aesthetic, poetic device in legends.

Perhaps the Hebrew poetry of the Old Testament would yield to analysis as cyclical paragraphs.

This completes the list of paragraphs in this chapter. The list is not exhaustive; your language may have paragraph types not discussed here. But the discussion up to this point should give you, the analyst, a feeling for what a paragraph is in relation to discourse level and sentence level.

Many of the paragraphs discussed here may have counterparts with the order of tagmemes reversed or changed in some other language. Such paragraphs may be given the names used here, or be given new names.

G. Paragraph cohesion

Most studies of discourse cohesion have concentrated on narrative discourse. There has been almost nothing on expository discourse. One study of explanatory paragraph cohesion by Professor Peter Fries has proved interesting and fruitful.

Professor Fries, following a suggestion by Halliday and Hasan, divides sentences into themes and rhemes. Then he shows that well-constructed paragraphs repeat their topics in the themes of the sentences and develop their ideas in the rhemes.

The theme is everything in a sentence up to the first main verb, disregarding the verbs in formulaic structures such as quotation formulas, cleft introducers and such. The rheme is the rest of the sentence. The themes and rhemes of the following sentences will help.

THEME	RHEME
Although the determiner is optional, it almost always when the phrase is embedded.	occurs

THEME	RHEME
In English, the theme	is the first part of a sentence.

THEME	RHEME
It is questionable whether this theory languages.	would apply to other

THEME	RHEME
We have already pointed out that the theme rheme in a sentence in English.	precedes the

In the last example above, the theme-rheme division might be posited before 'pointed.' Because of this ambiguity, if the cohesive material is put after the 'pointing,' it is weaker in its cohesion function.

The principle of paragraph cohesion (in English) requires that the theme of each sentence of a paragraph must mention the topic(s) of the paragraph. The rhemes should develop the thoughts of the paragraph. As an example, let us use an explanatory paragraph given earlier in this chapter.

THEME	RHEME
Another reason some managers fail to go up the ladder	is their failure to learn to delegate authority.
As effective young managers, they	learned to get things done by their own efforts.
They	had their fingers on all the departments under them and were personally responsible for success or failure.
But as a manager gets promoted he	reaches a level where he must change and learn to delegate responsibility.
He	must promote a team effort among the managers under him.
If he meddles at some lower level he	is not just meddling in a department, he is meddling in another manager's work, and it causes real problems.
If a manager is to continue up the ladder of promotion, he	has to make a radical shift, and some fail to make the change.

Technical English, in my experience, benefits from overt paragraph cohesion in the themes of sentences. If something is hard to read, lack of cohesion will often be part of the problem. As linguists, when we write our technical linguistic papers, it is very easy to write as the ideas come to us and forget about keeping the cohesion straight. My hope is that these ideas on cohesion will help us all write better papers.

How does your language achieve cohesion? Does it use recapitulation effectively? James Butler (personal communication) said that in his Tzutujil translation of nonnarrative material, he has to decide on what the topic of each paragraph is and then mention that topic in every sentence, whether the topic was Jesus' life or death, our thoughts or actions or responsibilities, and so on. Even though good expository or explanatory material is difficult to obtain in many minority languages, any study of cohesion in nonnarrative discourse should be rewarding.

Bibliography

Fries, Peter. 1980. Theme and rheme and paragraph cohesion. Forum lecture at the Summer Institute of Linguistics at the University of Oklahoma, August 5, 1980. Also given at the 1980 meeting of LACUS at Rice University, Houston, Texas, August 12-14, 1980.

Grimes, Joseph E. 1978. Papers on discourse. Dallas: S.I.L.

Halliday, Michael A. K. and Ruqaiya Hasan. 1976. Cohesion in English. London: Longman Group Limited.

Healey, Alan. 1972. Are there grammatical paragraphs in English? MS.

Jones, Linda Kay. 1977. Theme in English expository discourse. Lake Bluff, Illinois: Jupiter Press.

Larson, Mildred Lucille. 1978. The functions of reported speech in discourse. Dallas: S.I.L. and U.T.A.

Longacre, Robert E. 1968. Philippine languages: Discourse, paragraph, and sentence structure. Santa Ana: S.I.L.

_____. 1976. An anatomy of speech notions. Lisse: The Peter De Ridder Press.

_____. 1978. An apparatus for identification of paragraph types. Notes on linguistics 15. Dallas: S.I.L.

_____ and Frances Woods. 1976. Discourse Grammar. 3 vol. Dallas: S.I.L. and U.T.A.

Waltz, Nathan E. 1976. Discourse functions of Guanano sentence and discourse. In Longacre and Woods, 1976.

Chapter 14

Discourse level

Discourse level is the highest level in the grammatical hierarchy. Its units encompass any monologue from a few seconds to many minutes long. We are interested mainly in the longer monologues, such things as stories, arguments, speeches, sermons, and so on.

The structures of well-formed discourses reveal something about how people think or how they expect to be entertained, informed, or persuaded.

Not every speaker of a language produces well-formed discourses. Among our own people, some can speak and make better sense than others. Hence, you should expect differences among speakers of another language. The problem is to know which is most commonly used.

People who have conducted literacy programs and have seen the rise of native-authored written materials have noted that differences between oral literature and written literature arise in only a few years. So the caution here is that the analyst should analyze oral and written discourses separately and then compare them. (Written literature has to omit gestures of face and hands, intonation, and timing, so it has to have more links, pronouns and noun phrases.) (See Duff, 1973, N.O.T.)

A. Narrative discourse

Narrative discourse is the easiest discourse to acquire. A narrative discourse is a story told to entertain the listeners (and sometimes to teach social mores).

There are at least three varieties of narrative discourse. The easiest one to find is legendary narratives, folktales, tales told so often that everyone knows them. These stories are important to anthropology, but they often contain a minimum of performative material, such as names, places, times, and any other identificatory items. Folktales are so familiar to everyone that the teller can leave so much out that the outsider studying the language cannot follow or understand the story. And some analysts have found that legendary narrative is a distinct discourse type.

The second kind of narrative discourse, and the most valuable kind, is the narration of personal experiences, the narration of past events in the speaker's life or family. Here we get accounts of the time I (or someone) got lost or got hurt badly, or took a trip, or got arrested, or got denounced before the law; what happened when we moved, or got married, or went to school. These stories have been told a few times, but they are not common knowledge, so they will include more details, more cohesion.

The third kind of a narrative is a tour narrative; the story of a trip, for example, where there is not one overall plot but a series of scenes, each with descriptive material and a few events. After one scene, the action goes on to another place and another scene. The resulting narrative is like a string of beads, and isn't too interesting to the analyst.

Contentwise, narrative discourses do not consist of only narration. Most cultures like to have the narration broken up by quoted conversations. English is like this: a straight narrative is heavy and dull. We like some conversation to break the monotony and liven it up. Some analysts have found narrative discourses in which there is a narrative block, then a conversation block, another narrative block, another conversation block, and so on. Some have found that quoted conversation is important to getting a story started, to highlighting certain events, to marking the climax of the story, or to ending a story properly.

Narrative discourse

± Title	± Aperture	± Stage	± Narrative episode^n
clause	sentence	paragraph	paragraph
sentence	paragraph	discourse	discourse
phrase	clause	sentence	sentence

± Narrative peak	± Inter-peak^n	± Narrative post peak	± Closure	± Finis
paragraph	paragraph	paragraph	sentence	clause
discourse	discourse	discourse	paragraph	sentence
sentence	sentence	sentence		phrase

The title is expounded by a short clause, phrase, or sentence fragment, such as 'the time I got lost', 'the time we planted corn', 'the lousy tiger', and so on.

The aperture is expounded by a clause or sentence, such as 'my brother or sister here has asked me to tell about the animals in the woods', or 'I'm going to tell about when I was young and I went to school', or something similar.

The exponent of the aperture is fuller and less cryptic than the exponent of the title. It is a sentence or a paragraph that helps get the story started.

The stage is expounded by a sentence or paragraph containing descriptive clauses, clauses with past-completive action, identification clauses, or noun phrases. Examples might be: 'There was a man. He had two sons. He worked on his farm and his sons helped him,' or 'Once upon a time there was an animal that came up and ate our sugar cane,' or 'Far away, in another land, there are people who...,' or 'Long ago when I was young and went to school,' and so on. The main point is that, in general, the exponent of the stage sets the scene by pinning down time and place, and introduces the participants. Usually, this involves no events, but in a few cases, people have found the narrative of some background events in the stage.

The episodes are expounded by paragraphs and embedded discourses. Episodes are the major chunks of the discourse, and the breaks between episodes are signaled by major changes in time, place, cast of characters, or event chains.

The interpeaks are additional episodes that fall between the two peaks. They may be very short or very long, depending upon the plot.

In a well-constructed story, the episodes are chosen and constructed to build up the interest, tension, and/or suspense, until the peak episode is reached. The peak episode's exponents are often marked by a change in sentence length, a change in pace, a change in the amount of quoted material, a change in the number of characters, and other such phenomena.

Some narratives in some languages end with the peak plus a closure and finis, but in some cases, a postpeak is necessary.

In Mayan languages, the postpeak is expounded by a recapitulation of the whole story so far, sort of a retelling of the story. In a Philippine text, the postpeak was expounded by an embedded discourse in which everything was set straight and back to normal. In a fable, the postpeak is expounded by the moral of the story.

Closure is expounded by a sentence or paragraph that sort of winds everything up and ends the story.

And finis is expounded by 'that's all', 'that's all my talk', 'finished'.

B. Expository discourse

Expository or explanatory discourse is aimed at instructing the listeners--explaining something new, presenting one's ideas and viewpoints, no matter how emotion-laden it may be. It is found in sermons, political speeches, reports to the village or to the linguist about new ideas, debates, argument, and so on. In some village situations that are face-to-face societies, expository discourse may not be well developed be well developed and may be hard to elicit.

Expository discourse comprises several related points, each one developed in its own way. The points follow some pattern and add up to make the total impact of the discourse.

Expository discourse

± Lead-in	± Intro-duction	+ Expository point^n	+ Conclusion	± Finis
sentence	sentence	paragraph	sentence	phrase
paragraph	paragraph	sentence	paragraph	clause
		discourse	discourse	sentence

The lead-in, if present, gives background material that leads up to the real introduction. It may consist of some short narrative or expository paragraph or discourse.

The exponent of the introduction introduces the topic, theme, and/or setting of what is to follow. It is usually an explanatory paragraph or a sentence. In English, we expect the thematic sentence for the discourse to occur in the introduction.

Each expository point is expounded by an explanatory paragraph, an embedded expository discourse, or, sometimes, by other syntagmemes. Each point is a step in the explanation or argument, so it must contribute in some way to the overall aim.

The sequence of expository points usually shows some logical progression from old to new, from known to unknown, from evidence to conclusion, and so on. A study of the sequence of points in native texts might yield valuable cultural insight, how people think about things.

The conclusion may be expounded by a summary of the discourse, by a restatement of the main theme, or by some important subsequential material. It serves to bring the discourse to a proper end.

The finis is expounded by 'finished,' or 'that's all,' or the like.

All the chapters in this book are expository discourses, with each new syntagmeme section constituting an expository point. Here the aim is simply to present an inventory of helpful ideas, and the organization is according to complexity and ease of presentation.

C. Procedural discourse

Procedural discourse is aimed at telling a person how to do something. Like the procedural paragraphs it comprises, it is second-person oriented, although the person may be encoded in first-person inclusive plural or third-person indefinite subjects. The basic premise is that if you want to achieve something, this is what you do.

Procedural discourse

± Title	± Aperture	+ Procedure^n	± Closure	± Finis
clause sentence	sentence paragraph	procedural paragraph procedural discourse	sentence	clause sentence

Since the procedural discourse is similar to a narrative discourse, the title, aperture, closure, and finis exponents are somwhat similar to the same tagmemes in narrative discourse.

The exponents of the procedures are procedural paragraphs, embedded procedural discourses, or, occasionally, a 'procedural' sentence. Procedural discourse boundaries are marked by shifts in time, place, cast of participants, or activity.

In English, most of our procedural discourses are very stylized in the form of recipes, kit assembly instructions, chess instructions, home-repair instructions, knitting instructions, sewing instructions, income-tax-return instructions, and the like. They are often accompanied by drawings, schematics, and sample patterns to help the doer to visualize correctly what he or she is aiming for.

In eliciting procedural discourse, avoid doing it abstractly, away from actually doing the procedure. You may get a procedural discourse mixed with an expository discourse. You may get the third-person indefinite verb forms instead of direct imperatives.

D. Hortatory discourse

Hortatory discourse, or behavioral discourse, is a discourse aimed at changing the behavior of the listener, or getting him/her to do something. So it includes commands, requests, suggestions, hints, cajoling, threats, warnings, illustrations, evaluations, and promises. It normally occurs at weddings where parents instruct the newlyweds, in instructions to youngsters going to school for the first time, going to work for someone else for the first time, beginning to court the opposite sex, and in sermons in church and in village assemblies. A hortatory discourse must not be confused with an emotional expository discourse. A hortatory discourse is trying to persuade people to change their behavior, or to do something; an expository discourse is simply conveying information, be it emotion-laden or not.

The social status of the speaker/writer and the social situation influence how direct he/she can be. An old chief or a parent can use direct imperatives. Lesser individuals use suggestions and requests. A preacher can use some assortment, depending upon his personality and the culture.

Hortatory discourse

± Intro- duction	+ Hortatory point^n	± Conclusion	± Finis
sentence paragraph	hortatory paragraph hortatory discourse expository paragraph expository discourse narrative paragraph narrative discourse	sentence paragraph	clause sentence

The array says nothing about how the hortatory points are organized. But one strategy is to present the problem and a general exhortation in the first hortatory point; then to present an orderly succession of contributory arguments and exhortations in intermediate hortatory points; and to finish with a hortatory point that sums up the arguments and gives specific exhortations.

Another strategy is to use very mitigated exhortations in the early points and to build up to more explicit exhortations in the later points.

The succession of points may follow a chronological sequence or a logical sequence or a sequence of increasing complication, relevance, or generality.

Sometimes the peak hortatory point will be penultimate and the final point will be a rather friendly, mitigated, wind-down sort of a point.

Study the preferred order of points for various kinds of hortatory discourses in your target language.

Since a series of exhortations is boring, a speaker will use mitigated exhortations, narrative illustrations and explanatory material to lighten the exhortation load. In fact, a sermon may be all explanatory, with just a hortatory paragraph at the end.

E. Dramatic discourse

Dramatic discourse is narrative discourse told only in quoted material without quotation formulas.

The exponents of the marginal tagmemes are the same as those of the corresponding tagmemes in narrative discourse, except that here, dramatic or compound dramatic paragraphs may expound the stage and closure.

Since there are no quote formulas, the identification of speakers has to be made plain by the use of vocatives and kinship terms in the quoted material. Descriptive and narrative material can occur in the settings of the paragraph, but usually a thoroughgoing dramatic discourse omits all nonquoted material.

Larson (1978) posited dialogue discourse for Aguaruna, which is similar to dramatic discourse but has minimal quotation formulas and more background (not quoted) material.

Dramatic discourse

$\pm$ Title	$\pm$ Aperture	$\pm$ Stage	$\pm$ Dramatic episode^n
			dramatic paragraph
			compound dramatic paragraph
			dramatic discourse

	+ Dramatic peak	± Dramatic post peak	± Closure	± Finis
	dramatic paragraph	dramatic paragraph		
	compound dramatic paragraph	compound dramatic paragraph		
	dramatic discourse	dramatic discourse		
	without quotation formulas	without quotation formulas		

F. Activity discourse

Lawrence Reid posited an 'activity discourse' genre to account for 'what we do' discourses that report on customary activities. An activity discourse is similar in some ways to procedural and to narrative discourse. It has chronological linkage and event/activity forms for main verbs. But unlike narrative, it does not refer to any specific point in time or to any specific actors. And, unlike procedural, it does not imply that it is telling someone how to do the activity.

If you elicit an account of a customary marriage ceremony, or of a customary planting or harvest ceremony, or of how to make certain food, tools, or clothing, you are likely to receive an activity discourse. If you elicit a text on how to make bread away from the kitchen counter and not actually about how to make bread, you may get an activity text—how we usually make bread.

Activity discourse

± Title	± Disourse topic	± Activity^n	± Closure	± Finis
noun phrase	verb phrase	narrative paragraph explanatory paragraph activity discourse	clause sentence paragraph	minimal clause 'that's all'
		Person may be first, second, or third. Tense or aspect is habitual, noncompletive, and so on.		

G. Epistolary discourse

There is one further discourse type that has to be learned. It is epistolary discourse, the discourse of letters and of radio telephone communication.

Each epistolary point is expounded by narrative material (news of self and family), by expository material (explanations, clarifications of points in previous letters or conversations), by behavioral material (advice to family members), or by petitions (requests, which are a kind of behavioral discourse). Most letters or conversations contain a number of different kinds of epistolary point exponents.

Verbally, this kind of discourse must be used on radio telephones. It is interesting to hear children at boarding school learning to talk by radio to their parents. It is clearly a learned behavior; it doesn't come naturally.

In written form it is the discourse of letters. Here, again, people must learn to write the addressee's name and to sign one's own name, and wait weeks or months for a reply.

Epistolary discourse

± Salutation	+ Epistolary^n point	± Closure	± Signature
	sentence paragraph discourse		
	narrative, advice, or request		

H. Surface-structure matrices of discourse types

1. Longacre placed the first five discourse types in a matrix as shown on the next page. The various features are numbered uniformly for discussion purposes.

a. The personal pronouns most often used are first and third for narrative discourse; all first and second for dramatic; second person imperative or first person inclusive habitual or third person indefinite are characteristic of procedural discourse; third person is characteristic of expository discourse; and second person imperative, first person inclusive hortative, or third person characterize hortatory discourse.

b. Narrative discourse is mostly concerned with subjects encoding agent and experiencer. Dramatic discourse has almost all kinds of clauses and emphases. Procedural discourse focuses on the clause-level objects (encoding patients); it emphasizes the process and product more than the person(s) performing the procedure. Expository discourse uses more equative clauses, descriptive clauses, logical sentences, and paragraphs. Hortatory discourse has many of the features of expository discourse, but has added imperative and hortatory clauses.

c. Narrative discourse uses past tense or a historical present tense to talk about past events. Dramatic discourse contains all kinds of tense and moods. Procedural discourse uses second person imperatives, timeless present tense, or a general future tense. Expository discourse uses various tenses, and hortatory uses various imperative, hortative, and jussive moods.

d. Linkage in narrative discourse is by recapitulations and by repeated lexical forms. Dramatic discourse is linked by the back and forth verbal exchanges. Procedural discourse is linked by time margins and condition margins (or their equivalents). Expository discourse contains logical linkage that uses sentence topics, parallelisms, and conjunctions. Hortatory discourse has much the same linkage as an expository discourse plus, perhaps, more logic margins.

Longacre's surface-structure matrix of discourse types

	nonprescriptive	prescriptive
chrono- logical framework	NARRATIVE 1. 1/3 person pronouns 2. A/E as subject 3. past tense (present) 4. linkage by recapitulation and repetition - - - - - - - - - - - DRAMATIC 1. multiple 1/2 person interplay 2. many kinds of clauses 3. all tenses 4. linkage by repartee	PROCEDURAL 1. 2 person (12, 3) 2. P as object 3. present/future/imperative 4. linkage by recapitulation in time and condition margins
nonchrono- logical framework	EXPOSITORY 1. 3 person pronouns 2. equative/descriptive clauses 3. various tenses 4. linkage by sentence topic and parallelism	HORTATORY 1. 2 person (12, 3) 2. imperative clause 3. imperative/jussive/hortatory moods 4. linkage by sentence topic, and parallelism and by conditional, cause, and purpose margins

2. Keith Forster suggested that the four main discourse types should be placed in a 2 x 2 matrix based on agent versus nonagent and chronological versus nonchronological, or logical, form.

Forster's surface-structure matrix of discourse types

	Agent oriented	Nonagent oriented
Main-line verbs are event verbs and have chronological linkage	Narrative discourse	Procedural discourse
Main-line verbs are nonevent verbs and have logical linkage	Behavioral discourse	Expository discourse

Forster multiplied these four discourse types by another 'projected' versus 'nonprojected' vector.

Forster's matrix of projected and nonprojected discourses

	Projected	Nonprojected
Narrative	Prophesy or plans	Narrative (usual past tense)
Procedural	Procedural (usual instruction type)	Activity (report on customs)
Behavioral	Hortatory	Eulogy, or praise, or rebuke
Expository	Orientation Budget	Expository (usual type)

Note how Reid's 'activity' discourse is incorporated here as a nonprojected procedural discourse.

Forster also added another matrix for further subdivisions of behavioral discourse.

Forster's matrix of behavioral discourses

	Projected	Nonprojected
First person	Political campaign speech	Boasting
Second person	Hortatory	Rebuke or Praise
Third person	Nominating speech	Employee reference

Forster posits another vector, called 'tension.' Discourses can be +tension or -tension. A narrative discourse with tension has an involved development with an exciting peak and denoument. A narrative discourse without tension is quieter, deriving its beauty and interest from character development, descriptions of scenes, and such. Most procedural discourses are minus tension, but can be plus tension where there is conflict and risk in the procedure. The same can be said of behavioral and expository discourses.

I. Deep-structure matrix of discourse types

When we look at the social setting and intent of the various discourse types, we come up with a similar two by two matrix. (See below.)

1. Narrative discourse is about the speaker's history or someone else's; it is concerned with agents and events which occurred in a temporal succession some time past. A narrative is told chiefly to entertain, but often, also, to teach.

2. A procedural discourse is about processes and products. Agents are out of focus. The procedure is about events that are to occur in a temporal sequence, but the exact time is left flexible. It is for whoever wants to do the procedure to achieve the desired end result.

3. The expository discourse is concerned with its subject matter and the logical connections concerning it. The person involved is not in focus. Time is not focal. Its purpose is to explain, instruct, and inform.

4. Hortatory discourse is aimed at persuading a person or persons to change their behavior. So it is concerned with the addressee as second person and uses logic and illustration to achieve its aim.

Longacre's matrix of deep-structure discourse types

	nonprescriptive	prescriptive
chrono-logical	NARRATIVE (deep) 1 or 3 person agent oriented past time time linkage to entertain	PROCEDURAL (deep) nonspecific person patient oriented projected time time linkage to tell how to...
logical succession	EXPOSITORY (deep) no necessary person subject matter oriented time not focal logical linkage to instruct, inform concerning...	HORTATORY (deep) second person addressee oriented mode in focus time not in focus logical linkage change your behavior

Echerds's matrix of discourse encoding

	Deep Narrative	Deep Procedural	Deep Expository	Deep Hortatory
Dramatic Surface	more vivid	more vivid	more vivid	more vivid morality play
Narrative Surface	matching	more vivid 'A day in the life of'	more vivid	more vivid fable, parable
Procedural Surface	rare — a story told as a	matching	more vivid	more vivid
Expository Surface		procedure/ expository structure	matching	more vivid parable
Hortatory Surface				matching

295

J. Encoding matrix

Discourse surface structures are usually not in a one-to-one relation to deep structures. The result is a mixing of discourse signals, such as narration with expository admixture. We can show this mismatching of encodings in a matrix (see above).

The surface discourse types and deep discourse types can be ranked according to their vividness. Dramatic discourse is the most vivid, with narrative close behind. Procedural and expository discourse are in the middle, and hortatory is the least vivid. Stephen Echerd devised the preceding matrix of encodings to show the mismatching of deep and surface structures. (This is only one of the several matrices that Echerd visualizes.)

On the above matrix, the diagonal boxes are labeled 'matching', for in these boxes, deep structure and surface structures are matched.

Boxes above the diagonal are encodings that are more vivid than the matching boxes. Thus, to tell a story in dramatic discourse is to enliven the story. To give a procedure in the form of a narrative is to make it more vivid. To teach or exhort using a story or a drama makes the teaching and exhortation more interesting, hence the use of fables and morality plays.

However, there is a difference between a dramatic discourse with a narrative intent and a dramatic discourse with a teaching or exhorting intent. In the mismatching encodings we get blended discourse types. There are signals of the mismatching in the choice of words and particles, in the choice of thematic material, in the choice of sequencing of paragraphs, and so on. The blending of discourse types and the frequent cross-type embeddings make the search for pure paragraphs difficult in English.

K. Determining constituent boundaries

Finally, let us review the signals that help us divide discourses up into their constituents. Sometimes we call this 'chunking' a discourse.

    1. Narrative discourse divisions are shown by:
        Change in time, place, cast, activity
        Verbs of going, coming
        Introduction of new participants, reintroduction of old
            ones

    2. Procedural discourse divisions are signaled by:
        Change of time, activity
        Places where alternative procedures branch
        Places where an embedded procedure begins and ends
        Change in topic

3. Expository discourse divisions are signaled by:
      Places where new topic is begun
      After a summary statement, or before
      There is a hierarchy, or a relationship among the texts

4. Hortatory discourse divisions are signaled by:
      Each new point
      Each new text
      Each new illustration

5. Dramatic discourse divisions are signaled by:
      Change in time, place, participants, activity, topic,
         as signaled by cues in quotations

6. Epistolary discourse divisions are shown by:
      Each change of topic

L. Overlay structures

We are accustomed to a linearly ordered outline structure in discourse, with only a short summary at the end. There is another pattern, called overlay structure, that is preferred by many societies. In an overlay structured discourse, the speaker goes through his story or argument several times sketchily, but filling in new details each time through. For example, here is a text from New Guinea Pidgin, cited by Grimes:

Plane I
  1 Once upon a time our ancestors were living.
  2 Mr. Schutz arrived for the first time,
  3 and they became curious,
  4 and they thought him to be an ancestral spirit.

Plane II
  5 Yes, formerly when my ancestors, the men of Nobonob, saw the new white man, they came up to their village.
  6 And around this time came Mr. Schutz for the first time.
  7 He came on a mission to them.
  8 And some of the old men saw Mr. Schutz,
  9 and they were not clear
  10 whether they saw him as a man (whether they were looking at something like a man).
  11 They said,
  12 "Hey, we saw this man of a different kind,
  13 and we think
  14 he is a ghost belonging to our people."
  15 These ancestors of ours had this idea.

Plane III
  16 And they saw Mr. Schutz, and they said, "As for him (marked theme), our former parents died and went to be in the place of their ghosts.
  17 As for him, this one man has come.

18 So we have seen this man.
19 He is a ghost from our people."
20 They had this idea, and they did not believe Schutz's words.
21 They did not think he was Schutz.
22 Him a man?
23 No. They thought he was a ghost man and nothing else.
27 So, later on, there they were...

Notice how Plane II repeats Plane I but expands on it. Then Plane III repeats the last part of Plane II.

Here is another text that is a narrative text with an expository or hortatory intent, taken from Bororo (data by Thomas Crowell, cited by Grimes).

1. I arrived. At that time then some Brazilians said, "A jaguar mauled your cow." The Bororos said this too. At that time then, early in the morning, I saw her.

2. They said for me to go see her. I went to her. I looked at her lying by the side of the rice machine.

3. Those who went with me to see her ran to get me. They said, "Come look. That cow of yours arrived, but she's really in bad shape." I went quickly. I looked at her. She was fallen. She was fallen at the side of the machine. I saw the claw marks on her wrist, ankle, arm, chest, and neck. He really messed her up. He really messed her up. Her mother stood nearby. Her mother really produced big calves. As for her mother, the paw of the jaguar got her here on the shoulder. Here he got her. Therefore he hurt that mother when he left off attacking her child. Early the next day then the calf died.

4. It took a while for me to get to see the work of the jaguar. On the day I arrived, then the calf arrived in the village. Therefore I said that she would not die. But this was wrong. Therefore then she really died. It was bad for me. It was bad for me.

Note how each plane adds new information.

This way of story telling or of arguing has its own beauty, and a skillful speaker will manipulate the planes to achieve what people consider to be beautiful discourse. We should not downplay it. For one thing, it slows down the rate of information flow and raises the redundancy, making it easier to follow and react. And in expository discourse, its redundancy is used to make its impact greater.

Overlaid narrative discourse

± Stage	+ Narrative plane^n	± Closure	± Finis
paragraph sentence	narrative discourse narrative paragraph	paragraph sentence	phrase clause sentence

Overlaid expository discourse

± Introduction	+ Expository plane^n	± Conclusion	± Finis
sentence paragraph	expository discourse expository paragraph	sentence paragraph	phrase clause sentence

Sometimes, each plane may have a different theme as well as recurring themes.

In summary, the overlay strategy is another effective way to tell a story, give a message, or make a point. Each overlay plane has its own theme, and the themes are cumulative. The end result has more impact than a straight outline strategy would give.

Bibliography

Duff, Martha. 1973. Contrastive features of written and oral texts. Notes on translation 50.1-13. Dallas: S.I.L.

Forster, Keith. 1977. The narrative discourse in Border Cuna. In Longacre and Woods, Part 2, pp. 1-23.

Grimes, Joseph E. 1972. Outlines and overlays. Language 48.513-24.

_____, ed. 1978. Papers on discourse. Dallas: S.I.L.

Jones, Linda K., ed. 1979. Discourse studies in Mesoamerican languages. 2 volumes. Dallas: S.I.L. and U.T.A.

Larson, Mildred Lucille. 1978. The functions of reported speech in discourse. Dallas: S.I.L. and U.T.A.

Leenhouts, Inge. 1978. Overlays in Loron discourse. Papers in linguistics, ed. by Joseph E. Grimes. Dallas: S.I.L. and U.T.A.

Longacre, Robert E. 1968. Philippine languages. Santa Ana, California: S.I.L.

_____. 1976. An anatomy of speech notions. Lisse: The Peter de Ridder Press.

_____, and Stephen Levinsohn. 1978. Field analysis of discourse. Current trends in textlinguistics, ed. by Wolfgang U. Dressler. Berlin: Walter de Gruyter, pp. 103-22.

_____, and Frances Woods, eds. 1976. Discourse grammar, studies in indigenous languages of Colombia, Panama, and Ecuador. Dallas: S.I.L. and U.T.A. (3 volumes).

Reid, Lawrence A. 1968. Notes on Central Bontoc discourse and paragraph structures. MS.

_____. 1970. Central Bontoc: sentence, paragaph and discourse. S.I.L. publications in linguistics and related fields, no. 27. Norman: S.I.L. and The University of Oklahoma.

Chapter 15

Discourse features

In addition to the 'chunking' of discourses, we need to look at the 'threads' of discourse. We borrow the term 'threads' from Joseph Grimes's book and use it to apply to the features that run through a discourse.

A. Kinds of information in narrative discourse

In his book, The Thread of Discourse, Joseph E. Grimes (1975) describes three kinds of information in the backbone of a narrative discourse and five kinds of information in the nonbackbone. These are: events, participants, and participant identification in the backbone; and setting, background, evaluation, collateral information, and performative information in the nonbackbone, or background.

1. Events

Events are the activities that are chosen by the narrator to include in his narrative to make up the story line or backbone of the narrative. If all nonbackbone material were eliminated, the backbone series of events would still give the basic story.

The events usually occur in linear but unequally spaced time order. Flashbacks are possible, but most flashback material is a part of the background information and is usually given with special nonnarrative tenses or aspects. There may be gaps of time between events, and events may take different amounts of time.

In narrative discourse the event line is part of the backbone. In procedural discourse the products or activities are part of the backbone. In expository and hortatory discourses the ideas or facts are a part of the backbone.

There are two ways to define the backbone of a discourse. The first way is to define it in terms of surface grammatical features, in terms of main clauses (with some exceptions permitted). This view says that the speaker/writer had a choice in deciding what elements to push forward and what elements to downgrade in dependent clauses.

The second way is to define the backbone to include any clause, or part of a clause, that advances the story, description, or argument, no matter where the clause occurs, in independent, in dependent, or in embedded clauses.

A comparison of the results that the two definitions give you for a discourse should give you some insight into how the language functions, especially if the two definitions give very different answers.

2. Participants

The participants are the persons, animals, or spirits who are involved in the events. There are primary participants whom the story is about, or who participate in all or most of the story. Then there are secondary participants who come on the scene in certain places and then go out of the story. Tertiary participants are present in some parts of the story, but participate in only a few events. They are often related as kinship or as business associates of a primary or secondary participant.

Participants may shift in importance in different episodes. Secondary participants (or even tertiary participants) may become primary participants in another episode. And primary participants may become secondary or tertiary participants.

Props are the inanimate objects that figure in the plot of the discourse but do not do anything. Persons can also be props if they are just in the scene but are inactive. In contrast, participants act and interact in the plot.

3. Identification of participants

The identification of participants is an important part of discourse. In English we have certain preferred ways such as: 'There was a king who... The king did... He...' or 'A friend of mine once...' or 'George Washington once did....' We use an indefinite article plus a noun, then the definite article plus the noun, and then the pronoun. Or we can start off by naming a kinfolk or by naming a well-known person. Other languages have similar but different ways to introduce participants.

Once the participants are introduced, we need to know how to keep track of them if there are two or more. We need to know how to move them off stage and how to bring them back on stage.

Participants may act as individuals or as a group, and it is common for regrouping participants into new and different groups and segregating participants out into individuals again to occur in a narrative. How are these processes signaled?

These are all questions that enter into identifying the participants. And the rules may be different for primary versus secondary versus tertiary participants. And in some narratives, a participant may shift from being secondary to being primary, or vice versa.

These first three kinds of information belong to the backbone. The following kinds of information belong to the nonbackbone. They fill the narrative out and make it more interesting or informative.

4. Setting

Setting includes the time and location for the events. Setting is often conveyed by verbless clauses, or by time and location margins. It tells where and when the events took place.

At the beginning of the discourse, there is often a special paragraph that gives the setting. But the setting may change in the course of the narrative, and new setting information is needed. How is it given?

5. Background

Background is similar to setting, but it explains the why of certain participants or events. Background includes all explanatory material. Some narrators include lots of background, some very little. The amount of background material may vary in quantity or in type as the narrative progresses.

Background can sometimes contain accounts of previous events which are not a part of the present story but shed light on the present story. Such background is often called 'flashback.'

6. Evaluation

Evaluation information is the author's communication of who is hero, who is traitor, what is good and proper, and what is wrong or of questionable value. Much of the evaluative information is in adjectives, adverbs, and nouns (and sometimes verbs), such as 'good', 'nice', 'pretty', 'intelligent', 'capable', 'hero', 'friend', 'mother', 'father', 'succeed', 'win', 'be right', versus 'sneaky', 'villainous', 'ugly', 'stupid', 'inept', 'desparado', 'enemy', 'bad companion', 'fail', or 'be tricked'. In general, the narrator needs to let his hearers know how the participants in the story are to be rated in relation to each other. Evaluation is a part of the larger science of 'Pragmatics'.

In some texts, some participants are left unevaluated or are ambiguously evaluated, as in a mystery story. They receive their evaluations as the mystery is solved.

7. Collateral

Collateral information tells what could have happened but did not. Collateral may be absent in many narrative texts, but some authors, and some language groups, like a lot of collateral to spice up the story. Collateral information can occur as predictions, commands, or expected sequences of events which are in contrast to what did happen in the story. Negative clauses are usually collateral, especially in antithetical sentences where there is a reversal of expectancy. Rhetorical questions often raise possibilities of what might happen. Then as the story unfolds, some other possibility is followed.

8. Performative

Performative information is the information that lets the hearers (readers) know when and where the narrative is set and who the participants are. It involves proper names, standard dates, relative dates, place names, adverbs of distance and nearness, and the like. It overlaps extensively with setting, background information, and identification of participants.

Performative information also includes any remarks or questions aimed at the hearer (reader) and not a part of the story. Some Mayan texts, for instance, stop just before the peak and ask the hearer, "What do you think happened next?"

Performative information is most obvious in foreign stories in which we can't tell who is referred to or when or where the events took place--simply because we don't recognize the person and place names. The performative information in the story doesn't connect with us.

There is some performative information in presumed cultural items or habits, too. Often one needs to know the culture to understand a story.

B. Other features

1. Sometimes, it is profitable to study the aspects and tenses of the verbs in a discourse. In some languages, each different kind of discourse will have its preferred constellation of aspects and tenses, and different discourse types may be signaled by the aspects and tenses used. Verb inflections may signal backbone versus nonbackbone clauses. Or they may signal primary events from secondary events or events involving principal participants from events involving other participants. The range of possibility here is great, depending upon the richness of the verbal affixes.

Another valuable study is the tracing of the occurrences of special little morphemes that do not seem to have much meaning. They may signal important events or peak events.

Sentence margins often aid in making constituent breaks, but they also may signal important features of discourse.

The order of sentence constituents may be correlated with position in a discourse or with shifting scenes in discourse.

The occurrence of an overt subject that is otherwise optional may be connected with participant identification or shifting scenes.

These are all interesting and appropriate questions to study, and many will lead to a better understanding of the language.

2. The study of the ranking of information is important. In some languages, the distinction between old information and new information is important. Usually, old information has to be encoded in dependent clauses, as recapitulation clauses, while new information is in independent clauses.

In some languages, foregrounded material must be in independent clauses and backgrounded material in dependent clauses.

Analyses of primary versus secondary information, or highlighted versus nonhighlighted information have been helpful in some languages. Longacre has developed these levels of information extensively in Amerindian languages (see Jones, 1979).

3. Larson discusses the surface structures of discourses in terms of grouping, coherence, and prominence (Larson, 1978, p. 155 ff). Under 'grouping', she discusses the various clauses, sentences, and paragraphs that occur in each distinct discourse type. These are the comments that should be placed at the bottom of a bidimensional array--notes about exponent classes. Coherence includes lexical and grammatical linkage: the participant references, recapitulation, lexical repetition, and conjunctions. And prominence deals with the ways features are highlighted in each discourse type; the use of quotations, aspects and tenses, independent versus dependent clauses, overt subjects in clauses, moods, and sentence margins.

4. Another avenue of study that is useful for nonnarrative texts is the study of themes. Themes may be global, running through the whole discourse. Other themes are local to points and paragraphs. Beekman and Callow (1974, p. 267 ff) discuss the organization of themes at different levels and how they are interrelated.

The hierarchy of themes must be looked at in both ascending and descending order. One begins by stating the themes of individual sentences or paragraphs. Then these are combined into themes for larger paragraphs. These are then combined into themes for sections and for the whole discourse. Once the overall theme for a discourse has been determined, one can go back down the hierarchy checking the suitability of the smaller themes. Are the themes of the sections compatible with the overall theme? Within a section, are the themes of the paragraphs compatible with the section theme? And so on.

This going up the hierarchy of themes and coming back down may have to be repeated a few times, but the result is a good analysis of themes. Beekman and Callow give extensive rules for combining themes. This subject is treated in more detail in the courses on translation principles.

Also in the study of themes, you may find one or two or three main overt themes going through the discourse. There may also be other more covert themes that appear as strands in the text, such as background cultural beliefs or norms. They may involve the speaker's involvement or responsibility (or noninvolvement and nonresponsibility).

5. Discourses must be studied from two viewpoints. The first approach is discourse type determination and breaking discourses into constituents. The study of episode or point breaks and the signals of constituent boundaries are important facets of language, as are the beginnings and endings of discourses.

The second approach involves finding all the 'threads' discussed in this chapter. 'Thread' information cuts across grammatical boundaries and levels at times and intimately involves grammar at other times.

Both approaches are useful.

C. Recent studies

Since Grimes's book, there have been other relevant studies of various aspects of discourse. We will look at three of them, Hopper and Thompson's study of transitivity as it relates to foreground, Ellen Prince's study of participant identification, and Austin Hale's pragmatic approach to narrative discourse.

1. Hopper and Thompson have studied the relationship between transitivity and discourse background and foreground. They posit ten parameters for transitivity. These are:

Two or more participants (Agent and Objective)	versus	One participant only
Action	versus	Nonaction or stative
Action completed	versus	Action not complete
Punctual aspect	versus	Nonpunctual, durative
Volitional agent	versus	Nonvolitional agent
Affirmative	versus	Negative
Realis mode	versus	Irrealis mode
Highly potent agent	versus	Low potency agent
Totally affected objective	versus	Not totally affected objective
Objective individuated	versus	Objective not individuated

(I have changed some of their terminology.)

Hopper and Thompson give another chart to determine the individuation of the objective.

306

Individuated	‖	Nonindividuated
Proper noun (phrase)	‖	Common noun (phrase)
Human, animate	‖	Inanimate
Concrete noun (phrase)	‖	Abstract noun (phrase)
Singular number	‖	Plural number
Count noun (phrase)	‖	Mass noun (phrase)
Definite, referential	‖	Indefinite, nonreferential

Hopper and Thompson then study verbs and clauses in various languages and show that most languages have morphology or particles to show the contrasts listed above. Then, checking texts in some different languages, they found that usually, the most transitive verbs occur mostly in the foreground of a story and the low-transitivity verbs occur in the background.

Their hypothesis is true also of English, where the overt marking of transitivity is minimal. Checking all the contrasts showed that the English clauses of highest transitivity occur in foreground and clauses of lower transitivity occur in background.

One important finding for English speakers is that in many languages the passive or passivelike clauses are more transitive than active or activelike clauses. (In English we feel that the passive is less transitive.)

2. Ellen Prince has clasified the participant references in a narrative into seven classes. Here are her classifications:

a) The following participant references need no elaboration.

    1. References to textually-evoked referents. These refer to referents already on-stage and are usually only pronouns or are deleted. They are the most frequently mentioned referents, and their mention gives cohesion to the text.

b) The following participant references need minimal elaboration.

    2. References to situationally-evoked referents. These are the references to participants in the immediate situation, and include reference to first and second person (you and I) and references to other people or props near at hand (that chair, John here). These references need little elaboration and are frequent in conversations.

3. References to unused-new referents. These refer to referents that everyone knows, such as well-known people, well-known places, well-known things, such as 'Shakespeare,' 'the post office,' and 'nylon hose.' The speaker can introduce these participants with no further elaboration.

4. References to contained-inferrable participants. These refer to referents that are introduced as members of a set that has already been introduced, such as 'We have three children. The eldest is in college.'

5. References to noncontained-inferrable referents. These refer to the referents that can be easily introduced as related to something already introduced, such as 'The class meets in room 101. The teacher is always very prompt.' (Every class has a teacher.) These need minimal elaboration.

c) The following need careful elaboration.

6. References to brand-new, anchored referents. These refer to referents that are brought in from the outside, but are definite and are related to something already on-stage, such as 'my friend in Boston,' 'John Smith, a psychologist in my home town,' (where 'John Smith' is brand new, and 'a psychologist in my home town' is an unused-new participant.

7. References to brand-new, unanchored referents. These refer to referents that are introduced with no connection to anything on-stage, and the references are often indefinite, such as 'I asked a mechanic about it,' 'I saw a tourist,' 'We called a doctor.'

The references of the class one, 'textually evoked,' are usually reduced to pronouns or generic nouns or one-word names. They usually occur as subjects of clauses. Generally, 'textually evoked' references refer to referents that have earlier been introduced by references of one of the other classes.

The referents of the middle classes can occur as subjects but usually they occur as objects, indirect objects, benefactees, locations, and so on, at least in English.

The latter classes seldom occur as subjects but almost always as nonsubjects. English speakers use existential clauses, cleft and pseudocleft sentences, and run-on sentences to keep from introducing brand new referents as sentence-initial subjects, except at the beginning of stories.

Prince tested her classification with some recorded English conversation and found that her classification held up well.

3. Austin Hale takes a pragmatic approach to narrative discourse, and posits four aspects of discourse: 1) Focal content or plot, 2) Files, 3) Constituent structure and 4) Backbone structure.

a) The focal content or plot concerns the teller's strategy.

b) The files represent the information stored in the hearer-reader's mind as the story unfolds. There is a file for each participant. It is opened when the participant is introduced and is augmented whenever the participant is mentioned or described. Similarly, there can be files for props and locations that are relevant to the story. Each mention of the referent calls up the whole file as it is constituted at that time in the hearer-reader's mind. Files correspond to the vertical traces in a detailed span chart.

c) Constituent structure includes all the grammatical structures at all levels that make up the story.

d) And backbone structure is the cohering part of the story. It is carried forward by event verbs.

Hale shows how there is a pecking order among the facets of discourse. Focal content considerations can distort the files, the constituent structure and the backbone. The teller's strategy may involve such distortions for suspense or surprise. The requirements of the files can override normal constituent structure expectations and backbone considerations. The constituent structure can distort the backbone, placing backbone verbs in subordinate clauses or leaving them out by elision, and so on.

You should see the original papers to see more of what these authors have presented. Their ideas may prove helpful to you in your analysis of texts.

G. Discourse charting

Discourse features are best studied by means of charts of discourses. There are various kinds of charts, and the investigator needs to know what features he wants to study and what chart to use to study them.

1. Basic charting

The basic plan of a chart is that there is a separate line for each clause in the text. You number the clauses in a text and number an equal number of lines on the chart. The clauses may be written out on their respective lines in a column at one edge of the chart; or they may be written in different columns according to their classification. It is good to have the clauses written out somewhere in the chart.

Then vertical columns are drawn and labeled with the features being investigated.

So, in summary, we want a line for each clause with the clause written on that line somewhere and a column for each discourse feature.

2. Span charts

Span charts are one easy kind of chart. First, consider the span chart below of a narrative about a squirrel.

The sentences on the span chart are divided into clauses and each clause is on a separate line. In our chart we plotted participants, props, and evaluation material. We could have plotted more props, time, verb aspects and tenses, connectors, clause or sentence constituents, or anything we had wanted to study, had the paper been much wider.

Span charts may be made of nonnarrative discourses as well. In expository discourses one would plot topics and themes. In procedural, one would plot products, ingredients, processes, and times.

3. Thurman chart

Robin Thurman, in Papua New Guinea, devised a chart for displaying the kinds of information described by Joseph Grimes. We call it the Thurman chart.

Normally the Thurman chart takes a wide piece of paper. To make the chart narrower we omitted writing out the full clauses in the left-most column (before the events column). Note also, that since many entries are too long for the width of the column, we adopt the convention that the entry begin in the proper column and run over into columns to the right. So where an entry begins tells where the entry belongs.

A Thurman chart is interesting in that it shows the distribution of information which might give some insight into how much of each type of information is normal, and how it is introduced. But, by and large, this chart has not paid off well.

4. Longacre-Levinsohn chart

The third type of chart is attributed to Robert Longacre and Stephen Levinsohn in Colombia. Since the distinction between dependent and independent clauses is so often important in classifying information, this chart puts dependent clauses in two columns and independent clauses in another separate column. The independent clause is in the middle column. Dependent clauses preceding the independent clause are placed in the left-hand column, and dependent clauses following the independent clause in the right-hand column.

A span chart for a story about a squirrel

Sentence number	CLAUSE	PARTICIPANTS	PROPS	EVALUATION
1.	My story is about a a squirrel	a squirrel		
2.	This squirrel was walking in the woods.	this squirrel	woods	
3a.	After walking a while	∅		
b.	he heard a strange struggling noise	he	noise	strange struggling noise
c.	coming from a nearby tree.		tree	
4a.	When he went to see	he		
b.	what it was		a	it
c.	he saw a lizard	he	lizard	
d.	pulling something from under a root of the tree.	∅	root of tree	something
5a.	When the squirrel reached the lizard,	squirrel	the lizard	
b.	he said, cheerily,	he		cheerily
c.	Whatever are you doing, friend?		you friend	friend
6a.	The lizard answered rather grumpily,		the lizard	rather grumpily
b.	I'm getting honey.		I	honey
7a.	The squirrel said,	squirrel		
b.	That is good.			
c.	I will help you	I	you	
d.	get the honey,			honey
e.	and we will eat it.	we		it
8a.	The lizard said,		the lizard	
b.	All right.			
9a.	So the squirrel got down	the squirrel		
b.	and helped him.	∅	him	
10.	Together they pulled out the whole honey nest.	they		honey nest
11a.	When they finished	they		
b.	pulling out the honey nest,	∅		the honey
c.	they sat down and ate it,	they ∅		it
d.	looking at each other	∅		
e.	and licking their lips.	∅ their		

A Thurman chart of the story about a squirrel

Clause no.	EVENT	Partici-pants	Identi-fication	Setting	Background
1.		|-|-|	-a squirrel	My story is about a squirrel	
2.	was walking	|-|-|	-this squirrel	in the woods	
3a.	walking	|-|-|	-∅		a while
b.	heard	|-|-|	-he	coming from a nearby tree	a strange struggling noise
c.					
4a.	went to see	|-|-|	-he		what it was
c.	saw	|-|-|	-he	a lizard	
		|-|	__a lizard		
d.	pulling	|-|	__∅	a root of a tree	something from under
5a.	reached	|-|-|	-the squirrel		
		|-|	__the lizard		
b.	said	|-|-|	-he		cheerily
		|-|	__you, friend		whatever are you doing
6a.	answered	|-|	__the lizard		rather grumpily
b.		|-|	__I		getting honey
7a.	said	|-|-|	-the squirrel		that is good
c.		|-|-|	-I		help
d.		|-|	__you		get the honey
e.		|-|	__we		eat it
8a.	said	|-|	__the lizard		All right
9a.	got down	|-|-|	-the squirrel		
b.	helped	|-|-|	-∅		
		|-|	__him		
10.	pulled out	|-|	__they		the whole honey nest
11a.	finished	|-|	__they		pulling out the honey nest
		|-|	__∅		nest
c.	sat	|-|	__they		down
	ate	|-|	__∅		it
d.	looking at	|-|	__∅		
		|-|	__each other		
e.	licking	|-|	__∅		their lips

A Longacre-Levinsohn chart of the story about a squirrel

	Dependent Clause	Independent Clause	Dependent Clause
1		My story is about a squirrel.	
2		This squirrel was walking in the woods.	
3	After walking a while,	he heard a strange struggling noise	coming from a nearby tree.
4	When he went to see what it was,	he saw a lizard	pulling something from under a root of a tree.
5	When the squirrel reached the lizard,	he said cheerily,	Whatever are you doing, friend?
6		The lizard answered rather grumpily,	I'm getting honey.
7		The squirrel said,	That is good, I will help you get the honey and we will eat it.
8		The lizard said,	All right.
9		So the squirrel got down	and helped him.
10		Together they pulled out the whole honey nest.	
11	When they finished pulling out the honey nest,	they sat down	and ate it, looking at each other and licking their lips.

Investigators in South and Central America have found the Longacre-Levinsohn chart to be most helpful in seeing how different kinds of primary and secondary information are handled.

5. Summary

In summary, effective use of all the charts will usually involve some juggling of material, some shifting around of material and reclassifying it, or some modification of the chart to fit one's needs. These charts can be used to study how pronouns are used, how participants are introduced and reintroduced, how various verb forms are used, when certain particles occur, and how cohesion is achieved.

But remember, a chart is only a tool, not an end in itself. Make it serve your needs.

Bibliography

Beekman, John, and John Callow. 1974. Translating the word of God. Grand Rapids, Michigan: Zondervan Publishing House.

Beekman, John, et al. 1979. The semantic structure of written communication. Dallas: S.I.L.

Fillmore, Charles J. 1975. Santa Cruz lectures on deixis, 1971. Bloomington: Indiana University Linguistics Club.

Grimes, Joseph E. 1975. The thread of discourse. Janua Linguarum Series Minor, 207. The Hague: Mouton and Co.

_____, ed. 1978. Papers on discourse. Dallas: S.I.L. and U.T.A.

_____. 1978. Narrative studies in oral texts. Current trends in text linguistics, ed. by Wolfgang U. Dressler. Berlin: Walter de Gruyter. pp. 123-32.

Hale, Austin. 1983. A discourse pecking order. Research in text theory, ed. by Robert E. Longacre. Berlin: Walter de Gruyter.

Jones, Linda K. ed. 1979. Discourse studies in mesoamerican languages. Dallas: S.I.L. and U.T.A.

Larson, Mildred Lucille. 1978. The functions of reported speech in dis-discourse. Dallas: S.I.L. and U.T.A.

Longacre, Robert E. 1968. Philippine languages: discourse, paragraph, and sentence structure. Santa Ana, California: S.I.L.

_____. 1976. An anatomy of speech notions. Lisse: The Peter de Ridder Press.

_____ and Frances Woods, eds. 1976. Discourse grammar: studies in indigenous languages of Colombia, Panama, and Ecuador. Dallas: S.I.L. and U.T.A.

Prince, Ellen F. 1979. On the given/new distinction. Fifteenth Regional Meeting of the Chicago Linguistic Society. Chicago: The University of Chicago Press. pp. 267-78.

Index

... 22
+ 16
± 16
∓ 16
22
∅ 22
? 22
( ) 24, 25
* 25
abbreviations 17, 22
abilitative 56
ability 240, 241
ablative 105, 123, 107
absolutive 54, 59, 139
abstract 167, 307
Abulas 183
academic 146
accidental 56
accompaniment 56, 107, 138, 163
accompanying motion 56
accusative 49, 54, 123, 139
acquiescence 257, 260
action 37ff, 160ff, 257, 306
action-process verbs 161, 162
action verbs 161ff
active 54, 55, 122ff, 144, 215ff
active instrument 170
activity 161, 195, 286ff, 296ff, 301
actor 135
added explanation 23
addition 64, 94
addressee 290, 294
adjectival 128
adjective 52, 70
adjective phrase 19, 20, 28, 95-99
adjective stem 40ff
adjectivized 150
adjectivized clause 61
adjectivizer 41
advancements 139-43
adverb stem 41
adverbializer 41
adversative 196
advice 290
aesthetic 278
affected 163, 306
affected agent 169

affirmative 306
affix 22, 113
afterthought 182, 186
age 50
agent 125, 167, 169, 225, 240, 242, 291, 292, 294, 306
agentive 162-69
agreement 16, 134, 135, 154
Aguaruna 288
allative 105, 136
allomorph 63-67
allomorph description 67ff
allomorph statement 68
allophone 63ff
allosyntagma 10
alternation 229, 230
alternative 80-82, 88-90, 97, 98, 100, 103, 110, 145, 194-97, 245, 250, 251, 272, 296
Amarakaeri 129
Amazon-jungle English 23
ambient 129
American Indian 154
amplification 59, 204ff, 235
analysis 3
animate 123, 159, 160, 163, 225, 307
answer 211, 257, 260, 270
antipassive 59, 140
antithesis 196
antithetical 83, 84, 195, 196, 272
antonym 228, 229, 240
aperture 283, 284, 286, 288
apodosis 198-200
apparatus 242
apposition 92, 102, 150
appositional 88, 90, 92, 103, 109, 150
appositional noun phrase 29
appositional summary 79, 80, 91
archaic 146
arguments 225, 241, 284
Arnhemland 154
array 15ff, 27ff
article 70
articulation 63ff
Asaro 188
aspect 56ff, 117, 226, 304, 305
aspectual 195, 213, 218, 219
aspectual sentence 195

aspectual verb phrase 117ff
assimilation 63
associative noun phrase 14
asterisk 25
attestation 248
attribution 236, 237, 239
attributive 77, 87, 90, 91, 96, 97, 101
attributive noun phrase 46
augmenter 52
augmentive 56
Australia 154
auxiliary 113ff
avolitional 56
aware 240
awareness 56
axis 50, 74, 75, 104ff, 151 223
Bach and Harms 162
back looping 34
backbone 144, 301ff, 309
background 144, 245, 285, 301, 303, 305
Baird 244
Ballard 225, 243
Barai 208, 209
basic 165, 226
be-kind-to-the-reader 18
bearer 168, 225
Beekman 305
behavior 294
behavioral 245, 248, 252, 270, 271, 286, 290, 292-95
benefactee 53, 308
benefactive 108, 110, 136, 163, 165, 182, 185, 226
bidimensional array 2, 15-16, 27ff, 138, 305
Binukid 18ff, 27ff
bitransitive 121-123, 138
Blackfoot 142
blocking circumstance 238
body motion 127
Bororo 298
bound 104
boundaries 244, 245, 296
bounds 2
branch 27
brand new 308
breaks 12
Buck 194
buildup 245, 255
Bunn 50
Butler 140, 144, 280

cajoling 286
calculus 225ff, 243
Callow 305
Capanahua 157-59
cardinal 93
case 49, 156ff, 164
case frame 164ff
case frame matrix 164-65
case grammar 162
case marked phrase 76
case marker 154
cast of characters 244, 284, 286, 296
category 11, 17
causation 195, 232, 239
causative 36, 59, 161, 220, 221
causative motion 125
cause 179, 238
causer 240
caution 202
cessative 56
Chafe 159-61
change of state 160
character 284
chart 8, 309-14
checking 13
Cheyenne 160
Chomsky 113
Chorti 149
chronological 244, 246, 287, 289, 291, 295
chunking 296, 301
circumstance 178, 184, 238, 278
circumstantial 233
clarification 290
Clark 141
class name 1
clause 121ff, 243, 309, 310
clause-level 17, 60, 136, 137, 175, 182
cleft 210, 211, 308
climactic 246
climax 278
clitic 22, 60, 151, 198
close-knit 113
closed class 48, 113
closure 252, 283, 286, 289, 290, 299
coherence 305
cohesion 11, 16, 154, 265, 279, 280
collateral 301, 303, 304
collocation 157

colon 222
color 70
column 309, 310
comitative 163
command 146, 202, 286, 303
comment 248, 256, 263
comment paragraph 256, 263, 264
common 307
comparative 52, 206, 207
comparison 229
complementary 53
complementizer 162
complete 306
completive 55, 284
complex 109, 258
compound 42ff, 85, 118, 245, 258, 259, 261
compound glosses 22
compound stem 42ff
conative 214
concession clause 151, 152
concessive 178, 184, 195
conclusion 246, 264, 266, 267, 272, 275, 276, 285, 287, 288, 299
concord 154
concrete 160, 307
condition 152, 177, 184, 223, 240, 250, 291
conditional 95, 143, 198, 199, 233
conditionality 231
conjoin 226, 242
conjunction 52, 242, 291, 305
Conrad 225, 243
consonant-initial 54
constituent 27, 134, 309
constituent cuts 34
constituent trees 27ff
construction 5
contained inferrable 308
contiguous 9
contingency 232, 239
continuing 257, 260
continuous 55, 113, 230, 231
contraction 235
contrafactual 195, 199, 200
contrafactuality 233
contrast 180, 185, 197, 226, 228, 244, 256, 272, 273
contrasting 11
contrasting exception 197
contrasting parallel 197
contrastive 4

conversation 121, 256, 283
Cook 161, 163, 164, 171
coordinate 77, 79, 87-91, 97, 101, 103, 195, 196
coordinate patient 170
coordinate source 170
copula 130ff, 211, 212
core 36ff
correlative 232
coterminous 230
count 307
count noun 69, 159
counterbalancing considerations 197
counterproposal 257-60
counterquestion 257-60
counterremark 257-60
coupling 226, 238
course 225, 242
covariance 232
covariant 205
cross reference 9, 154
Crowell 298
custom 253, 289
customary place 37ff
cyclical 256, 278
Daga 94, 115, 116
data 12
data book entries 23, 24
dataful examples 18
date 100, 304
dative 49, 123, 163, 170
day 100
deactivative 161, 162
debate 284
decimal 93
declarative 69, 144
declarative description clause 28
deep 226, 295
deeper semantic level 171
deep structure 171, 243, 294, 296
definite 70, 307
degree 234
deictic 19, 70, 89, 236
deity 89
deixis 70, 236
deletion 64
demonstrative 70ff
dependent 151, 152, 223, 305, 310, 313
dependent clause 151
deprocessive 161, 162
derivation chart 161

derivational 36, 59
derivational affix 36ff
derived 36ff
derived adjective stem 40, 41
derived adverb stem 41
derived noun stem 37ff
description 130, 264, 265
description clause 28
description noun phrase 18ff, 69, 71
descriptive 130, 245, 283, 284, 291
descriptive complement 128
desiderative 56, 116, 146
designation complement 126
desire 241
destination 12
determiner 18ff, 70, 86, 87
diagnostic 10
diagram 158, 159, 243
dialogue 256, 257, 259, 261, 269
dictionary 156
difference 4, 9, 10
digits 94
diminutive 48, 56
direct quotation 190
direction 105, 136
directional 58
disclaimer 60, 173, 174, 192
discourse 282, 301ff
discourse genre 170, 292
discourselike paragraphs 245
displaying examples 21ff
dissimulation 64
distinctive features 14, 15
distinctive names 151
distribution matrix 111, 112
ditransitive 121, 123
do 117
doer 37ff
dots 22
double underline 18
dramatic 259-61, 288, 289, 292, 295-97
dual 48
Duff 282
dummy 121, 129, 211, 212, 214
duration 56, 106
durational 136
durative 56
Echerd 171, 225, 295, 296
echo 183
editing data 5

efficient cause 232
Eidsvoog 244
elaborate 248
elicited data 5, 286
elision 64
embedded 39, 42, 173, 224, 284, 286, 296
embedding 42, 255
emic 9, 164
emotion 56, 225
emphasis 70
emphasize 52, 56, 72, 89
emphatic 56, 70, 89
encoding 296
Engel 8, 50, 210
English verb phrase 113
environment 63, 67, 129
epenthesis 66
episode 283, 284, 288
epistolary 245, 290, 291, 297
equal 229, 242
equation sentences 210ff
equational 131
equative 291
equivalent 131, 234, 241
equivalent paraphrase 234
ergative 54, 59, 139, 140
ergativity 54
etic 154
evaluation 70, 208, 209, 212, 257, 260, 286, 301, 303
evaluative 246
event 245, 274, 289, 294, 301
evidence 248, 265, 266
evidential reasons 252
examples 13, 17, 19, 267, 268
exception 228
exchange 259, 261, 291
exclamation 173, 174
exclusive or 198, 242
execution 268, 269
exemplification 236, 248, 267
exhortation 245, 252
exhorting 296
existence 245
existential 133, 308
expect 56, 238, 241
expected outcome 238
experiencer 163, 165, 167, 169, 225, 242, 291
explanation 23, 290
explanatory 244, 248, 255, 265-67, 279, 280, 284, 285, 302

explanatory paragraph 15
exponent 1, 2, 16, 18, 19, 27, 34
exponentiation 27
exposition 246, 255
expository 245, 248, 270, 271, 279, 280, 284, 285, 290, 291-95, 297, 299
expounds 27ff
fable 284
facility 240
factive 163
farness 56
features 301ff
female derived noun stem 48, 49
feminizer 48, 49
field English 23
field notes 24
file 309
file card 3, 6
filler 3, 11
Fillmore 55, 70, 162, 163, 164
final 60, 143, 144
final cause 232
final verb 60, 182
finis 283, 285-90, 299
first person 53, 246, 291, 294
first person inclusive 286, 291
first person plural 250
fixed word order 154
flashback 301, 303
focal 309
focus 18, 24, 70, 147, 294
Foley 135
folktale 282
foot 94
force 163
forces of nature 167
foreground 305, 307
foreseen cause 239
foreseen result 202, 233, 252
formula 190-94, 214-22, 243, 277
Forster 292, 293
four-box tagmeme 2, 16
fourth person 53, 154
frame 244
Frank 225
Frantz 142, 154, 156
free 104
free translation 7, 21, 23

Fries 72, 76, 279
frustrated 238-40
frustrating outcome 197
frustration 238
full example 17, 18, 24, 25
full stop 22
function 1, 10, 11
function gloss 23
function label 1, 17
Furby 9, 14
fusion 65
future 143, 291
Garland 112
genders 48, 49, 154
general 56
general-purpose preposition 77
generic 160, 235, 241, 244
genitive 49, 123
gesture 257
give 117
gloss 7, 21-23
goal 122, 163, 167, 169, 225, 242
Godfrey 225
Golin 51, 57
Gradin 118
grammatical level 5
grammatically conditioned allomorphs 67
greater 229, 242
Grimes 297, 298, 301, 306, 310
grouping 305
Guanano 278
Guerrero Amuzgo 194, 195
guess and check 3, 12
habitual 56, 250
Hale 306, 309
Halliday 279
hand 94
harmony 66ff
Hasan 279
head 69ff
hierarchy 1, 34, 163, 297, 305
highlighted information 305
Hindi 169, 170
hint 286
historical 291
historical past 55
history 246, 294
honorific 51, 87-90
Hooper and Thompson 141,

306, 307
hortatory 146, 244, 252, 266, 286, 287, 291, 292, 294, 295, 297
Huckett 71
human 159, 160, 307
hyphen 21, 22
hyphenate 22
hypothetical 143, 271
hypotheticality 231, 239
identification 237, 284, 301, 302, 304, 306
identifying participants 302
idiomatic 118
Iduna 71
illustration 236, 286, 294, 297
impending future 55
imperative 60, 146, 166, 250, 252, 291
imperfect 143
impersonal 250
implication 231, 239, 242
inactive 55
inadvertently 56
inanimate 123, 248, 302, 307
inanimate force 167
inception 56
inchoative 56, 161
inclusive or 198, 229, 291
incompletive 55
indefinite 70
indefinite time 177-84
independent 305, 310, 313
indicative 143
indirect object 53, 135, 308
indirect question 193
indirect quotation 190 191, 221
individuated 306
induction 265, 266
infinitive clause 152, 213ff
infix 22, 23
inflected 53
inflected preposition 110
inflected subordinating conjunction 53, 152
inflection 304
inflectional 36
information 145, 301
inhabitant derived noun stem 39, 40
Inibaloi 152, 243
initiating utterance 257, 260

initiation 252
innately possessed 69
inner benefactive 166
inner locative 166
inner periphery 157-84
inside-the-clause 135
instigator 163
instruction 286
instrument 24, 38, 106, 107, 137, 162, 167, 170, 225, 242
instrument advancement 142
instrument promotion 59
instrumental 109, 163
intensifier 74, 95, 96
intent 240, 241, 296
interest 284
interpeak 283, 284
interrogative 60, 144, 194, 270
intersentence relationships 244
intervening circumstance 238
intransitive 127, 128
introduce 173, 174, 244
introduction 14, 15, 18, 80, 81, 92, 103, 197, 236, 237, 272, 285, 287
introductory paragraph 14, 15
Ireland 123, 198
irrealis 143, 306
Jeh 118
Jones 210, 305
jussive 146
juxtapose 187, 201
juxtaposed sentence 187
Kaje 45, 119
Kalamian Tagbanwa 171
Katz and Fodor 157
kinship 50, 86-88
Kiowa 48, 189
knowledge 237
Kobon 61
Koiari 112
label 11, 17
Landerman and Frantz 156
Larson 246, 256, 288, 305
Latin 48, 123, 154, 198
lead-in 285
lead-up 245
Leal 34, 225
legendary 282
legendary narrative 121
less 229, 242

letters 290
level 5, 12
level skipping 34
Levinsohn 310, 313
lexical decomposition 156ff
lexical properties 159
Li 135
ligature 18
likeness 241
limiter 70, 72
link 78, 79, 81, 82, 91-93, 101, 103, 126, 196, 201, 207
linkage 291, 305
location 105, 110, 122, 125, 132, 136, 182, 185, 214, 242, 303, 308
location phrase 102, 103
locative 105, 163, 167, 169, 225
logic 248, 294
logical 179, 195, 226, 231, 245, 252, 285, 287, 291, 292
logical entailment 248
logical reason 252
Longacre 2, 3, 11, 34, 118, 166ff, 171, 173, 176, 193, 204, 210, 213, 222, 225, 226, 244, 256, 278, 291, 292, 295, 305, 310, 313
look ahead 60
Loos 157
Lubeck 149
man 94
manner 107, 108, 114, 122, 213, 214, 242
margin 17, 173, 174-86, 304, 305
marginal 138, 262
marker 191, 192, 194
masculine 48, 49
mass 307
mass noun 69, 159
matrix 4, 10, 11, 45, 46, 111, 112, 153, 171, 291-94, 296
Mayan 117, 134, 149, 284, 304
McElhanon 51, 52
McKinney 45, 119
McMillen 52, 110
measure 166, 168, 169, 242
medial 60, 143, 144
member 242

merged sentence 118, 213ff
metaphorical extension 55
metathesis 65
mezzanine 222
mismatching 296
mistaken idea 239
mitigated exhortations 253
Mixe 114, 115
modality 163, 226, 240
mode 245
modifier 49, 69, 70, 100, 173, 174
modify 150, 158
monologue 5, 282
month 100
mood 53, 60, 113, 143, 226
Mopan Maya 114, 141, 142
moral 284
morality play 295
morpheme 36, 304
motion 115, 125, 245
motivation 252
multiplier 94
Murane 94, 115, 116
name 14, 16, 89, 90, 133, 134, 304
name phrase 29
name of syntagmeme 14, 16, 27
narrative 187, 188, 244, 245, 255, 268, 271, 273, 274, 278, 282-84, 286, 289, 290-97, 299
narrative discourse 170, 282-84
narrative past 55
narrative sequence 188
nasalization 66
nearness 56
negated antonym 234
negated extremes 235
negated higher degree 234
negation 228, 229
negative 57, 95, 96, 137, 303
negative link 84, 85
nervous system 167
neuter 48
neutral 163
New Guinea English 23
New Guinea Pidgin 297
new information 305
node 27
nominalized clause 147-49
nominalized verb 69
nominalizer 36ff
nominative 49, 139

nominative-accusative 54, 139
nonaction 306
nonactive 54, 55
nonanimate causer 170
nonanimate noun 160
nonbackbone 301, 302
nondescending 34
nonfocus 18
nonhighlighted 305
nonnarrative 255, 280
nonprescriptive 295
nonprojected 293
nonreferential 307
nonreportive 234
nonrestrictive 73, 150
nonsequential 226, 238
nonspecific 241
nonsubject 308
nonverb 48ff
nonverbal 257
nonvolitional 306
notebook 6
notes and rules 16
noun 48ff
noun attributive 77
noun class 154
noun head 69
noun phrase 28, 69ff, 158, 284
noun stem 37-45
nuclear 3, 4, 9, 134, 138, 173, 186ff
nucleus 17, 48-61
number 93ff
object 53, 108, 109, 122, 135, 158, 163, 213, 217, 225, 291, 308
object advancement 139
object demotion 141
object incorporation 59, 141
object marker 135
objective 163, 306
obligation 58, 216, 240, 241
obligation aspect 58
obligatorily possessed 50, 159
obligatory 1, 9, 16, 27, 134
old information 305
Olson 208, 209
onomatopoeic 45
open class 9, 48, 113
opposite 238, 240
optative 56, 146
optional 1, 9, 16, 27, 134
optionally possessed 50
oral literature 282

order 10, 158, 304
ordering 48
ordinal 93
orthographic 244
outer location 226
outer peripheral 173, 174
outside-the-clause function 135
overhead line 21, 24, 25
overlaid 299
overlapping 230, 238
overlay 297
overt object 124
owner 167, 169, 225, 226
pace 284
Pacoh 206-208
Papua New Guinea 118, 182, 203, 310
parable 295
paragraphs 244ff, 305
parallel 202, 203, 227, 245, 272, 273, 276, 291
parallel structure 202ff
paraphrasable 213
paraphrase 203, 204, 234, 235
parenthesis 24. 25
parsing 34
participant 59, 241, 246, 284, 296, 297, 301-3, 307
participial 214ff
particle 70, 113
passive 59, 124. 139, 158, 216ff, 307
passive experiencer 166
passive instrument 170
past tense 291
path 166-68, 242
patient 135, 163, 166, 168-70, 226, 242, 291
pattern 244
pattern point 1
Payne 66
peak 246, 248, 252, 283, 284, 289
pecking order 309
perceived description 193
perfect 143, 200
perfective 144
performative 173, 282, 301, 304
period 22
peripheral 4, 9, 12, 173, 186, 246
permission 241

322

permutable   27, 174, 175, 180
permutation   14ff, 16
permute   72
person   291
person hierarchy   154
person marker   52ff
personal experience   282
persuade   294
Peru   129
petition   245, 290
Philippines   11, 135, 171, 247, 248, 284
phobic   56
phonology   54
phrase   69ff
phrase search matrix   86
physical sensation   168
Pike and Pike   2, 16, 17, 114, 138
pilot project   6
place   244, 284, 286, 296, 297, 304
plan   268
plane   297, 299
Platt   163, 166
plot   309
plural marker   48, 307
Pocomam   244
poetic   278
point   285, 287, 290, 291, 297
Pokomchí   50, 210
political oration   252, 253
political speeches   284
possessed   75, 76, 159
possessed head   76
possessed noun   50, 73, 76, 159
possession   75, 76, 132
possession marker   50
possession phrase   73-76
possessor   76, 132
possessor axis   74, 75
possessor noun phrase   73-75, 87
possessor relator   74, 75
possibility   56, 241
Post   18
postmodifier   18, 19, 72, 96
postpeak   283, 284, 289
postpositional   104
potent   160, 306
potent noun   160
potential   56
practical orthography   48
preacher   253
preceding cause   239

predicate   134, 147, 225, 240, 241
prediction   303
predispositional   215
preferred order   72
prefix   36ff, 44
preliminary   248, 252, 266, 267, 272, 273, 275, 276
premodifier   18, 19, 71
preposition   52, 53, 104ff, 154
pre-positional   104
prepositional phrase   69, 104ff
prescriptive   295
present   291
price   167, 168, 225
primary   302, 305
primary exponent   34
primary information   305
Prince   306, 307, 309
prior time   151, 175, 184, 250
procedural   244, 249, 250, 266, 274, 286, 289, 291-96
procedure   3, 286
process verb   160ff, 291, 294
product   168, 226, 291, 294
projected   293
prominence   143, 305
promise   286
promotion   143
pronominal affix   53
pronoun   51, 69, 88, 89, 291, 308
prop   302
proper   307
proportional covariance   232
proposal   257, 260
proposition   212
propositional   225, 243
protasis   199, 200
pseudocleft   210, 211, 308
pseudopassive   154
punctiliar   55, 136, 230, 231, 306
purpose   138, 179, 185
qualified   115
qualifying   76, 115
quality   70
quality derived noun stem   39
quantifier   72, 76, 93
quantity   70, 72, 76
Quechua   156
queries   145
question   211, 257, 260, 270
question mark   22

quotation 168, 189, 237, 246,
    256, 257, 259, 269, 272,
    277, 283, 297, 305
quotationlike 194
quoted 226, 284
radio 290
Ramos 171
random 160
range 166, 168, 226, 242
rank 159
ranking 305
reading 27
realis 143, 306
reason 138, 151, 179, 185,
    195, 201, 202, 248, 272,
    275, 278
recapitulation 59, 176, 204,
    244, 280, 291, 305
receiver 37
recipe 286
recipient 59
reciprocal 59, 219, 220
reciprocity 227
reduction 64
reduplicated 83, 98, 110
reduplicated noun stem 45
reduplicating noun head 83
reduplication 44, 83
reference 305, 307
referent 53, 71, 135, 307
referential 307
reflexive 59
regrouping 302
Reid 289, 293
reinforce 248
reinforcement 252
rejection 257, 260
relational 49, 53, 60
relationship 243
relative action 56
relative clause 19, 20, 72,
    73, 150
relativized 150ff
relator 49, 74, 75, 104ff,
    151, 223
relator-axis 104ff, 175ff
relevance 55
religious term 156
remark 257, 260
repartee 256
repeat 291
repetition 4, 11, 12, 59, 305
repetition aspect 58
replacement 66

replacive 83, 90, 93, 98, 99,
    102, 109, 110
report 284
reportive 234, 236
request 286, 290
residue 4, 6, 12
resolving utterance 257, 260
respect 50
response 173, 174, 257, 269,
    270
restrictive 150
restrictive relative clause 73
result 37ff, 180, 185, 195, 201,
    202, 271, 272, 275, 276,
    278
resultative 161
reversal of order 43
rheme 279
rhetorical 234, 270, 271, 303
rhetorically 239
role 16, 135
root 48
route 105
Ruch 171
rule 16, 63
Saksema 170
salutation 291
sample sorted slip 8
scope 157-59
score 94
script 244
search matrix 86, 112, 153,
    292-95
second participant 257
second person 53, 246, 286,
    291, 294
second person plural 252
secondary 302, 305
secondary exponents 34
secondary information 305
selection hierarchy 163
Selepet 51, 52
semantic component 157
semantic content 243
semantic derivation 160
semantic gloss 23
semantic theory 157
semitransitive 123, 154
sensation 191, 192, 221, 222,
    236, 237
sentence 173ff, 305
sentence introducer 173
sentence length 284
sentence-level 175, 182, 243

324

sentence margin 173ff, 304
sentence modifier 173
sentence topic 181, 184
sentencehood 272, 277
sentencelike 272
separability 53, 113
sequence 188, 226ff, 238
sequential 230, 250
serial 79, 80, 90, 91
series 109
sermons 121, 252, 284, 286
setting 144, 244, 245, 246,
    250, 257, 259, 261, 264,
    268, 270, 271, 274, 277,
    285, 301, 303
shorthand 67
signature 291
similarity 180, 185
simile 236
simple 257, 262
simple sentence 186
simultaneous 176, 184, 189,
    250, 252, 272, 274
simultaneous time 151
singular 48, 307
situationally evoked 307
size 70
social situation 253
social status 287
sort 7, 8
source 163, 168, 169, 226, 242
space 21
span 241, 310, 311
span chart 309
Spanish 48
specific 56, 160, 235, 241, 244
speech 236, 237, 282
spirit 160
spreading 66
stage 283, 284, 288, 299
state 160, 168
state verb 160, 161
statement 201-5, 214
stative 56, 144, 306
status 253
stem 36ff
Stemberger 65
step 250, 274, 275
stimulus 269, 270
story 282
story line 245
Strange 188
strategy 287, 309
stress 46

structural difference 10
subclass 11, 67
subject 1, 53, 109, 122, 134,
    158, 225, 291, 304, 305,
    308
subject enhancement 140
subject person marker 57, 134
subjunctive 143, 177
subordinating conjunction 52,
    53, 60, 151, 152, 175
subsequent 177, 184
substitute action 238
succession 231, 238
suggestion 286
summary 208, 210, 236, 264, 267
    273, 297
summary chart 14
superlative 52
superscript 242
supposition 271
surface 295
surface structure 243, 296
suspense 284
syntagma 3
syntagmeme 1-3, 11-14, 27
tactile 105, 137
tag 183, 186
tag question 183
Tagalog 135, 171
tagma 3, 9
tagmeme 1-4, 10, 27ff
target step 250
taxonomic 3
teach 135, 296
telic 217
temporal 55, 226, 230, 232,
    248
temporal clause 151
tense 53ff, 113, 226, 291,
    304, 305
tension 284, 294
tentative labels 11
term 241
terminal 56, 248, 252, 274
terminating utterance 257, 260
terminus 245, 246, 250, 259,
    261, 270, 277
tertiary exponents 34, 302
text 5, 248, 255, 256, 263, 264,
    267, 272, 273, 275, 276,
    278, 297
textually evoked 307
thematic vowel 64

theme   135, 244, 279, 280, 285, 305
thesis   196
third person   53, 246, 248, 291, 294
third person indefinite   250, 286, 291
Thompson   141, 306, 307
threads   301, 306
threat   286
three-box tagmeme   16
three dots   22
three-line format   21
threshold   173
Thurman   310, 312
time   99, 100, 106, 109, 110, 122, 136, 163, 175-77, 184 187, 188, 231, 244, 245, 284, 286, 291, 294, 296, 297, 301, 303
time frame   250
time oriented   188
time phrase   99
timeless   250
title   283, 286, 288, 290
Tongan   141
topic   70, 135, 181, 185, 244, 245, 271, 280, 285, 290, 291, 296, 297
topic-comment   130
topic marker particle   70
tour narrative   283
transductive   34
transfer   168, 169
transitional   246
transitive   124, 125
transitivity   306
transitivizer   36
translocative   105, 137
tree   27ff
Trique   222
Tzutujil   140, 141, 144, 280
Ulrich   114
unaffected agent   169, 170
undergo   168
undergoer   59, 163
underline   25
undesirable alternative   198
undesirable foreseen result   233

unexpected outcome   197
uninflected   219ff
unintentional   56
universal quantifier   231
universe   229, 242
unused-new   308
unwittingly   56
Uspantec   52, 53, 58, 110
utterance   257, 260
Van Haitsma   114, 115
Van Valin   135
variability   16
variant   14ff
Vendler   158, 159
verb   53ff
verb cluster   113
verb phrase   113
verb-phrase level   136, 137
verb stem   36, 37
verbal   121
verbalizer   36ff
verbless   121, 130
vernacular   7, 21
Vietnamese   118, 206
vivid   295, 296
vocative   173, 174
voice   53ff, 59ff, 139
volition   56, 167, 306
vowel-initial   54
Waltz   278
warning   198, 233, 248, 252, 266, 267, 286
Watson   206, 207
wave   16
Weber   158
wedding   252, 286
Wilson   183
Woods   225, 244, 278
word   48ff
workchart   8, 9
write   12
write-up   14ff
written literature   282
year   100
yes-no question   144, 194
zero allotagma   22
zero level   34
zero morpheme   22